Jack
and Old Jewry

THE CITY OF LONDON POLICEMEN
WHO HUNTED THE RIPPER

Amanda Harvey Purse

Published by Mango Books
www.mangobooks.co.uk
18 Soho Square
London W1D 3QL

and Old Jewry

THE CITY OF LONDON POLICEMEN
WHO HUNTED THE RIPPER

Dedication

For Derrick Roy Purse

As this book will hopefully show, there is much behind a name, and 'Derrick Purse' is certainly more than just a name, for he has shared with me the many headaches that these Victorian people, described within these pages, had to offer in the censuses. He has given his time to share some of the research trips with me and been there when I needed to mull over ideas.

Considering the following pages are about certain people and their families, it feels only right that this book is not just the accumulation of fifteen years' study of the City of London Police for me, but thanks to Derrick Purse it has felt like a real father and daughter project. Because of his involvement, he has made this book something I will truly cherish for all my life for so many reasons.

So again, this book is for Derrick Roy Purse... my Daddy.

Contents

Acknowledgements

There are so many people I want to thank for their help with this book, so if I unintentionally miss anyone out I'm truly sorry.

Firstly, I would like to thank Adam Wood of Mango Books for understanding instantly that I never intended for this book to be another factual book where details are put before the reader, but wanted it to feel as if the author and reader are learning this information together. Thanks also to Adam for his agreement that this information should be 'out there' for people to know.

I would like to thank all the people involved with the City of London Police Museum who have allowed me to take photographs of items both on display and behind the scenes. They also allowed me to see a folder which contained information leading me to discover the first name of the policeman who took John Kelly, Catherine Eddowes' partner, to Golden Lane Mortuary to identify her. This information has not been found before, and allowed me to fully research this officer's life.

I would like to thank Neil Bell and Robert Clack for permission to quote from their article about Detective Constable Edward Marriott's pension in issue 115 of *Ripperologist* magazine (July 2010). Thanks are also due to Neil Bell and Jake Luukanen for permission to use the information that PC Edward Watkins had worked his beat 'left-handed' on the night of 29th September 1888, and that there had been roadworks near the Fire Station in St James Place, from their article 'As Far as Mitre Square' in *Ripperologist* issue 71 (September 2006).

A number of people working at various archives and other facilities deserve special thanks, and these include the staff at the National Archives, Old Bailey, British Library, City of London Cooperation, the Barbican Library, Cripplegate Institute, Wolverhampton Archives, various churches throughout London, Islington Cemetery, Ladywell Cemetery, Manor Park Cemetery, Brompton Cemetery, West Ham Cemetery, Romford Cemetery, Municipal Cemetery, Camberwell Cemetery, City of London Cemetery, Metropolitan Heritage Centre, Thames Magistrate Court, Library and Archives of Freemasonry, South West Heritage Trust, Scotland's Church Trust, Tower Hamlets Local History Archives and Library, West Sussex County Council, Hatfield's History records, London Road School History records, Guildhall, and of course the Guildhall Library.

Special mention must be made of the help given by Laura at the London Metropolitan Archives, who organized many, many different files for me to look through on my many visits. I'd also like to thank Haydn at Abney Cemetery, who went above and beyond to help through emails and my eventual visit.

I would like to thank all the people who work for the London Hospital Museum, who not only were friendly and very kind, but also gave permission to publish photographs of Frederick Foster's maps of Mitre Square. One of these is on public display, and a second is not often seen. They also kindly supplied copies of files they hold on the Jack the Ripper case.

Thank you to Paul Begg for his information on PC Alfred Long, including his medals, death certificate and children.

I am grateful to Alan M Clark for his permission to include his artwork of Catherine Eddowes in life, as we should all remember her.

Now for some personal messages. I would like to thank my father for the many reasons given in the dedication, and also my dear husband Benjamin Harvey, who is not just a constant support in my life and every writing project I undertake, but he has an ability to give me confidence just by listening to me and understanding me, which is not always an easy thing to do. He has told me that he always knew I was fated to write and to finally write a factual book on the Ripper's crimes, and didn't quite know why I had put it off until now, because in his eyes it was in my bones as I don't just enjoy history but I care about the people that are part of history too. He has listened to me read every chapter of this book to him, and his comments were not just interesting, but above all they were honest, and now I can't help but smile when I mention a policeman's name and my husband states 'Wasn't he the guy that...'

Without my husband, I would not be the author I am today... Yes Ben, I have finally admitted 'I am an author!' Thank you.

Finally, I would like to thank the readers of this book. By reading the information within these pages you have helped me to pass on history, which is all I wanted to do. Perhaps these grave plots without a headstone can be more than mere patches of grass to us; these places that have changed so much over the years, with the past being slowly forgotten, can mean something more.

We can now all appreciate the people behind the guessing game of 'Who was Jack the Ripper?' their lives and their own part of history.

Foreword

by Tracey Smith

When Amanda asked me to write a Foreword to her book, my first thought was 'Why me? What could I offer to enhance the reader's experience?" I admit to thinking long and hard before deciding I do have a very relevant and personal reason that links me to this book.

Jack the Ripper, a name infamous in the annals of not only British, but world crime... of course I have heard of him and his crimes, there cannot be many people who are unaware of him. I had no more than a passing interest in his story, but that was all to change when I discovered my very real connection to the case. My great, great, great, great grandmother was Catherine Eddowes, one of the unfortunate victims of Jack. This discovery has led me on a very personal and often painful journey through the past to find Catherine's story.

If you want to know about Jack you are spoilt for choice with books, articles, exhibitions and guided walks to choose from, but what if you want more than the gruesome details of the murders? What if you want to find out the very real stories of his victims, the women who suffered so brutally at his hands, or the stories of others who were involved and deeply affected by those heinous crimes. The policemen who found the victims dealt with an increasingly angry and frightened public - what of their stories?

My journey to find Catherine's story was a very personal one but along the way I found others who have stories as well. These crimes may have happened so long ago and we may never know for sure who Jack really was, but we can look into the lives of so many others who are largely overlooked in Jack's story. There are descendants out there like me who are keeping their ancestors' life stories going, so that in the history of Jack the Ripper they do not get overlooked.

So that's why I have written this brief introduction to this book. It is written for the largely forgotten people, for the victims, and mostly for Catherine, my great, great, great, great grandmother, with love and respect.

TRACEY SMITH
Granddaughter x4 of Catherine

INTRODUCTION
The Secrets of London

'If the lions drink, London will sink'

London: a home of political standing and financial business. A tourist land of sights such as the Millennium Wheel, the London Dungeons and the Sea Life Centre. The city which has the famous River Thames flowing through it, today filled with tourist boats, speedboats and the occasional Yellow Duck going backwards and forwards along the waterside.

With its glass buildings reaching higher and higher into the sky, the continuous fast food restaurants and busy human traffic, London can seem a very modern place.

However, one of the most marvellous things about London, the great capital, is that if you look deeper, maybe just by an inch or two in certain areas, you can see its history.

Look to the east, to the iconic image of Tower Bridge and the haunting history of the Tower of London; look to centre stage towards St Paul's Cathedral, a symbol if ever there was one of 'the phoenix from the flames',[1] and finally to the west, and to the home of the government, a place we all 'remember, remember' on the 5th of

---

1   The original St Paul's Cathedral burned down in the Great Fire of London of 1666.

1

November[2] each year.

History is everywhere within this wonderful city, but even after you have seen all the well-known landmarks there will always be more to see the next time you visit, because you cannot have a city this old without it holding a few secrets, and if you know where to look, the secrets are still there for us to see today...

'If the lions drink, London will sink' is one of the classic sayings about London. It refers to the quite large faces of lions with their open mouths which line the river along from the gothic-styled Houses of Parliament: if the water ever reached the level of these lions' mouths, then London will supposedly collapse under the pressure. Thankfully that has never happened.

In Fish Street Hill there is a sculpture that commemorates the Great Fire of London called the Monument. It stands 62 metres high and is located exactly 62 metres from where the *great* fire started in Pudding Lane; it also stands on the area where the first church caught in the Fire, St Margaret's, was set alight. Sir Christopher Wren designed this monument[3] as he did 66 churches within the City of London including St Paul's Cathedral, considered his masterpiece,[4] but some do not know that he didn't get it all his own way. Wren wanted to have King Charles II standing proudly on top of the Monument, but the King was not delighted with the idea, as he did not want other people thinking the King of England actually started the fire.

King Richard I, known as the 'Lionheart', designed a chapel within All Hallows Church, where ironically his *heart* is said to be buried

---

2   The poem that starts with the line, 'Remember, remember the 5th of November...' is used to describe a gang who wanted to change the world by blowing up the Houses of Parliament with King James I therein. The most famous of this gang is Guy Fawkes, as it was he who was caught with the barrels of gunpowder in the cellars of the Houses of Parliament. The poem was used as a warning to everyone from then to now that treason in England should never be forgotten.

3   Completed in 1677.

4   In fact, Sir Christopher Wren is buried inside St Paul's and on his gravestone is inscribed in Latin: 'Reader, if you seek his monument - look around you'.

5   Alternatively, some believe his heart could have been placed in France.

somewhere in the grounds.[5]

The monarch that famously said she had 'the heart and stomach of a king and of a King of England too', Queen Elizabeth I, amazingly only has one statue in London - above the vestry door of St Dunstan's in Fleet Street - even though she reigned for 44 years.[6]

The Church of the Holy Sepulchre has had its own moments in history. For example, it was in this church that the bell rang to inform everyone in the nearby area when a criminal had been hanged at Newgate gaol. Captain John Smith of Pocahontas fame is buried in the south west corner of its churchyard, and the church is even mentioned in the nursery rhyme 'Oranges and Lemons'.

After the London Stone,[7] which the Romans used to measure distances from, the second oldest relic in London stands over 60 feet tall and was placed on the Victoria Embankment in 1878. It is called Cleopatra's Needle and came, unsurprisingly, from Egypt, but did you know that this large needle is not only an ornate obelisk but is actually used for another purpose, and that there is something wrong with it? Firstly, it is a very elaborate time capsule, holding a Victorian newspaper, railway timetable, a Bible and even photographs of what were considered to be the twelve best-looking women in England at the time. Secondly, if you look at the base of the needle you will see two sphinxes added to fit with the Egyptian theme, but their role is to protect an item so they be should facing out from it, not facing towards it...

Staying with the Embankment, the Duke of Buckingham asked that the streets around that area to be named after him so we now have George Street, Villiers Street, Duke Street and Buckingham Street. In 1878, the Embankment was also the first area to have electric street lamps.

Charing Cross train station is not only one of the busiest stations in London but also one of the most famous, being used in many films

---

6 While her father King Henry VIII's only statue in London stands on the gatehouse of St Bartholomew's Hospital as a reminder that the King gave the hospital to the City of London.

7 This stone is situated near St Paul's Cathedral in the City of London.

and books. It is named so because *charing* means 'bend in river' and the *cross* signifies the final one of twelve crosses that King Edward I designed along the route of his wife Eleanor's funeral cortege which travelled from Nottingham to Westminster. The cross had to be moved when the station grew in size, and now a statue of King Charles II stands in its place while a copy of the cross is displayed outside.

In Trafalgar Square, King Charles I's statue looks down Whitehall, ironically where he was beheaded. This statue was intended to be melted down once he was executed, but it was stolen before this could be achieved and hidden in a garden until Charles' son was crowned and it was given back, to be positioned where it still stands today. It is said that Charing Cross station is the place where all distances from London are measured, but it is actually from this statue instead.

The first recorded victim of the Great Plague, Margaret Ponteous, was buried on 12th April 1665 in Covent Garden's St Paul's church, otherwise known as 'the actor's church' because of all the free plays which were held inside. She was a pauper, but her death was commemorated in a generous way as remembrance for all those who died of the plague.

The famous Eros in Piccadilly Circus is an oddity as most people think of it as being a statue, but in reality it isn't; it is a memorial fountain for the Victorian Earl of Shaftesbury. It is not even of Eros, the Greek god of love, but of the Angel of Christian Charity. Nevertheless, it was the first monument ever to be made from aluminium. During the Second World War it was taken away for safe keeping but most people did not realise that when Eros was placed back in the middle of the busy Piccadilly Circus, he was placed the wrong way around.

Everyone knows the image of the tower which holds the famous bell Big Ben, but did you know halfway up the tower is a prison cell? In the 19th century the famous suffragette Emily Davison, who cleverly hid in a broom cupboard in the Houses of Parliament on the night of the 1911 census so that she could then write on the census where she was, was held within this tiny prison cell.

There are many myths floating around London and its past, one being that Queen Boudicca is buried underneath Platform Eight at King's Cross train station, but others think she is buried in Primrose Hill.

You can see Queen Boudicca in statue form by Westminster Bridge. She was placed there in 1902 as an symbol of 'defending London', but considering Boudicca hated the city and tried to burn it down it is a little odd to have a statue of her. The little door at the bottom of the statue leads to the subway of utilities for London, the longest part of which runs from the Houses of Parliament to Blackfriars Bridge.

Even the Victorians got history wrong, for in the Tower of London there is a plaque placed because Queen Victoria requested it to mark where the scaffold was upon which Anne Boleyn lost her head. However, the plaque is in the wrong place by over fifty metres.

Everyone knows of the image of Marble Arch, now standing in the middle of a large roundabout, but do you know the reason why it is there? It was intended to be a part of an entrance in Buckingham Palace, but because the arch was too small to allow carriages through it was moved to now stand near the plaque to Tyburn Tree.[8]

At an historical place like the Tate Britain, you could be mistaken for thinking they would never get anything wrong. However, if you were to look above the entrance of the museum, you will see Britannia looking over you. Such a prominent vision of Britishness, you wouldn't want to get this statue wrong would you? For example, placing the spear and shield in the wrong hands... but this is amazingly what happened.[9]

These are just a few little examples to show that London is full of little facts and bits of information which, if you can spot them, will tell much more of the city's history than you would first imagine. For

---

8   Tyburn Tree was a wooden triangular structure which sat on three legs, which allowed over twenty criminals to be hanged at the same time. See Amanda Harvey Purse: *Victorian Lives Behind Victorian Crimes: It's a Hanging Job Now.*

9   When the creator noticed his mistake, it was too late and there is a myth that he threw himself into the Thames over it.

instance, the novelty of having two police forces.

Not many capital cities can boast that they have two police forces, very different in nature and values, with different regulations and protocols. However, London is indeed one of those cities and while the Metropolitan Police is perhaps the more recognised of the two forces, there is a younger police force which had its own 'Bobbies'[10] who have walked their beats within the square mile for one hundred and sixty four years.

You may think that the smaller, younger force - the City of London Police - has always stood within the shadows of its larger and more famous counterpart, the Metropolitan Police, but this book will hopefully show you that this was not always the case.

This book describes why we have the City of London Police force, how it evolved from its small beginnings to having an active involvement in probably the most curious and notorious unsolved case there has ever been, the crimes later known as the 'Jack the Ripper' murders.

On the morning of 30th September 1888, the City of London Police force went from being a close bystander in the world's famous serial murder case to actually having an active part with the death of one single woman, a woman that otherwise would have disappeared into history had it not been for the revolting manner of her death at the hands of an unknown fiend, who had possibly killed several times previously, but had seemed, in the public's view anyway, to get away with it under the very nose of the neighbouring Metropolitan Police force.

From then on, the two London police forces had to work together, but that had not always been the case. In fact, in the early years it was very taxing for both forces to work in close proximity to each other. These difficulties, some say, led to the reason why Jack the Ripper was able to kill twice in one night...

There is another, perhaps more important aim of this book, and

---

10 The word 'Bobbies' comes from Sir Robert Peel, the creator of the Metropolitan Police force. It is also from where we get the word 'Peelers'.

that is to bring the City of London Police officers who were involved in the investigation of that horrid and infamous crime more alive to you, the reader. For these men were more than just names in police reports turning yellow with age, more than names in inquest statements locked away in vaults, and more than names briefly mentioned in newspaper articles.

They were living, breathing men, who decided to have a career within a force that was meant to protect the capital's square mile, probably never thinking for one moment that they would be caught up in such a haunting and murderous crime.

To that end, the life stories of certain City of London Police officers forever entangled with Jack the Ripper are examined in these pages, from their births, their marriages and children, and finally to their own deaths.

Because there was only one of the generally accepted victims of Jack the Ripper killed within the boundary of the square mile, it is easy to imagine that the Metropolitan Police had nothing to do with the murder of Catherine Eddowes, the City of London victim. However, later in this book the author examines the life stories of two Metropolitan Police officers who will be forever linked with the death of Catherine Eddowes and the subsequent investigation for their own unique reasons.

PART ONE

THE HISTORY OF THE CITY OF LONDON POLICE

CHAPTER ONE

The Criminal Streets of London

'Jack the Ripper has killed again,
is there anything he can't do?'[1]

The City of London Police is sometimes seen to an outsider, to always be in the shadow of its much larger neighbour, but the truth of the matter is that the City Police has lived through its own quite substantial and illustrious history; so much so, that it is worth a moment of your time.

Early records show that the first form of the City of London Police was in the hands of its citizens in the form of a Watch or Ward Committee. These committees were run voluntarily, and were similar to the Special Constabulary which existed to help police our streets through Wartime. The words 'Watch and Ward' generally meant a day or night guard within the whole group of watchmen that guarded many of the companies in the City boundary.

At first, these watchmen guarded the City from attacks commencing outside the City walls.[2] These Roman walls had gates, seven in total,

---

1   Mary Kelly in *Dead Bodies Do Tell Tales – A Jack the Ripper Novel* by Amanda Harvey Purse.

2   Some parts of the City walls are still visible today, especially along the so called 'London Wall' near the Museum of London, where the medieval walls sit quite peacefully among the glass buildings of the modern era.

with names you might recognise: Aldersgate, Aldgate, Bishopsgate, Cripplegate, Ludgate, Moorgate and Newgate. These were at one point locked up at night, with those living within the city's boundary under a curfew, with a bell being rung from St Martin's Le Grand church to announce the closing of the gates and a bell rung from St Thomas of Acon church in Cheapside to announce their reopening in the morning.

The actual City, the middle area of the whole of London, had a strengthened walled area resembling a garrison or castle with its battlements and towers which stretched from the Tower of London all the way towards the Blackfriars area.[3] Like any walled castle, it also needed a ditch. This is where we get the name of the area Houndsditch, for it was common at one stage to throw the dead dogs from a local hunt into the ditch. This was soon paved over to allow more homes to be built for the ever-growing population.

Over the years, the duties of the watchmen changed, to protect properties and arrest any offenders breaking in. There is a truncheon held at the City of London Police museum[4] dated from 1737; painted in red and gold, it is the oldest truncheon held at the museum. This truncheon was paid for by the Company of Bakers for their own watchmen to use, and was designed in such a way that should it be used it would leave an imprint on the criminal, allowing the public and other watchmen to know where the criminal had been, and what he had been up to.

London has always been difficult to police, but in the 18th century things were made harder by the high population of people living and working within the area. The City, physically, was bursting at the seams with people. This led to an elevated crime level, bringing to attention many prominent criminals such as Mr Jonathan Wild,

---

3   Probably built between the 2nd and 3rd centuries. *London: The Illustrated History* by Ross, Cathy, and Clark, John, eds. (2008). London: Allen Lane.

4   The City of London Police Museum is now located in Guildhall Library. It is free to visit but a donation is always accepted.

possibly the most famous criminal of the era.

Mr Wild was so prominent that he was still being written about well into the 19th century, with the celebrated author Sir Arthur Conan Doyle having his Sherlock Holmes compare Professor Moriarty to Wild in his novel *The Valley of Fear*.[5]

Born in Wolverhampton around 1683, Jonathan Wild was the first born to a poor family. His first trip to London was in 1704 when he worked as servant, but he was quickly dismissed so returned to Wolverhampton, but would revisit London in 1708 and this time remain. What he did in those first two years after coming back to the Big Smoke is unknown, but in 1710 he was sent to Wood Street Counter[6] in the City of London for a debt he couldn't repay.

Sentenced to four years, he spent one year in 'the hole', an underground cell that was lacking in space, air and light, but because of his time spent there he met dishonourable jailers, who at first had Jonathan running odd jobs for them for which he got paid, and he managed to repay the debt for which he was originally imprisoned. However, working for the jailers he acquired 'the liberty of the gate', which meant he was released from prison at night to help catch other criminals. While out on one of these trips Wild met Mary Milliner, a woman of illicit and immoral earnings. This is where Jonathan started to learn the true depths that the criminal underworld of London could go.

He was released from prison in 1712 and went to live with Mary in Covent Garden.[7] While she became a 'madam' to many younger prostitutes, Wild started his own criminal career, beginning slowly at first but eventually moving into Cock Alley in Cripplegate, Charles Hitchen's area.[8] He began a huge rival unlawful empire, in which

---

5   Doyle, Sir Arthur Conan: *The Valley of Fear*. First published in Britain in the *Strand Magazine*, September 1914.

6   The Wood Street Counter or Compter was a small prison within the City. Originally built in 1555 as a debtor's prison, it also held people who were drunk and disorderly.

7   Jonathan Wild in *Encyclopaedia Britannica*, 11th edition.

8   Charles Hitchen was another criminal who ran protection rackets for brothels and had his own gang of pickpockets.

he got gangs of thieves to steal certain items, wait for them to be published as stolen and then he would appear to 'find' these same items, making himself a hero to the public. Wild was quite clever: as long as he was never actually holding the stolen goods, the police could never arrest him.

Wild then decided to work with Hitchen rather than against him, in order to obtain more money, more quickly. This partnership was short lived, however, as Wild did not like the way Hitchen was treating other people. Wild managed to save enough money to run a 'Lost Property Office' at the Old Bailey opposite Newgate Gaol, and this time Wild's actions changed: instead of him waiting to hear of something being stolen, the public were now coming to him asking for help getting their goods back, so he began to keep records. He would write which thief had stolen what item, and if the thief had enough criminal history behind him to be hanged should Wild need to cover his tracks.[9]

It was at this time that the Privy Council asked for Wild's help in controlling crime. The public also loved him because he managed to 'somehow' return stolen goods when the official form of police couldn't.

His criminal ways were eventually exposed by an enemy he had gained along the way, Sir William Thomson, who was one of the City's recorders, lawyer and politician, but more importantly, he was himself corrupt.

Thomson arrested Wild because the latter had helped a fellow criminal named Richard Johnson escape from custody. He was found guilty of corruption, and hanged on 24th May 1725. Wild's execution was a highly anticipated event and was watched by many, including a young man named Henry Fielding.

As well as being a popular and famous writer,[10] Henry Fielding should be mentioned here, as without him and his money, the birth

---

9   It is said that the term 'double cross' came from Wild's record books, for he would put a cross by a thief's name who had worked for him, and then another cross if the thief had enough previous criminal history to hang him should Wild choose to.

10   Henry Fielding's most well-known novel was *Tom Jones*.

of policing as we know it would possibly never have come about.

Born on 22nd April 1707 in Somerset, Fielding was known for his dry wit, similar to Jonathan Wild. He wrote many pamphlets to try to improve standards in prisons, and attempted to stop public hangings after being disgusted at the sight of Wild's death.[11]

It was Henry Fielding, his blind brother, John[12] and four other friends who in 1742 came up with the idea of paying a band of men to hand out punishment for crime. This band of men became known as the Bow Street Runners as they were based at No. 4 Bow Street in London.

The Bow Street Runners never patrolled the streets or had a uniform, but they went up and down the country issuing warrants and summonses to many criminals, using their wits alone. Although they were very skilful in what they accomplished, they were not accepted by a large number of the public as they thought the government was trying to control them. The Runners lasted until 1829 when the Metropolitan Police force was formed.

Henry Fielding died rather suddenly in Portugal in 1754 after he had travelled thinking that the warmer climate would help cure his gout and asthma. When Henry died, his brother took over as Chief Magistrate, taking more control and advising police patrols that were a little closer to what we know today. He even came up with the idea of giving horses to officers.[13]

---

11 *The History of Henry Fielding Vol. 2.* New Haven Yale University Press.

12 John Fielding was known as the 'Blind Beak of Bow Street'.

13 Gerald Newman: 'Bow Street Runners' – *Britain in the Hanoverian Age 1714-1837: An Encyclopaedia.* London: Taylor and Francis.

CHAPTER TWO

The Start of Policing
as We Know It

'Keep them peeled'[1]

London was forever growing, and some believed that with this a change was needed in the policing of the city. It was Robert Peel who was tasked with creating a new 'police force'.

Born on 5th February 1788 at Chamber Hall in Lancashire, Robert was the son of a textile manufacturer, also named Robert, who had made a name for himself as an industrialist and Member of Parliament. Robert Peel Jr was sent to the local grammar school in Bury, ending his education at Christ Church in Oxford, where he studied law, classics and mathematics. He was a part of the military service in the Manchester Regiment and then the Staffordshire Yeomanry Cavalry, following his father into politics as the MP for Cashel.

Peel prepared many fine speeches which made him well known, and he was considered one of the stars of the Conservative Party. He became Home Secretary in 1822 and it was at this time that he was asked, because of his military background, if he could transfer this

---

1   The first time this saying was used was in 1833 as a way to keep your eyes wide open or 'skinned' to look for something. Hendrickson, Robert: *The Facts on File of Encyclopedia of Word and Phrase Origins.*

knowledge to the policing of London.

He resigned as Home Secretary when George Canning was elected Prime Minister, as Canning favoured Catholic liberation while Peel was against it. When Canning died just four months later, Peel returned as Home Secretary under the new Prime Minister, the Duke of Wellington.[2]

Peel himself was elected Prime Minister twice.[3] His first term was from 1834 and lasted just one year, because he was intensely disliked by the young Queen Victoria. Being young and also new to her role as Queen, she was the only monarch to publicly dismiss the government. When Robert Peel was elected Prime Minister for the second time, the Queen decided to stay quiet.[4]

Peel quite openly said "the country has entirely outgrown its police intuitions", as he thought that the whole of London should be served under one police force. However, he was fearful that the City might not agree, so his first step was to order an investigation into the procedures of the police force that was already in existence. This was quite a shrewd idea, because it automatically highlighted everything that was wrong within the City force. So, armed with the findings of this investigation, he presented his Bill 'for the Improvement of the Police of the Metropolis' on 15th April 1829.

Another shrewd idea was to discount the area of the City of London within his Bill. This was because the City had recently changed its ruling and, with Peel probably knowing that he was not well liked in the House of Lords who governed the City, he sensed that the whole Bill might not be passed. However, an unexpected problem was that some saw the Bill as unclear in its aims and motives,[5] so after a period of revision the Bill was passed and the first Metropolitan

---

2 While working for the Duke of Wellington, Peel was known as the Conservatives' 'number two'.

3 Robert Peel was the first Prime Minister to sit to have his photograph taken, which today hangs in the National Portrait Gallery in London.

4 Stephens, H. Morse: *Sir Robert Peel, A Memorial Biography.*

5 One Member of Parliament even thought that the Bill was only for Night Watchmen rather than both Night and Day Watchmen.

Police officers walked their beats on 29th September 1829.

On 29th June 1890, Peel was riding on Constitution Hill when his horse threw him off and stumbled on top of him. He died three days later from the injuries sustained, at the age of 62.

Robert Peel was proud of his new 'Peelers' for obvious reasons, but despite all his planning he did not foresee the problem these brand new officers of the Met would bring to the City within a short space of time.

It was said that a few officers of the Met were taking advantage of the fact that the City was still manned by watchmen, and that they only guarded certain areas in certain hours. The Met officers were telling criminals to go over the boundary, into the City, in order to avoid arrest.

The City of London did not like change, and did not like the idea of being governed by one person. They thought this would open themselves up to corruption again. However, there were arguments from the few thousand who actually lived within the square mile that robberies and other crimes were taking place when the streets were not being patrolled.

Sir Matthew Wood listened to these people and in 1834 tried to pass his 'Bill for more effectively enforcing the due execution of the Office of Constable in the City of London and the Liberties', but the Court of Common Council brushed it to one side without much fuss. The same happened in the years 1835, 1836 and 1837, until in 1838 the Council themselves slightly changed the Bill in their favour. Although this was also discounted, it showed the way the City was thinking, that they did not under any circumstance want to be a part of the Metropolitan Police force.

Born on 2nd June 1768, Matthew Wood was the son of a serge maker from Exeter. He studied at Blundell's School before he had to leave in order to help with the family home, as by that time his mother Catherine had died and his father was ill. Matthew became an apprenticed chemist, first working with his cousin and then moving to London to set up his own business.

While in London, Matthew joined societies in order to increase his standing such as the Worshipful Company of Fishmongers, and he later became a member of the Court of Aldermen of the City of London. He married Maria Page and had six children.[6]

He became Lord Mayor of London in 1815,[7] holding the role for two years until he was made a Member of Parliament in June 1817,[8] keeping that seat until his death in 1843.

After a lot of debate and discussion Wood's Bill allowing the City of London to have their own police force was passed, which displeased the Court of Common Council who would lose some of their power within the City as a result.[9]

On 17th August 1839, the City of London Act was passed, which meant that any previous attempts to unite the Metropolitan and the City Police forces were now redundant,[10] but it wasn't until 11th November 1839 that Daniel Whittle Harvey was made the first ever Commissioner, and officially the City of London Police as we know it was born.[11]

Born on 10th January 1786, Daniel Whittle Harvey was schooled as a lawyer, becoming a Member of the Inner Temple in 1818. Although he studied hard and his grades were decent, he was refused entry to the Bar twice. He first ran for Parliament in 1812, unsuccessfully,[12]

---

6   One of his children was John-Page Wood (born 1796), who became a vicar for the Church of England in Essex. John-Page Wood's daughter Katherine, known as Kitty O'Shea, had a relationship with the Irish leader Charles Stewart Parnell which led to the downfall of his political career.

7   City of London Corporation: Lord Mayors of the City of London from 1189.

8   *London Gazette*, 11th June 1817.

9   In an act of childish revenge, the Court of Common Council did the one thing they still had power over. They cut the salary of whoever was going to be the first Commissioner of the City of London Police from £1,000 to £800 a year, an attempt to discourage anyone that wanted the job. This almost worked.

10 Although in 1863 the Metropolitan Police force came close to taking over jurisdiction of the City of London after the failure of the City Police to keep order as Princess Beatrice passed through the City.

11 London Metropolitan Archives records.

12 FWS Craig: *Britain Parliamentary Election Results 1832-1885*.

but ran again in 1820 and won the seat of Colchester.[13]

Harvey founded *The New Observer*, which quickly changed its name to *The Sunday Times*, in which he voiced his opinion of the state of affairs of the country or his opinion of certain people, whether they were famous or not. This attitude caused him a few problems, including being imprisoned for libel when the newspaper claimed King George IV to be mad.

When he became the first Commissioner of the City of London Police, Harvey also became Registrar of the Metropolitan Public Carriages, meaning he was chief watchdog of all cabs driving within the City of London.

One of the first cases the Commissioner had to deal with occurred on 16th December 1839, when one William Lees was being hanged for the murder of his wife. Harvey had to take on the traditional role of the City Marshall and commanded the convoy to the hanging scaffold.

In the early days of the force, uniforms changed relatively quickly. The murder of Constable Robert Culley during the Coldbath Fields Riot of May 1833 was still firmly in the public's minds, and it was thought that his uniform had a part to play in that he was probably not noticeable enough in the midst of the riots.[14]

There were often complaints made by constables over the cheapness of the uniforms; these men would probably not have complained at all, for a uniform and a wage was better than life without it in the Victorian era, but the bad weather[15] and very long hours endured by those on the beat often resulted in illness.[16]

---

13 In actual fact, after winning this seat the votes were proved to be worthless but he was re-elected six years later for the same seat.

14 When the Coldbath Fields Riots at which Constable Culley was killed occurred, the public still had doubts over the police force, believing them to be spies of the government. The verdict at Culley's inquest was unbelievably returned as 'justifiable homicide', with medals awarded to the jury and banquets held in celebration.

15 Constables were not allowed to carry an umbrella.

16 Within the police records held at both London Metropolitan Archives and the City of London Police Museum, it can often be seen that new recruits worked for a few months, possibly a year, before most visited the police surgeon, who signed them off for a month because of illness.

The truncheons often broke, the capes splintered and shredded with the bad weather and the seams ripped frequently. The situation improved when each officer was issued with a dark coat, which was good for keeping the constable warm on cold nights, with a truncheon pocket included. The coat bore the City's shield on the collar, and constables were also issued with two pairs of trousers, one cape, one hat,[17] a button brush (for the buttons had to be shining before the constable set out on his beat), a red-and-white striped armlet,[18] and two pairs of boots or a boot allowance.

A dark coat/blue coat with belt cost £15 6s 3d; trousers 9s 3d; a cape 5s 6d; a hat 12s and a pair of boots 12s 6d.[19]

The helmet given to constables was in the style of a fireman's helmet, and to distinguish between the Metropolitan and City forces the latter affixed their own coat of arms in black and gold, whereas the Met stuck to the Brunswick star of the Victorian crown. The helmet had a chinstrap that had to be worn at the point of the chin because this was meant to stop the helmet being pulled over the constable's head, which could cause injury or worse.

Whistles were not used at the time of Catherine Eddowes' murder, despite what is often seen in the many films and documentaries,[20] as the City of London Police did not employ whistles on regular use until a year later, in 1889. They did, however, use whistles during crowd disturbances. Acting Commissioner Henry Smith brought up the subject in 1889, possibly after looking at the Metropolitan Police force's use of whistles, when he commented: "Whether in favour of or against the proposition and referring to any instance in which whistles would, in their judgement, have proved more useful

---

17 Initially made from leather, which looked clean and presentable, but the heat held within them made them uncomfortable to wear. The hats were changed to Beaver crowns which coped better with the heat but looked unkempt and were easily broken. This resulted in a change back to leather ones with better ventilation and a hat cover.

18 Armlets were normally worn on the left wrist to show that the constable was on duty. A sergeant wore the armlet above the elbow, although this was changed to the right wrist later on.

19 City of London Police record, City of London Police Museum.

20 In fact, PC Edward Watkins ran to the nearest nightwatchman to raise the alarm.

in obtaining ready assistance in cases of need than the rattle now carried."[21]

After it was agreed that whistles were more useful than the wooden rattles which the City force had been using as the sound travelled further, constables were given instructions of how to carry them as a part of their uniform:

> Whistles, some of which have been issued today... are to be, when the great coat is not worn, affixed by the hook to the second button hole of the tunic from the top and the whistle itself passed in about the second button from the waist.[22]

Another item in the constable's armoury were handcuffs. These are still used today, but in the Victorian era the constables had many different styles available to them, although they mainly used two basic styles of handcuffs - the 'figure of eight' and the Darby cuffs. They were both made for the City of London Police force by Hiatt and Co., who were based in Birmingham.[23]

Both styles used a barrel lock that was unlocked by a heavy, durable key. The use of the 'figure of eight'[24] was mainly for the transferring of prisoners from station to station or court to court. A prisoner would be attached to one of the cuffs by the wrist, with the other end being controlled by the police officer. They were mainly used in this way because the officer could easily transport the prisoner around due to the sturdiness of the cuff. The Darby cuffs, however, where used mainly when the constable was out on his beat and needed to secure both of a prisoner's hands.

Bullseye lamps were next on the list. The name came from the magnified glass lens on the outer side of the lamp, allowing the light from the oil reservoir behind to shine through. On night beats, the smog-filled streets and lack of street lighting meant that a Bullseye

---

21 *City of London Police Station Number Six Order Book*, 21st May 1889.

22 *City of London Police Station Number Six Order Book*, 9th January 1890.

23 The City of London Police also used the same company for other metalwork such as pistols and occasionally helmet plates.

24 The 'figure of eight' handcuffs were also called 'come alongs' and sometimes in later years 'nippers'.

lamp was essential, but they did have their down side: as the lamp had metal handles on the back by which it could be clipped onto a belt,[25] allowing the constable to have both hands free, it must have weighed quite a lot as the constable was walking around on his beat. There was a flume to let the oil fumes out, which must have been horrible for the constable to breathe in. Lamps were filled with just enough oil to provide the constable with light for the duration of his beat, but if a constable fell short there was always spare oil stored at fixed points, to be used only if he was on a longer than normal beat.

With their close proximity to Bishopsgate Police Station, it has been suggested that T. Joyce of 43 Bishopsgate Without provided the Bullseye lamp for the City of London Police.[26]

Daniel Whittle Harvey then turned his attention to recruitment. By today's standards, we would be a little shocked that the Commissioner complained that "Men, dwarfs in height and old in years, of divers bodily deformity, mentally weak and with little or no character had no hesitation to apply."[27]

Constables were to be 40 years of age or under when they joined the force;[28] their height had to be five foot seven inches or more, they had to be able to read and write, and they had to be able to keep account of themselves and be physically well.

Harvey's idea was to increase the wages, which had earlier been reduced to match that of the Metropolitan Police, as he wanted to reward officers who worked hard, with the opportunity to cut wages as a form of punishment for those who did not work so diligently.

Constables' wages were broken down into five stages, the lowest stage being 17s 6d per week to the top stage of 22s 6d per week. This extra money more than likely went on renting a property within the City, for if a constable could not stay within a station or one of the

---

25 A leather strap was added behind the lamp in 1885 to stop oil stains on the constable's uniform and prevent him getting burned.

26 It was first suggested in Mervyn Mitton's *The Policeman's Lot*.

27 Harvey, Letter to Police Committee dated 24th April 1861 (City of London Police Museum).

28 This changed in 1861 to be under 32 years of age.

many police homes,[29] they had to reside within the City boundary to which they were bound by the terms and conditions of being a City of London Police constable.

Daniel Whittle Harvey liked to maintain control: for the first seven years he personally interviewed all the new recruits, a total of over three thousand men. He liked the idea of hiring people from the army as they would be used to the way he wanted to run the police force. He even travelled in public hansom cabs so that he could keep an eye on his men at work.

When new recruits started they were given a 'beat book' or card, which told each constable which area he had to walk his beat and the time in which he was given to complete this task. A constable was not, under any circumstances, allowed to talk to anyone that might make himself late on his beat. The idea behind this was to allow the station sergeants to know exactly where each policeman was at any given time.

While out on each individual beat the constables had to mainly look out for crimes being committed, but they also had other duties[30] such as the amount of rubbish in certain areas and whether it needed cleaning or not, make sure the pavements were as clean as they could be, push on any lurking hansom cabs or carts, and even check whether the glass of a gas lamp was cracked or not.[31] If a constable was seen talking to anyone he shouldn't be while on a beat, especially a woman, they were 'pressured' into behaving well otherwise a dismissal could be in order.

---

29 One of which was situated in Smithfield opposite St Bartholomew's Hospital, a place where one of the policemen involved in the Ripper investigation lived.

30 PC Edward Watkins' duties in Mitre Square included inspecting the coal hole of the building belonging to Heydemann and Co., on top of which he found the body of Catherine Eddowes.

31 It has been suggested that two of the street lamps within Mitre Square, the scene of Catherine Eddowes' murder, were not working that night.

CHAPTER THREE

Police Stations and Police Beats

'Goodnight Old Cock'[1]

In order to build their stations, the City of London Police had to approach the largest landowners within the City boundary. One of these was the governors of St Bartholomew's Hospital, who at first were reluctant to offer the former Greyhound public house opposite the hospital in Smithfield, but ultimately they leased this for 43 years to the Police Committee for an expensive sum of £140 a year.

In late 1839 this became the first ever City of London Police police station, but oddly it was named Station Number Two. Prisoners would suffer from the terrible cold conditions within the cells, especially those who had tried to commit suicide by jumping into the Thames, as they were placed in the cells still in their wet clothes.

In 1840, the City of London Police leased the area which became Moor Lane Police Station, otherwise known in the records as Station Number One. Building work started in the cold month of November and finished in June the following year.

Moor Lane Police Station could house a total of 40 policemen at any given time. It had five prisoner cells in the back yard, the gate of which was left open during the day. This allowed family members or

---

1 The last haunting words of Catherine Eddowes as she left Bishopsgate Police Station, recorded in PC George Hutt's inquest statement.

friends to walk into the yard and right up to the cells, passing food to the prisoners or more than often rum or gin.

Number Three Station was situated in the old watch house in Black Horse Court in Fleet Street. This station was so small and dark that candles had to be kept burning both day and night in the main charge room.

Station Number Four was sited at 62 Watling Street, until notice was given on the lease.

Number Five was at 91 Great Tower Street.[2] This station was not far from the Tower of London, and would house a few familiar names in the Ripper case, which will be mentioned in later chapters.

The final station, Number Six, was Bishopsgate. It stands today opposite Liverpool Street train station, at 182 Bishopsgate. As you walk past, you could easily think that it is quite a modern-looking police station, and you wouldn't be too wrong as it was in fact rebuilt in 1939. It was here that Catherine Eddowes was taken after she was arrested for being drunk the night before she died.

Bishopsgate Police Station had a history of its own long before Catherine Eddowes ever set foot inside. On 30th December 1865 the City of London Police force opened their own hospital, which was attached to the station, holding four wards with a few nurses and a matron who operated under the inspection of the divisional surgeon, at the cost of £3,750.[3] The building works of this new venture did not go unnoticed. A neighbour, Mr Chadwick, made a few 'complaints of notice' that stopped work for four whole months.[4] The money for building the hospital was donated by Dr George Borlase Childs (1814-1888), who was the City of London Police's own surgeon at the time.

Born in Liskeard, Cornwall, George Childs went to Liskeard Grammar School where he had his first taste of the world of medicine. His liking for this work carried on at Aldersgate School of Medicine in the City, when he also worked within Westminster

2 *Dickens' Dictionary of London 1888.*

3 The hospital was built by Messrs Myers and Sons using Portland Stone.

4 *London City Press,* 22nd December 1864.

Hospital. He later was appointed House Surgeon at the Margate Sea Bathing Infirmary before he had enough money to run his own practice in London.

Whilst a surgeon at the Metropolitan Free Hospital he worked on deformities of the foot, and was one of the first doctors to suggest dividing the muscles of the foot to help the curvature of the spine.

As well as being the Surgeon in Chief of the City of London Police, at the same time Childs was the Chief Surgeon for the Great Northern Railway and the City of London Militia, 4th Battalion of the Royal Fusiliers, and was also a medical officer for the Cape Mounted Rifles and a member of and President for the Militia Surgeons' Society.

He retired in 1886 after a fall from his horse left him deaf, living at 1 Aldridge Road Villas until he died on 8th November 1888. He is buried at Kensal Green Cemetery.[5] A portrait of Dr Childs is held at the City of London Police Museum for public viewing.

A hospital dedicated to the use of policemen was well-received. It was the first of its kind, for all City Policemen to use free of charge as an incentive to join. Patients known from the investigation into the murder of Catherine Eddowes include PC Edward Marriott, who was taken to Bishopsgate Hospital in 1908 after being injured by a horse and van, suffering concussion and a scuffed arm. He was discharged, but a year later, after being found unconscious by a beat constable, it was discovered that Marriott suffered from epileptic seizures which Dr Fredrick Gordon Brown, divisional surgeon at Bishopsgate Hospital, stated were "a consequence of his injury on the 19th November 1908."[6] Marriott was subsequently discharged from the force, after 23 years' service, on a pension of £74 4s 4d.[7]

---

5   *Copy of the General Report of G. Borlase Childs, on the Dress of the City Police Force*, 8vo, London, 1801; *Copy of a Report on the Probable Duration of Life of the Men in the City Police Force, with General Observations on the Medical History of the Force*, 8vo, London, 1863.

6   Brown, F.G.: City of London Police Medical Department Report on DC Edward Marriott, 1st April 1909.

7   Bell, Neil and Clack, Rob: 'Detective Constable Edward Marriott', *Ripperologist* magazine issue 115, July 2010.

Next to the hospital record book, which is on display at the City of London Police Museum, is a curious turquoise-blue uniform, which looks very plain and appears to be made of some kind of very itchy material.

This symbolises a form of punishment that is rarely spoken of, and which might seem harsh at first, but when compared to losing your job, an income and the benefits of being a City Policeman it is quite a modern way of thinking really. If a policeman was found drunk on duty or late on his beat times he could, if the person issuing the punishment thought highly of the officer in question, be told to dress in this blue uniform to indicate that he had done something wrong and they would have to make their way over to Bishopsgate Police Hospital and clean out the bed pans of the patients, who probably knew the punished policeman. Sometimes, the punishment would only last a few days or weeks for the embarrassment to take its desired effect, but there was one policeman that had to undertake bed pan duty for two months.

It is said that if you are on the 9th Floor of Bishopsgate Police Station at night today, you might meet a ghost of a nurse who worked within the hospital as she goes screaming down the long hall. The most interesting question about this is why is she screaming? What had happened? I am guessing, nothing particularly good.

The hospital was forward-thinking, as a similar idea, the NHS, wasn't created until 1947. In fact, before the NHS the police force was also the public's form of ambulance service. If you had an accident and needed hospital treatment, you could be picked up in a form of a rug and carried along by two policemen at either end of you and they would walk you all the way to the nearest hospital. Sometimes, if the police didn't grab you right or could not manage the weight, you could find yourself dropped to the pavement!

This form of ambulance service was used until 1907, when City Commissioner William Nott-Bower paid for the first electric ambulance at the cost of £15,000, which included crushed velvet seats and some walnut panelling. This enhanced your chances of surviving and getting to hospital without suffering further injury or bleeding to death on the way!

This was also the year that Nott-Bower saw another idea being used in other countries and changed it to fit the City of London's needs and to help the ambulance service - the telephone box. This is probably more famous now for being a certain Doctor's 'Tardis', but that was always in the Metropolitan Police colour of dark blue, which came a little later. The City of London Police telephone boxes were originally painted a light baby blue colour.

There are not many of these light blue telephone boxes left in the City, but if you look closely you might still see one, such as the box often missed by busy workers near the side entrance of Liverpool Street train station. There is another telephone box outside St Botolph without Aldgate and Holy Trinity Minories Church.

If you do happen to miss these two, there is always one sitting proudly within the City of London Police Museum, where guides are often asked by a visitors of a certain age whether they have 'the Doctor' inside.

These telephones boxes had three official uses, and one unofficial use. The first was for members of the public that had been a victim of, or a witness to, a crime to be able to telephone a police station directly. This helped the police get to the scene of the crime more quickly, as the public now didn't have to go all the way to the nearest police station or wait until they saw a policeman on his beat.

The second use was for officers on their beats. If the light above the telephone box was flashing, the officers knew there was a new order to be given out and they should contact the Call Room to get the information.

The third use was from 1907 to 1948, when the City Police Ambulance Service used the boxes to receive directions to someone in need, and this was also the main reason why these boxes stocked a first aid kit in them.

The unofficial use for these boxes was when officers on early duty would buy sausages and bacon from nearby Smithfield Market and come along on their first beat of the day and place their dinner in the base of the telephone box, where it could not be seen. The cast iron of which the box was made would act as a sort of fridge, so the food could be kept fresh all day long until the same officer finished his shift and, using the cape of his uniform to hide his arm, would bend down and scoop up the food and cycle off home!

There has always been a history of cats working as rat catchers for the City of London Police, probably the most famous being 'Big Chap'. You can see a photograph of this rather large cat at the City of London Police Museum. He certainly lives up to his name, as the man in the photograph holding the cat appears to be somewhat struggling with the weight of him. Big Chap was a lovely looking tabby who was either good at his job or good at looking cute, earning the treats given to him by the staff.[8] In October 2008, the last of the City of London Police cats retired from Snow Hill Police Station, bringing to an end a century-old tradition of cats working for the force. The cat, Reagan, was rehomed to the City of London Police force from Battersea Rescue Home in 1997 with a fellow feline called Carter, their names taken from the TV series, *The Sweeney*.

The fact that they were both deaf has led some to believe it heightened their other senses and made them excellent hunters. Carter sadly died after eighteen months, but Reagan carried on for nine and a half years before his retirement. All the officers at Snow Hill adored Reagan and on his retirement he received a certificate commemorating eleven years' service in the force. He lives out the remainder of his years in Essex with his own Facebook page.

From 1884, Cloak Lane Police Station was operated by the City of London Police, so that by 1888 the force had stations at Bishopsgate, Bridewell Place, Cloak Lane, Moor Lane, Snow Hill and Tower Street.

The main headquarters of the City of London Police was at 26 Old Jewry, previously a merchant's counting house. Here they remained until 2002, when the headquarters were moved to Wood Street, which came along much later than the other Victorian stations. Designed to look like a Italian palace, it was refurbished in the early 1960s and is classed as a Grade II listed building because during the

---

8   Big Chap weighed at his heaviest 21lb 7oz.

refurbishment they found a series of Roman walls, some of which you can see within the reception.[9] Until the 1990s, Wood Street also held the Wakefield Mess Bar on the third floor, mainly used by the reserves within the force, where they would have a cheap drink - when off duty of course.

As well as being the City of London Police's headquarters since 1842, 26 Old Jewry was also the Commissioner's official dwelling as the first Commissioner was not allowed to have an official residence outside of the City boundary.[10] It also housed some of the Detective Department at one time.

Each policeman's beat would be under the control of a Section Sergeant, who would come on duty an hour before changeover between shifts[11] in order to learn whether there were any special duties ordered from the Main Office. Each Section Sergeant would have around twelve constables to command. One of the roles of a Section Sergeant was walking each beat with a Beat Wheel,[12] a wooden implement that could be wheeled around the beat with a timepiece affixed, measuring how long it took to walk one point to another. This allowed the Section Sergeant to know where a certain constable would be at a certain time, and if the constable wasn't at said point it meant he had come off his beat, which was against the rules, with the constable liable for punishment. Each beat was roughly the same distance; the City of London Police governed a smaller area than its larger counterpart, meaning a City policeman had a shorter beat to walk than the Metropolitan policeman.

---

9   There is a rather large black-coloured looking bomb within the City of London Police Museum, 'looking' being the right word as it was never a live bomb. Some students from a local college thought it would be fun to make a fake bomb and place it within the building site while Wood Street was being refurbished. It stopped work for three days.

10 Although the next Commissioner, Sir James Fraser, was allowed to do just that.

11 Shift times were roughly 6:00am to 2:00pm, 2:00pm to 10:00pm and finally 10:00pm to 6:00am.

12 There is one such wheel within the City of London Police Museum for you to view.

Each beat was drawn in a 'beat book' which was handed to each constable and assigned a number, so that when he came on duty a constable was given a beat number.

Day Beats took normally around half an hour, and constables on this beat had a number of duties, including ensuring that goods displays were where they should be and not overflowing into the street, that stall holders held the correct license, and even to direct traffic.

Night Beats would last about fifteen minutes, with the intention that the more frequent appearance of a constable on his beat would act as a deterrent to criminals.

An Act of Parliament passed on 23rd April 1887 allowed public houses in the City to open at five in the morning and to close at half past twelve the next morning - meaning the public houses were shut for only five and half hours - resulting in night police officers often having to handle members of the public who were drunk. Most were asked politely to move on and they would go, but if the drunken person was incapable of looking after themselves or causing a nuisance, a constable could arrest the said person and they would be taken to a police station. This happened to Catherine Eddowes the night before she died; on being released from the station she was given a warning rather than the other option - being charged and summoned to attend a court hearing at a later date.

The City of London Police Orders and Regulations Book stated that a constable should 'make himself perfectly acquainted with all parts of his beat with the street, thoroughfares, courts and houses within it'.[13] He was expected to get to know everyone on the beat, and everyone should know him.

The beats rota meant that each constable would spend four months on Day Beats and eight months of Night Beats in a year.

The Section Sergeant would walk all constables to the start of their beats, all together. Once the group arrived at the starting point of a each beat, that constable would drop away from the group, and the

---

13 *The City of London Police Orders and Regulations Book 1839-1894.*

constable who had been doing that beat on the previous shift would join the group to be eventually walked back to the station. Once back at the station the constables would then be checked again, in part to confirm they had not been drinking on the job. This would also be when constables would inform the Section Sergeant of anything that needed reporting, such as unlocked factories, unlocked coalholes and non-working gas lamps. The Section Sergeant would then pass this information on to the appropriate people, such as the Board of Works.

The Section Sergeant would also do unexpected checks on the constables, visiting them occasionally while they were walking their beat to check whether they were hitting points within their beats on time, if they had had a drink or doing anything else they shouldn't be. This did not always go down well with the constables.

Once the beat constables had passed the checks and given over their information to the Section Sergeant, they were then signed off the beat. It was normally at this time that the constables chose to sort out any problems with their uniform, whether it was to mend them, wash them or ask for replacements. They would also refill the oil in their lamps.

The City of London Police was all too aware that criminals were watching the beat constables and recording when they arrived at certain points on their beat. In fact, there is a theory that Jack the Ripper watched the police beats, allowing him to escape, often with only a few minutes to spare.[14] To combat this, the City Police allowed the beat constable to occasionally reverse their beat, although for short periods only, to stop criminals learning the new beat.

Constables were meant to arrive at their appointed stations about fifteen minutes before they were due to set off on their beats, allowing the Section Sergeant to check on them before sending them

14 In the case of the murder of Catherine Eddowes, the gap between the beats of PC James Harvey and PC Edward Watkins as they entered Mitre Square was at the most four minutes.

15 Some constables failed this from time to time. PC Louis Robinson, the constable who brought Catherine Eddowes to Bishopsgate Police Station the night before she died, was indeed one of these.

out. They should be sober, and clean, presentable[15] with a uniform to match. After passing this parade, constables were given any special duties which may have arisen on earlier shifts.

Police officers were meant to live within the City because if they were needed they were meant to be at hand quickly. To assist with this, the City of London Police eventually bought premises at Bishopsgate, New Street and Rose Alley for constables to live in, although at the time they were purchased the buildings were dilapidated.

These became known as City Police Dwellings Blocks A, B and C, with the luxury of a toilet, kitchen and a wash bath in each flat. Officers were for the first time charged rent for these homes, whereas previously they would live within police stations if unmarried or police homes for those with a family. There were police homes in Huggin Lane and St Anne's in Blackfriars, for example, places that were classed as slums.

CHAPTER FOUR

Other Crimes in Which The City of London Police Were Involved

'I can understand why you would think that, after all Jack the Ripper has made this area famous hasn't he? However he is not the only criminal around here'[1]

It is somewhat easy to think of Jack the Ripper as the only criminal within the Victorian era. Although this killer is certainly famous, he or she was not the only criminal of the time, and the murder of Catherine Eddowes was not the only crime the City of London Police had to deal with.

Below are a few examples.

In 1846, a murder occurred in a coffee house situated at 23 King Street, Cheapside. Over the years, the building had been a number of different workplaces reaching back to when it was first built in 1685, but from 1838 it was the Guildhall Tavern and coffee house, run by a Mr James Walters. Although it enjoyed a good reputation, as with all coffee houses at that time it was susceptible to pickpockets.

1   PC Teddy Collard to Amelia Christie in *The Strange Case of Caroline Maxwell* by Amanda Harvey Purse.

John Vincent Smith worked as a cook at this coffee house, and on 15th August 1846 he was preparing a duck, while Susan Tolloday, his wife's niece who worked as the kitchenmaid, was cutting beans. They started arguing, and when another maid came back from the larder Susan was in a panic, as blood flowed from her neck. A William Carr saw Susan running around holding her throat and screaming, but there was nothing he could do for her and Susan soon died.

Inspector Woodruffe was called in to investigate, and when he and fellow City Police officers arrived at the scene of the crime they found the murder weapon, a large knife which had been left at the scene.

John Smith was taken to Bow Lane Police Station where he confessed, claiming 'she drove me to it'. In court Smith said nothing when asked questions, and after hearing from all the witnesses the coroner returned the verdict of wilful murder against John Smith. This was quite an odd case for Inspector Woodruffe and his men, as normally when they were called to a coffee house it was for pickpocketing, not murder.[2]

Haymarket, near Regent Street, was a hive of activity in the late 1880s, being a popular haunt for ladies of the night. It was also a sordid place where the abduction of children into the prostitution trade was rife, and it had been for quite some time.

In 1858, for example, Heloise Thaubin was a young prostitute living at Arundel Court, near Haymarket. She had gone to bed at two o'clock in the morning, but when her commission agent, or 'minder', knocked at her door later that same morning there was no answer. He left, thinking she was already out walking. When he hadn't seen Heloise all that day he returned to her door and opened it, finding her lying on her bed, not moving. She was lying on her chest with her hands behind her back, with blood coming out of her mouth. When the doctor was called he said she had been badly strangled, as

2   Old Bailey records (t18460817-1582a).

the tongue was protruding.

Sergeant Joseph Huggett of the City Police was called in, and investigated the main suspect, a man who could not speak English. The man, who Huggett later discovered was Italian, was in his twenties with a flat face, short hair and no facial hair. This man had been seen leaving Arundel Court at seven o'clock, dressed in a loose coat and hat, his face bright red. It was quickly discovered that this man lived in Finsbury Square, where there were more witnesses stating the suspect was named Giovanni Lani, and that he had returned to his lodgings with scratches across his face.

He was discovered hiding on the *Pride of the Thames* at Greenhithe, with Sergeant Huggett and Inspector Park discovering several incriminating items including a bloodstained shirt. At the Old Bailey he was found guilty of Heloise Thaubin's murder and hanged on 26th April 1858.[3]

Cannon Street, in 1866 was, as it is today, set in the centre of the beating heart that is the City of London. It is the street which links St Paul's Cathedral to the famous Roman London Stone that still stands for any visitor to see today. The warehouse owned by leather merchants Messrs Bevington stood at 2 Cannon Street, close to Cannon Street Railway Station which had opened four months after a murder. Sarah Milson, the victim of the crime, was a 40-year-old widow living at Bevingtons' warehouse with her cook, Elizabeth Lowes.

On the night of 12th April, Elizabeth Lowes heard the sound of the doorbell, which Sarah went downstairs to answer. When she had not returned after thirty minutes, Elizabeth went downstairs to check that everything was fine. She found Sarah lying on the hallway floor, her face severely bloodied.

City PC James Stevenson, walking his beat, happened to be passing and was called by the distressed Mrs Lowes. Confirming that Mrs

3   Old Bailey records (t18580405-429).

Milson was dead, he fetched a local doctor named Dr May, who examined the body and found several extensive wounds to the head and face, including one which had fractured Mrs Milson's skull, and seven knife wounds made by a long, sharp knife.

With a little detective work the City Police discovered that the victim had a history of borrowing money. This time, however, it seemed as if Sarah had fallen short of paying the money back.

The police found some letters of Mrs Milson's within her items which discussed a man named George Terry. This man was easily tracked to St Olave's workhouse, where he explained that he was working on behalf of a woman named Mrs Webber, who had been the original money lender to Sarah, but there was a problem - George Terry could not write, so he asked an acquaintance, a Mr William Denton who also went by the name of William Smith, to write a letter to the victim for him. Smith was traced to Eton, and was arrested and taken to Bow Lane Police Station. He repeated the same story to the police: that Sarah Milson was in debt to George Terry, a drinking friend of Mr Smith, and it was while drinking that Terry asked Smith to write a threatening letter.

Smith claimed he was playing cards in Windsor with a man named Harris at the time of the murder. Although this alibi appeared flimsy, the police had to go with it until they were able to come up with two witnesses - a servant and a widower who lived in the property next to the scene of the crime - who identified Smith as the man they had seen in Cannon Street at the time of the murder.

Smith was committed to trial at the Old Bailey, but found not guilty because a Mr Harris confirmed Smith's story that he was playing cards with him on the night of the murder. Smith's last words to the court were that he was 'innocent as the babe unborn'.

Three years later, a Mr William Hale was charged with the murder of a man at Highgate. While being questioned by City Police Detective Potts, Hale said he had killed the man, and also the woman in Cannon Street. Although the detective wanted to reopen the Cannon Street case, Hale was classed as having an unfit mind and the case was not revived.

The Milson murder remained unsolved until eight years later, when Eliza Cross overheard her uncle Edmund Pope talking in his sleep, stating his was the murderer of the woman in Cannon Street. Although her family begged Eliza not to go to the police, on 4th December 1874 she felt she had to after receiving a letter from her uncle demanding money, so Metropolitan Police detective George Clarke travelled the twelve miles east from where the murder happened, to Erith in Kent.

When Clarke arrived, Eliza told him that the letter had come from Ashford. Clarke travelled to Ashford and asked the local postmaster for an actual address for Edmund Pope. The postmaster remembered the letter, but could not remember who sent it, or an address. Clarke did not give up hope, for Eliza had also told him that she had another uncle living in Folkestone, and Edmund could be living there. Clarke travelled further into Kent to the little seaside town of Folkestone, where he found not only John Pope, the other uncle, but discovered that his wife Martha was the sister of Elizabeth Lowes, the cook at the Cannon Street warehouse, and that John and Martha's son was Richard Pope, a policeman working in E Division within the Metropolitan Police Force.

On contacting PC Richard Pope, Clarke discovered there was another uncle in the family, an Edward Pope, who lived in Newchurch, Romney Marsh. Clarke arrived on 10th December, only to learn that Edward had died. The officer finally found Edmund Pope working on a farm in Ivy Church, but Pope offered an alibi which brought to an end Clarke's investigation. There was not enough evidence to apprehend Edmund Pope, but Clarke did tell his superior, Superintendent Williamson, who told Clarke to pass the information he had collected to the City of London Police. This he did, but the City force amazingly thought the case too old to continue with, and without a confession from Edmund Pope there was nothing they could do.[4]

4   Old Bailey records (t18660611-534). Case also mentioned in *The Escape Artist: The Criminal of the Imperial Times Newspaper* (The Victorian Detective Adventures of Amelia Christie Book 1) and within The City Crimes series of articles for *The Whitechapel Society Journal* August 2016, both by Amanda Harvey Purse.

1888 was a year which started like any other for the City of London Police, with nothing hinting at events to come.

On 9th January alone, five City officers appeared at the Old Bailey. PC Riddon, collar number 780, was called to give evidence in the case of Arthur Mills, who had obtained £10 by false pretences from William Wiseman. Mr Mills was found not guilty.[5] PC 389 John Bowey gave evidence in the trial of Robert Overland, who was accused of stealing tinned lobster from the warehouse of George Sanderson,[6] and PCs Daniel Packer, George Steves and Robert Bowton, along with Sergeant Edgar Welham, who had all appeared having arrested various criminals on a charge of coining.[7]

These were relatively common crimes, and 1888 would continue in the much the same vein. But in late September, the City of London Police were suddenly thrust into the hunt for the Whitechapel murderer when a 45-year-old woman was released from Bishopsgate Police Station, having been brought in drunk the evening before.

---

5   Old Bailey records (t18880109-173).
6   Old Bailey records (t18880109-174).
7   Old Bailey records (t18880109-182).

PART TWO

THE INVOLVEMENT OF THE CITY OF LONDON POLICE FORCE IN THE JACK THE RIPPER CASE

CHAPTER FIVE

History of Mitre Square and Golden Lane Mortuary

'Ripper's Corner'[1]

Mitre Square was where Catherine Eddowes was murdered on the morning of 30th September 1888, her death bringing the City of London Police into the investigation of crimes by the killer known to history as 'Jack the Ripper' - but only just.

Mitre Square is situated very close to the City of London boundary; in fact, if you were to walk from Mitre Square along Aldgate High Street today, within moments you would be faced with a cast iron statue of a dragon holding a shield which bears the coat of arms of the City of London, a marker indicating that you are entering or leaving the City of London boundary.

The area on which Mitre Square is situated was for many years occupied by the Holy Trinity Priory. Founded in 1107 or 1108 on the orders of Queen Matilda, wife of King Henry I, the Priory was known as 'the richest of London's Monastic House' at the time,[2] and continued to be so until the Dissolution of February 1532.[3] The Priory was situated along the City Wall, leading up to the gate of

---

1 The name by which modern researchers know the spot where Catherine Eddowes's body was found.

2 VCH1909 pgs. 464–475: 'Priory History' by Miss M Reddon.

Aldgate. The City Wall was at this time where Bevis Marks runs into Duke's Place today, the site of the gate being at the bottom of Duke's Place.

After the death of Queen Matilda in 1118, King Henry I sanctioned an enclosed lane from the City Wall to the Priory's buildings which became the basis for Duke's Place. He also granted them the Soke of the Cnihtengild Portsoken Ward in 1125, which meant that the Priory had control of the churches of St Botolph's Aldgate and All Hallows (St Gabriel in Fenchurch).[4]

In Saxon times, Aldgate was probably the gate mentioned as the 'East Gate' in the Anglo-Saxon Chronicle of 1052.[5] On one side of this gate was the church of St Botolph's Aldgate, with the Priory on the other. The first mention of the church came when it was received by the Priory in 1125.[6]

There was a fire in 1132 that engulfed most of the City, and in this particular area a part of the Priory and Gilbert's House opposite were burned.[7]

The Priory became noted for its popularity with royalty with the burial of two of King Stephen's children - middle son Baldwin and second daughter Matilda - prior to 1147.[8]

The connection with royalty continued with the baptism in 1155 of Henry, son of King Henry II and Eleanor of Aquitaine, followed the next year by the baptism of their daughter Matilda.[9]

Indicating how important the Priory also was to the City, Henry FitzAilwin, the first Mayor of London, was buried by the entrance to the Chapter House of the Priory in 1212, and four years later

---

3   On 11th February 1532 King Henry VIII decided to go against Rome and the Pope, and come up with his own religion. In doing so he dissolved many of the churches, monasteries and priories, claiming their possessions. This became known as the Dissolution of 1532.

4   *Cartulary xiv–xv Number 113*, held at Glasgow University Library.

5   Garmonsway 1954, pg. 181.

6   *Cartulary Number 871*.

7   *Cartulary Number 13*.

8   *Cartulary Number 14*.

9   Ibid.

Geoffrey de Mandeville, an English peer and the second Earl of Essex, was also buried in the Priory.[10]

The importance of the Priory continued into the 14th century, when the Papal Inquisitors, investigating charges against the Templars, visited the Priory and used it for meetings.

In 1349, tenements were added to the area, along Aldgate Street to the south and to the Priory in the north. This area included the gate to the churchyard of St Katherine Cree, which although situated in the churchyard of the Priory, was unconnected.[11] St Katherine Cree didn't claim rights to the Priory following the Dissolution by Henry VIII, meaning there was no parish for the area. This is why St James Duke's Place church was built in 1622, situated where the playground of Sir John Cass School is today.

After the Dissolution, Henry VIII gave the area to Thomas Audley, the Lord Chancellor, who rebuilt the Priory as his home before his death in 1544. The residence was then passed down to his eldest daughter, Margaret, and her husband, the Duke of Norfolk, hence the name 'Duke's Place', and it became known for its parties, one of which Queen Elizabeth I was invited to. The Duke was later executed for his involvement in the plots to put Mary, Queen of Scots on the throne of England.[12]

The area was recorded in Wyngaerde's "Panorama of London in 1543", which shows what remained of the Priory Church, including poles with traitor's heads on top nearby.[13]

The important Ogilby and Morgan's map of 1676[14] shows Mitre Square, although not yet so named, beginning to take the shape known in 1888. Duke's Place can clearly be seen, and the gap or passageway which would become Church Passage is now in place. This map also shows the introduction of the name 'Mitre' to the area, showing as it does the Mitre Tavern.

10 *Rot Hund*, I, 407,412, 418.
11 Cal Husting Wills I, 594, ii, 88, Schofield 1994, pg. 108-109.
12 Stow 1603, L, pg. 142.
13 Held at the Ashmolean Museum in Oxford.
14 Held at the Guildhall Library.

The Mitre Tavern plays a part in the myth of Mitre Square, according to *The Curse Upon Mitre Square AD 1530-1888* by John Francis Brewer. This fanciful story, written within a month of the murder of Catherine Eddowes, tells of a mad monk named Brother Martin, who had killed at the altar of the Holy Trinity Priory on the very spot where Catherine would later meet her end. Brewer writes of a legend that anyone standing at this spot at a certain time would receive a mortal visit from the spirit of Brother Martin. At the Mitre Tavern, a group of men joking about the legend decided to see if it was true, so at the end of the evening persuaded the barmaid to stand on the spot within Mitre Square. The group go to see if she actually went; the weather changes and lightning hits the ground, the group are unable to move away from the spot and the ghost strikes.

The site of the Mitre Tavern is today occupied by the Sir John Cass School, but this was not the first Sir John Cass School within this area. In 1710 the first school was built next to the church of St Botolph's Aldgate, founded by and named after Sir John Cass, an alderman of the City. When Sir John died in 1718, an oversight in his Will resulted in the School not receiving any money and it had to close. This was rectified thirty years later, and the Sir John Cass School reopened in 1748.[15]

There is a statue of Sir John in the Guildhall Art Gallery, sculpted in 1751 by Louis-François Roubiliac. There is also a watercolour of the school on its first site held at the Guildhall Library, painted in 1812 by R. Schebbelie, which shows how close it was situated to the church of St Botolph's Aldgate.

The elementary part of the school, the part we see within Mitre Square today, was built in 1908.

A fire in Mitre Court in November 1800 saw four properties at the junction of Mitre Court and Aldgate High Street engulfed in flames. Their destruction brought about the formation of a new street, as there was now a gap along what was Aldgate High Street (now part

15 Harben 1918, pg. 533.

of Leadenhall Street), and Mitre Street was born.[16]

A watercolour of St James Duke's Place church painted by J. Coney in 1812, held at the Guildhall Library, shows us not only what the church looked like but, because of its position (where the Sir John Cass School is today), the painting shows one corner of what would become Mitre Square, some seventy years before Catherine Eddowes would walk past the same spot, her body being found just off the painting to the right.

St James Duke's Place church became famous as couples could get married there without needing a marriage license, until the Act of Parliament in 1753 put a stop to this.[17]

Another map of the area, drawn by R. Schebbelie in 1825,[18] introduces familiar landmarks. St James Duke's Place church is still there, and the passage which PC Harvey would walk down to reach Mitre Square in 1888 is now actually mentioned as a 'passage', and the Great Synagogue on Duke's Place is also included. Mitre Street is on this map, as are King's Street and Heneage Lane.

One of the major questions surrounding the Eddowes murder is how the killer escaped Mitre Square, given the short space of time between the beats of PCs Watkins and Harvey. One suggestion is that he escaped through the sewers, and it is interesting to note that in 1953, while working on the sewers between Nos. 32 and 38 Duke's Place, workmen found a passage on the south side which led away from the Synagogue at an angle. Within this passage was pottery from the 16th and 17th centuries, indicating that this passage existed long before 1888.[19]

Looking at maps, this passage ran almost underneath Church Passage, which PC Harvey walked down from Duke's Place to Mitre Square, towards what is today Creechurch Lane. Did Jack the Ripper escape Mitre Square underground?

---

16 A plan of the fire damage can be seen in London Metropolitan Archives. CLRO, Comptroller's City Land Plans 540A.

17 Wheatley and Cunningham, 1891, pg. 532.

18 Held at the Museum of London.

19 Recorded by Noel Hume and held at the Guildhall Museum. 1953.

A painting of Heneage Lane by F. Sheppard in 1874 shows a number of houses with many windows and doors,[20] which you can easily imagine being checked by PC Edward Watkins as he walked his beat in 1888, and a 1884 watercolour by John Crowther gives a view of St James's Place and Sugar Baker's Yard looking north, which really gives us a good idea of what the streets would have been like for the policemen walking them. With narrow lanes and high roofed buildings, it must have seemed very dark during the day, let alone at night.[21]

In 1888 Mitre Square was fully formed and we are quite lucky that there are a number of maps we can use to aid us in a detailed description of the area, these being the Ordnance Survey maps of 1873, 1894 and 1913, a Goad's Fire Insurance Map made in January 1887,[22] and of course surveyor Frederick Foster's map which was completed in the aftermath of Catherine Eddowes' murder.[23]

Using these maps, we can see that the square was 22.5 metres by 21.33 metres. It had three entrances: Mitre Street, from which PC Watkins entered on his beat, was 7.62 metres in width; Mitre Passage, a small alleyway just big enough to push a small cart through as many stallholders presumably once did on their way to St James' Place, known as the 'Orange Market';[24] and finally Church Passage, named because of the close proximity of St James Duke Place alongside. This would have still been a small alley in 1888, being just 1.52 metres wide meaning it would have taken PC Harvey a matter of moments to walk towards Mitre Square and back again.

A photograph taken by William Whiffin[25] in 1925 shows how

---

20 Held at the London Metropolitan Archives, SC/P2/CT/01/103.

21 Held at the Guildhall Library.

22 Held at the British Library.

23 Held at the London Hospital Museum.

24 By 1888, two bollards were placed at the entrance to Mitre Square from Mitre Passage, stopping carts being pushed through this way.

25 William Thomas Whiffin was a highly-respected pioneer of London street photography. He was born in Poplar in 1878 and took over his father's photography business when the latter died. William Whiffin himself died in Poplar Hospital on 13th November 1957. An exhibition of his work was staged at the Tower Hamlets Local History Library and Archives in 2015.

dark and gloomy Mitre Square still was, even 37 years after the Whitechapel murders. The photograph, taken from the end of Church Passage, shows a horse and cart in the foreground, with what appears to be a set of removable steps leading into what would have been Horner and Sons warehouse. This is interesting, because while preparing his map of the square following Catherine's murder Frederick Foster suggested that there was a set of steps in the same position - could these have obscured the view of PC Harvey as he walked towards Mitre Square, stopping him from witnessing the murderer at work?

The big letters of "Kearley & Tonge" on their warehouse are prominent in Whiffin's photograph. Most of these Victorian warehouses were demolished in the 1970s and 80s, allowing more light into the square.

Church Passage was renamed St James Passage in 1939 and significantly widened around 1974.[26]

In more recent years Mitre Square has undergone a complete redevelopment, with new offices being constructed at the time of writing. With a footprint of some 279,000 sq ft, the offices comprise two lower ground floors, a ground level and 16 upper floors.[27]

Walking about this part of the City today, you would be hard pushed to spot any building or structure that was there in 1888 and would have been seen by the City of London policemen. However, parts of the history still remain. The Hoop and Grapes public house on Aldgate High Street still serves City workers and tourists alike, as does the Still and Star on Little Somerset Street. Survivors from the 1880s, these hostelries are possible candidates for the location where Catherine Eddowes became so intoxicated that she had to be locked up at Bishopsgate Police Station.

---

26 See the Jack the Ripper Wiki at wiki.casebook.org/index.php/Church_Passage.

27 www.cityoflondon.gov.uk/services/environment-and-planning/building-control/ our-projects/mitre-square.

The History of Golden Lane Mortuary and Surrounding Area

'A Palace for the dead...'[28]

The City's mortuary along Golden Lane was another important location in the City force's Jack the Ripper case, for this was where Catherine Eddowes was taken from Mitre Square. It is also the place in which she was identified, because until her partner John Kelly was taken to Golden Lane Mortuary by Sergeant Miles to view the body she was an unknown victim. So let's learn a little more about the area to which Catherine was transported to after her death.

Close to the Barbican area within the City of London, Golden Lane runs north-south, with Whitecross Street running parallel to the east.

In the early 1500s, Whitecross Street and the surrounding area was considered 'rotten' compared to other parts of the City of London, with all that was believed by some to be bad in the world at that time - breweries, alternative religious centres and unlawful trading markets - grouped together within this area of London.

Long before the Coroner's courtroom and mortuary was built in 1871, the site on Golden Lane was occupied by Loyd's Brewhouse from 1747, this being taken over by the Genuine Beer Brewery in 1804.

A painting of the Genuine Beer Brewery by the artist and engraver J.S. Barth in 1807 shows how busy Golden Lane was at that time, with many carts and horses lining the street. The brewery certainly stands out in the painting, which shows it to be a creamy white while the rest of the buildings along Golden Lane were a dirty brown.[29]

A map made by Horwood in 1813 shows the Genuine Brewery quite clearly, as well as nearby Beech Street and Red Lion. Ironically, the area which would become the mortuary, where souls of the City

---

28 Golden Lane Mortuary described in *The Times*, 27th October 1869 and *The City Press*, 1st October 1870.

29 Held at the Guildhall Library.

were placed in the late Victorian period, is called Angel Court on this map.

The Genuine Beer Brewery was demolished in 1824 under a private Act of Parliament,[30] and the development of the new City Bunhill burial ground began, finally opening in 1833.

The surrounding area of Golden Lane was heavily populated at this time by the Irish, as mentioned by a Mr Stone, the then keeper of the new burial ground, in an article in *The Times* of 16th August 1836. This was followed by writings by John Garwood, who stated that 'in addition one quarter of the Irish immigrants came from the province of Connaught and Golden Lane was the Chief Connaught Colony'.[31]

Between October 1833 and its closure on 14th August 1853, 18,036 people were buried at the City Bunhill burial ground,[32] mostly on a Sunday between 2.00 and 4.30pm. However, because of the large number of burials in such a small space, a special order was issued to the managers by the General Board of Health on 14th September 1849 stating there should be no more burials until the place had been inspected.[33]

This inspection took place a month later on 15th October.[34] One of those in attendance was Doctor of Medicine Gavin Milroy, whose opinion that the burial ground was "in such a state as to be dangerous to the health of the persons living in the neighbourhood thereof" appeared in the *London Gazette* the following day. The outcome was a series of regulations issued to the managers by the General Board of Health.

Firstly, the whole area apart from the footpaths had to be covered in quicklime. Secondly, there had to be just one body per grave, instead of the existing practice of building up the ground, burying

30 7GEOIV CAP32.

31 *The Million-peopled City:* John Garwood, 1853, pg.304.

32 TNA: PRO, RG8/35-38.

33 *Bulletins and other state intelligence*: Watts, 1850, pg.763.

34 *London Gazette*, 16th October 1849.

a number of people in the same grave. There also had to be a space of two feet and six inches between graves, and nobody was to be buried in a vault or catacomb without the coffin being first lined with six pounds of lead.[35]

Although these measures were adhered to, the City Bunhill burial was closed four years later.[36]

The unscrupulous reputation of the area surrounding Golden Lane was now quite firmly established, and in 1851 Henry Mayhew would visit the area and describe it as 'a bad, ruffianly, thievish place'.[37]

A painting by an unknown artist held at the Guildhall Library shows the Crown and Coopers' Arms on Golden Lane in 1869. In this watercolour, we can see that Golden Lane was lined with tall buildings, which had two residential levels above shops at street level.[38]

Social commentator James Greenwood visited Golden Lane a few years later, his 1874 book *In Strange Company* deploring the state of the area:

> Its thieves are the most desperate and daring in the world... it is the slummiest of slums.

> Terrible stories are still whispered about the worst of these Golden Lane lodging houses, of which there are seven that, in the aggregate 'make up' about five hundred beds every night...

> At the Golden Lane establishments, a lodger is *privileged* to go to bed as dirty as he likes.[39]

The City of London Mortuary and Coroner's Court Room stood on the southern section of the New Bunhill burial ground from 1871 until May 1941. In 1869 the Corporation of the City of London had awarded a budget of £13,000 to have a mortuary built with a postmortem room, a room for disinfecting and a station for

---

35 *Bulletins and other state intelligence*: Watts, 1850.

36 Order of Council, 25th November 1853.

37 *London Labour and London Poor*: Henry Mayhew, 1851, pg.237.

38 Held at Guildhall Library, catalogue number q476975x.

39 *In Strange Company*: James Greenwood, 1874.

ambulances.[40]

This was a princely sum for the time, but a complaint over the amount awarded stated that the new mortuary would be a 'palace for the dead' saw the budget reduced, so that, when the Coroner's Court was added to the mortuary in 1877, the total cost was £12,000.[41] The Coroner's Court dealt with inquests into those deaths within the City boundaries, while the mortuary received not only bodies found within the area but also those found in the Thames.[42]

The Cupid's Court burial ground, which was situated north-west of what was the New City Bunhill burial ground along Golden Lane, was turned into offices in 1896 after the bodies had been removed to Brookwood Cemetery in Surrey,[43] and today it is completely covered over by the Golden Lane Estate.

There was also a burial ground known as Thomas's burying ground, which was adjacent to the Cripplegate Poor ground,[44] north of the City mortuary. By 1896 these burial grounds had been built on with a large shoe factory,[45] which in turn was later demolished. Today, the area is a large open space surrounded by the Victorian Peabody Estate, which itself was built in 1883.

An official report on the Golden Lane mortuary in 1898 described it as 'a large well lighted and ventilated chapel or mortuary chamber containing slabs on which the coffins rest. A post mortem room was suitably fitted up. There is a store-room, in which is kept a hand ambulance for conveying bodies to the mortuary'.[46]

---

40 *The Times*, 27th October 1869; *The City Press*, 1st October 1870; and *The British Medical Journal* II, 1875. These ambulances were not what we think of today, but were coffin-sized caskets which were carried by two policemen, one at either end.

41 *Bodies of Evidence*: Burney, pg.87.

42 *The City Bunhill burial ground, Golden Lane*: MOL Archaeology Studies Series 21, 2006.

43 *The London Burial Grounds*: Holmes, 1896.

44 First used in 1636, Cripplegate Poor burial ground was a part of St Giles Churchyard and it closed many times during its history. Due to the cheap cost of a burial there, the ground was too full. It also suffered bomb damage during the War, which resulted in the open space we see today. *A History of Islington*: Cosh, 2005.

45 *The London Burial Grounds*: Holmes, 1896.

46 Report of the Medical Officer of Health for London County Council: London County Council, 1898.

WWII air raids between December 1940 and May 1941 saw the Barbican area heavily bombed, and the City of London's Coroner's Court and Mortuary was included in the devastation. The London County Council bomb damage maps show the whole of Golden Lane and Whitecross Street being damaged beyond repair.[47] A photograph taken of the Mortuary and Coroner's Courtroom at this time shows half of the courtroom completely demolished.[48]

The Mortuary moved for a short time to the Cripplegate Institute on the western side of Golden Lane,[49] then to Milton Court within the Barbican Estate in the 1960s. This was also where the City's Fire Station was housed at the time.

In 2002, agreement was reached with the authorities of the surrounding areas allowing the City of London authorities to use the mortuary in Camden, rather than pay out for the expense of keeping one of their own.[50]

In 1965, the Prior Weston Primary School was built on the site of the old burial ground, and the Fortune Park Children's Centre, built in 1995, now occupies the site where the Coroner's Courtrooms and Mortuary once stood. Golden Lane's haunting past reappeared during construction, when workmen found the remains of a body on the site. Despite almost certainly being an historic death, the remains had to be taken to the forensic department of the City of London Police for investigation before the body could be reburied.[51]

It is strange to think of Golden Lane having such a dark past when you visit it today, with the leaves blowing in the trees and children laughing in the park. However, its past is an important part of history, which allows us a peek into the place that we, researchers and students of the Jack the Ripper case, so strongly associate with Catherine Eddowes.

47 Saunders Maps, 2005, 50-1, 62-3.

48 Cross and Tibbs Collection. Held at the Guildhall Library, catalogue number M0018028CL.

49 Records of the Cripplegate Institute at the LMA.

50 Records held at the Barbican Library.

51 The City Bunhill burial ground, Golden Lane: MOL Archaeology Studies Series 21, 2006.

CHAPTER SIX

Catherine Eddowes

*'I must have drunk a lot, because I woke up inside
Bishopsgate Police Station cell, I knew it well. I had faded
memories of thinking I was a fire engine on Aldgate High Street
but that was it, I was singing quite merrily to myself when a
copper came and signed me out.'[1]*

On 30th September 1888, everything changed for the City of
London Police force with the death of one woman. This woman, who
should be remembered as more than just a victim of Jack the Ripper,
was a living, breathing human being.

By the end of her life sadly reduced to possibly working as a casual
prostitute, she claimed to go by the name of Mary Ann Kelly, but was
in reality called Catherine Eddowes.

Before we look at the lives of the City of London policemen who
were in some way connected to the investigation of the killing of
this woman, there is another life we should most certainly look at
first, and that is the woman who was found in Mitre Square, Miss
Catherine Eddowes herself. For, like the policemen of the City force,
there was more to her life than what happened to her in the early
hours of Sunday, 30th September 1888.

---

1   Catherine Eddowes speaks in *Victorian Lives behind Victorian Crimes Vol: 1 The Women
     who made Jack the Ripper famous* by Amanda Harvey Purse.

She is a part of history, but she was also a mother, partner and a daughter, and should be remembered also as such.

Catherine Eddowes was born on 14th April 1842 in Graisley Green, Wolverhampton.[2] Her father George was born in 1808 to Thomas and Mary Eddowes neé Barks (who had married on 6th June 1802 in Wolverhampton),[3] and was baptised on 1st August 1808.[4] George was the second child born to the Eddowes family, with sister Elizabeth having been born in 1807 and baptised on 17th May of that year.[5] Younger siblings were Mary (baptised on 6th March 1814)[6] and William (baptised on 29th October 1818).[7]

George Eddowes worked his apprenticeship at the Old Hall Works in Wolverhampton, and married Catherine Evans, who was working as a cook in a local hostelry called the Peacock Hotel,[8] on 13th August 1832 in Bushbury.[9]

George and Catherine had twelve children, five of whom were born before Catherine Jr: Alfred (born 1833),[10] Harriet (born 1834),[11] Emma (born 1835),[12] Eliza (born 1837,[13] although she is missing on the 1841 census) and Elizabeth (born 1838).[14]

In the 1841 census, the Eddowes family were recorded as living at Graisley Green, Wolverhampton in Staffordshire.[15]

---

2   Birth record.

3   Marriage record.

4   Baptism record.

5   Ibid.

6   Ibid.

7   Ibid.

8   1841 census.

9   Marriage record.

10 Birth record.

11 Ibid.

12 Ibid.

13 Ibid.

14 Birth records.

15 1841 census.

Catherine Eddowes was baptised in the same church that father, uncle and aunts had been, St Peter's Church in Wolverhampton, on 26th April 1842.[16]

By the time Catherine's brother Thomas was born on 9th December 1844, the family had moved to London, his birth certificate recording their address as 4 Baden Place, Crosby Row, Bermondsey.[17]

Within five years the family had moved to 35 West Street, Long Lane in Bermondsey, where they were living when another brother, John, died from cyanosis convulsions on 18th March 1849 aged just three months.[18] The family were still in West Street, Bermondsey in the 1851 census, and the fact that George was still a tin plate worker seems to suggest that the family moved to London for his work. His wife Catherine was at that point 36 years of age, and had given birth to nine children, with George (born 1845)[19] and Sarah Ann (born 1850)[20] joining the family.

Emma and Harriet appear to have left home by the time of the 1851 census, in which eldest son Alfred is classed as an 'idiot'. Eliza, at the age of fourteen, was recorded as a domestic servant, while Catherine, Elizabeth and Thomas were scholars.[21]

Catherine Sr would give birth to two further children, Mary Ann in 1852[22] and William in 1854. Sadly, William passed away through convulsions at just four months old.[23] His mother was also quite ill at this time, and she died at the age of 42 on 17th November 1855 from phthisis (tuberculosis), from which she had been suffering since the beginning of the year. She passed away at home, which at this point was 7 Winters Square, Bermondsey.[24]

---

16 Baptism record.
17 Birth record.
18 Death certificate.
19 Birth record.
20 Ibid.
21 1851 census.
22 Birth record.
23 Death certificate.
24 Death certificate.

Daughter Elizabeth married labourer Thomas Charles Fisher at St Paul's Church, Bermondsey, on 21st September 1857. Her father, George, made his mark on the marriage certificate, but at some point in the three months following this happy event he may have died, because on 9th December three of his children - George Jr, Sarah Ann and Mary Ann - were admitted into Bermondsey Workhouse as 'orphans'.[25] Thomas joined them the following day, and he, George Jr and Mary Ann were ordered by the magistrate on 26th December 1857 to attend Bermondsey Industrial School to learn a trade. Sarah Ann would join them a year later.[26]

It can be presumed that at this time Catherine was sent to live with her aunt Elizabeth, her father's sister, as she was recorded as living with this relative in the 1861 census.

On 23rd January 1859, Eliza Eddowes married James Gold, a butcher, at St Barnabas Church, King's Square, Finsbury.[27] With their respective addresses given as numbers 5 and 20 Rahere Street, Goswell Road, it seems certain that they met through being neighbours.

On 7th November the same year, George Jr left the Industrial School to work as a shoemaker for a Mr Tebbetts of 5 Union Road, Coburg Road, Old Kent Road.[28] Thomas Eddowes left school eight days later, on 15th November, joining the regimental band of the 45th (Nottinghamshire) Regiment of Foot, otherwise known as the Sherwood Foresters.[29] Becoming Private 287 on 19th November 1859 at the age of fourteen and eleven months, Thomas was stationed at Preston, Lancaster, and gave his previous trade as a shoemaker,[30]

25 Workhouse records.

26 Workhouse records. That George Eddowes, father of the family, had indeed died towards the end of 1857 is uncertain; the author located a death record for a George Eddows (without the 'e', as recorded on his birth certificate) who was born in the same year and who died in 1860 in Wolverhampton. Did George leave his children to find more work back in his hometown?

27 Marriage record.

28 Records of the Bermondsey Industrial School.

29 Ibid.

30 Records of the 45th Regiment of Foot, 1859.

which indicates that the Industrial School at Bermondsey were training both George and Thomas Eddowes, and doubtless many other boys, as shoemakers at the same time.

On 11th November 1860, Emma Eddowes married James Jones, a tallow chandler, at the same church that her sister Eliza had married in the previous year.[31]

Catherine, meanwhile, was living with her aunt Elizabeth, uncle William and their three children at 50 Bilston Street. She was certainly there by 1861, as she appeared on that census, working as a 'scourer'.[32] It was suggested by another aunt, Sarah Croot (who on the 1881 census was living at 36 Bilston Street with her husband Jessie), that Catherine's uncle William worked at the Old Hall Works at this time, and that from time to time Catherine went to work with him as a tin plate stamper. To date no evidence of this has been found, but it is possible that Catherine only worked there as needed, and no formal employment was recorded.

George Eddowes Jr was working as an errand boy in 1861, living with his sister Harriet at 174 Goswell Street, Finsbury. Harriet claimed in this census to be married to one Robert Garrett, but in fact their marriage would not take place for another six years.

Thomas was discharged from the 45th Regiment after being classed as unfit for service in August 1861,[33] with the regimental surgeon J. Leary stating:

> This boy enlisted a year and half since, to be trained as a musician but from the delicacy of his chest he has been exempted from playing on the wind instrument. He has been frequently in hospital under the head of 'asthenia' and as it is not likely he will ever make an effective soldier, he is brought forward for discharge.[34]

Thomas was discharged at Chatham Hospital on 27th August 1861 after being diagnosed with pulmonary consumption.[35]

---

31 Marriage records.
32 1861 census.
33 Records of the 45th Regiment of Foot, 1861.
34 Ibid.
35 Records of the 45th Regiment of Foot, 1861.

It was said that in 1862 Catherine moved to Birmingham to live with her other uncle Thomas Eddowes, at Brick Hill, Bagot Street, sent there because she had stolen from her place of work. Again, there is no evidence to support this beyond an interview given by her sister Emma to the *Daily News* following Catherine's murder. In the same interview, it was stated that from Birmingham Catherine returned to Wolverhampton to live with her grandfather, also Thomas Eddowes. She would not stay there for long, leaving once again for Birmingham and, at the age of sixteen, meeting Thomas Conway.[36]

Thomas must have meant a lot to Catherine, for she would have his initials tattooed, rather crudely, onto her arm. He was a pensioner of the 18th Royal Irish Regiment, although when he enlisted and when drawing his pension he went by the name of Thomas Quinn.[37]

The couple moved around a lot, travelling to places in and out of Birmingham, apparently making their money by selling chapbooks, and it has been suggested that Catherine might have started working on the streets at that time. These cheap books were often called 'ballads', and were an inexpensive way for the public to read about the latest hangings, which were classed as entertainment. Catherine was even supposed to have sold a 'gallows ballad' about her own cousin's hanging in Stafford in January 1866 for the murder of Harriet Segar.[38]

During these travels Catherine gave birth to her first child, Catherine Ann Conway, who was also called Annie from time to time. She was the daughter that Catherine would later claim to intend visiting on the day before she died. Catherine gave birth to Annie on 18th April 1863 in Yarmouth Workhouse, Norfolk. Calling herself Catherine Conway, the new mother registered her daughter's birth on 13th May 1863.[39]

---

36 Interview with Emma Jones reported in the *Daily News*, 4th October 1888.

37 Recorded at the time of his death.

38 Catherine's cousin was Christopher Charles Robinson, born on 15th May 1847 and son of Mary Ann Robinson, late Colbourne but formerly Eddowes.

39 Birth Certificate.

Catherine's sister Mary Ann Eddowes left the Industrial School at Bermondsey on 18th April 1867 to work as a maid to a Mr McDougall at 11 Brooklyn Terrace, Peckham.[40] This position did not last and Mary Ann returned to the school seven months later on 16th November 1867.

Harriet Eddowes finally married Robert Carter Garrett, the man she was already claiming to be her husband in 1861, on 6th October 1867 at St Barnabas Church, Finsbury. At this time, the couple lived at 17 Fann Street, with Harriet giving her occupation as a fancy bag maker.[41]

Catherine and Thomas Conway made their way from Wolverhampton to London following the birth of their second child, Thomas Jr, in 1868.[42]

Mary Ann Eddowes left the Industrial School on 3rd February 1868 to work in service for Mr Harthuis, a watchmaker, at 5 Park Terrace, Sutton. Again, this employment did not last and she was back in the school by 18th February. She left the school again on 4th July 1868, this time to go into service for Mrs Jessie of 10 Gloster Terrace, Albany, Camberwell. Within six weeks she returned to the school, returning on 14th August 1868, before leaving yet again on 6th October to work for Mrs Simmons at 30 Surrey Street, Camberwell. Mary Ann returned to school on 5th January 1869, but two days later left again to work for Thomas Harress of 25 Cornwell Road, Brixton, and this is the last we hear of her.[43]

On 19th October 1870, Alfred Eddowes was admitted from Newington to St George's Workhouse, Mint Street, classed as destitute.[44] Sadly, his sister Sarah Ann Eddowes was admitted into the Imbeciles Asylum at Caterham a week later, on 26th October. A Mrs Elizabeth Fisher of 4 Acacia Terrace, Abbeywood, took Sarah in

---

40 Records of the Bermondsey Industrial School.
41 Marriage Certificate.
42 Thomas's birth appears not to have been registered. Year of birth from 1871 census.
43 Records of the Bermondsey Industrial School.
44 Workhouse records.

and the last address Sarah gave for herself was that of her sister's, Emma, at 16 Bridgewater Gardens, Aldersgate, London.[45]

On 15th August 1873, Catherine gave birth to Alfred George Conway at St George's Workhouse, Mint Street.[46] She gave her address as 119 Kent Street. Alfred was christened at the workhouse on 26th August 1873, and on the baptism record Catherine gave her address as 120 Kent Street - was she giving a false address and couldn't remember what number she had used before? Was there a reason that she had Alfred baptised, but none of her other children?

On 6th October 1876, Alfred Eddowes re-entered Mint Street Workhouse, with his previous address given as 4 Mint Street.[47] He suffered a bad run of luck in 1878, going in and out of the workhouse, firstly leaving on 11th March but returning on 3rd September. He stayed for five weeks before leaving on 7th October, only to return a week later on the 15th, his previous address recorded as 64 Tabard Street.[48]

Alfred continued to struggle in 1879, leaving the workhouse on 20th January but returning seven days later; he was discharged again on 13th September, only to return on 24th February 1880. This is the last we hear of him in workhouse records.[49]

In the 1881 census Catherine was still living with Thomas Conway and their two sons at 71 Lower George Street, Chelsea, but this was not to last and in the latter part of 1881 she and Conway parted. Catherine is said to have started working for the Jewish community in Brick Lane, while living in Cooney's Lodging House at 55 Flower and Dean Street.[50]

On 21st September 1881 Catherine appeared at the Thames Magistrate's Court, charged with being drunk and disorderly, and

45 Asylum records.

46 Workhouse records.

47 Ibid.

48 Kent Street was renamed Tabard Street in 1877.

49 Workhouse records.

50 Statement by the superintendent of 55 Flower and Dean Street reported in the *Daily News*, 4th October.

using obscene language. She was discharged without a fine by Magistrate Thomas William Saunders.[51]

In 1882 Annie Conway gave birth to Catherine's grandson, Louis Phillips,[52] and two years later had another child, whom she named Catherine, on 22nd September 1884. When registering the birth Annie gave her name as Catherine Phillips, even though she had not married her partner and the father of her children yet. They were living at 317 Weston Street, Southwark.[53]

On 5th March 1885, George Eddowes, Catherine's brother, died of a cerebral haemorrhage aged 39 at the Union Workhouse, Hemel Hempstead.[54] George was buried on 7th March 1885 at St Mary Churchyard, Hemel Hempstead.[55]

Annie Conway finally married the man who had fathered her two children, Louis Phillips, on 3rd August 1885 at St Mary Magdalene Church, Southwark. They were living at 14 Townsend Street, Old Kent Road at the time of their wedding, with Louis stating he was a Lamp Black Packer on the wedding certificate.[56] On 10th August 1886, Annie gave birth to son William at her home of 22 King Street, Bermondsey, with Catherine Eddowes recorded as being there at the birth.[57]

On 14th June 1887, at 5.15pm, Catherine was admitted into the Whitechapel Workhouse Infirmary with a burn on her foot. She gave her religion as Roman Catholic, and was sent to Ward E2. She was discharged six days later on 20th June 1887.[58]

In the years following Catherine's murder, her family left behind continued to grow.

51 Court records, 1881.
52 1891 census.
53 Birth certificate.
54 Workhouse records.
55 St Mary's Church Parish records, 1885.
56 Wedding certificate.
57 Birth certificate. Perhaps 22 King Street, Bermondsey, was the address to which Catherine might have been headed to on the morning of her death, not knowing that Annie had moved?
58 Whitechapel Infirmary records, 1887.

On 20th February 1889, Catherine's daughter Annie Phillips gave birth to daughter Ellen at her home of 21 The Grange, Bermondsey, the child being registered on 25th March.[59]

There are two interesting points here. Firstly, the mother gave her name as 'Annie' rather than her legal first name of Catherine - did she perhaps not want to be reminded of the name 'Catherine' so soon after the death of her mother?

Secondly, Annie giving birth to Ellen in February 1889 indicates that she was pregnant at the time of her mother's death, so when we picture her talking at the inquest, talking to the newspapers or even viewing the body of her own mother at the mortuary, we should imagine a woman suffering with grief and shock while being pregnant at the same time.

On 19th May 1890, Annie gave birth to Thomas and the family was recorded as living at 1 Paulin Street, Bermondsey.[60] A year later, on the 1891 census, the family was recorded at 13 Dix's Place.[61]

Harriet Garrett, Catherine's sister, was admitted to Holborn Union Workhouse at Mitcham on 15th September 1891, being discharged on 22nd August 1892, only to be re-admitted three days later. She left on 31st October 1893, and returned once again the following day.[62] Harriett sadly died on 17th November 1898 at Holborn Workhouse, the certificate recording the cause of death as apoplexy.[63]

In the 1891 census Catherine's sister Emma Jones was recorded as still living at 20 Bridgewater Gardens, Aldersgate,[64] and by the 1901 census was at 33 Bastwick Street, St Luke's. Her other sister, Elizabeth Fisher, was recorded in the same census with her daughter Amelia and family at Down's Place, Plumstead, while daughter Annie was living at 6 Haddon House, Russell Place in Southwark.

Catherine's former partner, Thomas Conway, was living in 1901 at

---

59 Birth certificate.
60 Ibid.
61 1891 census.
62 Workhouse records.
63 Ibid.

19 Park Street, St Margaret's in Westminster.[65] He died on 31st July 1908 at the age of 80 at St Olave's Union Workhouse, Parish Street, Bermondsey. Workhouse records record him as suffering 'senility and demented', and he was recorded as being an 'army pensioner of the 18th Royal Irish Regiment, Identity Number 350 of Lynton Mews, Bermondsey'.[66]

Thomas Jr, Catherine's son, sadly passed away on 31st October 1903, five years and one day to the date of his mother's death. He died of pulmonary tuberculosis at St George's Union Infirmary, on Fulham Road, Chelsea, his address given as Parker Street.[67]

Catherine Phillips, Catherine's granddaughter, married Thomas Hall on 8th June 1908 at St Mary Magdalene Church, Southwark. They were both living at 16 Madron Street, and both her brother and sister attended the wedding.[68] Sarah Hall, their first child, was born at Camberwell on 15th April 1909.[69] They would go on to have further children - Thomas, William and Joseph Lewis Hall.

Louis Phillips, Catherine's grandson, was living at 40 Westcott Street, Tabard Street in 1911,[70] while a year later Ellen Phillips, Catherine's granddaughter, married Joseph William Wells on 14th August 1912 at the same church in which her sister Catherine had been married,[71] and would go on to have six children.

On 26th June 1916, Thomas Phillips, Catherine's youngest grandson enlisted into the 2nd/24th County of London Regiment Battalion TF at Kennington,[72] becoming Private 721750. He was part of the European expeditions and was awarded the British War Medal and the Victory Medal for his part in the Great War. He sadly

64 1891 census.
65 1901 census.
66 Workhouse records.
67 Ibid.
68 Marriage certificate.
69 Birth record.
70 1911 census.
71 Marriage certificate.
72 County of London Battalion records, 1916.

died of an abscess on the liver on 19th August 1918, and is buried at Cairo War Memorial Cemetery in Egypt.[73]

Although it is possible to trace the descendants of Catherine Eddowes to the present day, the author believes that the living, breathing family deserve their privacy and as such intends to end this look at Catherine's family with one final event in the life of Annie Phillips, her only daughter.

Catherine Ann Phillips, née Conway, passed away on 15th July 1943, a whole 55 years after the death of her mother, at Lambeth Hospital. Her occupation was recorded as a paper sorter and her previous address as 107 Chaucer House, Tabard Street, Southwark.[74]

One last interesting note to make here is that Tabard Street used to be called Kent Street, the address Catherine Eddowes had given 70 years earlier when registering the birth of her son Alfred Conway.

---

73 Army records of Thomas Phillips, 1916-1918.

74 Death record.

CHAPTER SEVEN

Saturday, 29th September 1888

On the morning of 29th September 1888, Catherine Eddowes was with her partner, John Kelly, at 55 Flower and Dean Street. This was a common lodging house used by many, and was known as Cooney's.

The couple had spent the summer hop-picking in Kent, but due to a poor harvest had returned to London almost penniless. Arriving on 27th September, they spent the night at the casual ward in Shoe Lane. The following evening Kelly slept at 52 Flower and Dean Street, while Catherine went to the casual ward at Mile End, where she was known. According to an interview with the *East London Observer*, the superintendent there claimed she said to him, "I have come back to earn the reward offered for the apprehension of the Whitechapel murderer. I think I know him." The superintendent warned "Mind he doesn't murder you too," to which Catherine replied 'Oh, no fear of that'.[1]

Catherine and John wanted breakfast, but of course that meant having money to pay for it. It was agreed that Catherine would go to a pawnbrokers, Mr Jones on Church Street, with a pair of John's boots. When pledging these she gave her name as 'Jane Kelly'.[2] With the 2/6d received, the couple bought tea and sugar, and some food.

Between ten and eleven that morning, the couple were seen

---

1   *East London Observer*, 13th October 1888.

2   The pawn ticket was found on her person when her body was found in Mitre Square. Coroner's inquest (L) 1888, No.135, Catherine Eddowes' inquest, 1888, London Metropolitan Archives.

enjoying their breakfast in the kitchen of Cooney's lodging house by Mr Frederick William Wilkinson, the deputy of the lodging house.[3] He would state at the inquest into Catherine's death:

> I have known the deceased and Kelly during the last seven years. They passed as man and wife, and lived on very good terms. They had a quarrel now and then, but not violent. They sometimes had a few words when Kate was in drink, but they were not serious. I believe she got her living by hawking about the streets and cleaning amongst the Jews in Whitechapel. Kelly paid me pretty regularly. Kate was not often in drink. She was a very jolly woman, always singing. Kelly was not in the habit of drinking, and I never saw him the worse for drink. During the week the first time I saw the deceased at the lodging-house was on Friday afternoon. Kelly was not with her then. She went out and did not return until Saturday morning, when I saw her and Kelly in the kitchen together having breakfast. I did not see her go out, and I do not know whether Kelly went with her. I never saw her again.[4]

By the afternoon the couple were once again penniless, so Catherine decided to visit her daughter to borrow money, according to John Kelly's later testimony:

> I last saw her alive about two o'clock in the afternoon of Saturday in Houndsditch. We parted on very good terms. She told me she was going over to Bermondsey to try and find her daughter Annie. Those were the last words she spoke to me. Annie was a daughter whom I believe she had had by Conway. She promised me before we parted that she would be back by four o'clock, and no later. She did not return.[5]

However, Catherine did not know her daughter's address, Annie having moved several times to avoid her mother's regular visits for money. Whether this supposed visit was an untruth on the part of Catherine or John Kelly is unknown – perhaps she had resorted to casual prostitution in order to obtain money. Either way, after parting with Kelly, Catherine was not seen again until later that evening.

3   Mr Wilkinson's statement at Catherine Eddowes' inquest.
4   Ibid.
5   John Kelly's statement at Catherine Eddowes' inquest.

At around half-past eight, the attention of City PC Louis Robinson was drawn by a crowd of people surrounding a woman who later proved to be Catherine, slumped outside 29 Aldgate High Street. She was heavily drunk, a sign that she had indeed got some money from somewhere. Had she been drinking near where she was found, this could have been at either the Bull's Head Inn or the Hoop and Grapes, or a number of other public houses in the vicinity. It has been written that she doing an impression of a fire engine,[6] although there is no independent evidence of this.

As PC Robinson walked his beat along Aldgate High Street he soon arrived at the scene. The young constable had to push the people aside to get through the crowd, asking if anyone knew this woman but receiving no answer. He tried to help Catherine to her feet, but she fell backwards against the shutter of No. 29. PC George Simmons, whose own beat crossed that of Robinson, came to his assistance and the two officers half-carried Catherine for the few minutes' journey to Bishopsgate Police Station,[7] where they arrived at 8.45pm.[8]

Catherine was placed in front of Station Sergeant James Byfield, who attempted to take some details in order to complete the custody form. In her drunken state, this was a hard task. When asked her name, she replied "Nothing".[9] It did not take long for Sergeant Byfield to decide that this woman needed to be placed in the cells to sober up.[10] So at 8.50pm, PCs Louis Robinson and George Simmons watched as Catherine Eddowes was led away from the custody desk, her apron catching Louis's eye. He would later remember this apron, when the police were attempting to identify the body found in Mitre Square.[11]

---

6   Stated in Tom Cullen's *Autumn of Terror.*

7   Inquest testimony of City Constable 931 Louis Robinson.

8   Ibid.

9   Inquest testimony City Station Sergeant James Byfield.

10 Ibid.

11 Inquest testimony of City Constable 931 Louis Robinson. The apron would prove to be the clue which linked the woman found in Mitre Square to the drunk taken into custody by PC Louis Robinson.

At 9.45pm, PC George Hutt started his shift as Bishopsgate Police Station's gaoler.[12] Ten minutes later he performed his first check on all the prisoners that had been brought in the Bishopsgate Police Station before his shift. He first looked in on the sleeping Catherine Eddowes at 9.55pm.

These are the movements of Catherine Eddowes in the hours following her and John Kelly enjoying breakfast together at 55 Flower and Dean Street. Considering the life these two people had, it could seem as if this was a good start to their day, but just thirteen hours later she was now sleeping in the cells of Bishopsgate Police Station.

No matter how disheartening these events may seem, things were about to get a lot worse...

---

12 PC Watkins, who would later find Catherine's body in Mitre Square, started his shift at the same time, also from Bishopsgate Police Station.

CHAPTER EIGHT

Sunday, 30th September 1888

Less than an hour into the morning of 30th September 1888, the woman who had given her name as 'Nothing' to Sergeant James Byfield just over three hours earlier had woken from her drunken sleep.

PC Hutt, the station gaoler, would later testify:

> I visited her several times until five minutes to one on Sunday morning. The inspector, being out visiting, I was directed by Sergeant Byfield to see if any of the prisoners were fit to be discharged.

Finding her sober, Hutt released Catherine from her cell and took her to the custody desk, where she gave her name as Mary Ann Kelly and her address as 6 Fashion Street.

She asked PC Hutt the time and was told "Too late for you to get any more drink." On hearing it was almost one o'clock, Catherine exclaimed "I shall get a damn fine hiding when I get home." The unsympathetic constable replied "Serve you right; you have no right to get drunk," and at one o'clock opened the station door to allow her out. Asking her to pull the door to, Hutt heard Catherine respond "All right, Goodnight, old cock." These would be her last recorded words.

Hutt then watched her turn left in the direction of Houndsditch and off into the night.[1]

---

1   Inquest testimony of City Constable 968 George Henry Hutt. It is interesting to note, that if Catherine's intention was to get some money before returning to John Kelly, her sister Emma Jones was still living in Aldersgate, within the city and not that far from Bishopsgate Police Station. Emma Jones had been living in Aldersgate for quite some time so it could be possible that Catherine knew very well where her sister was. However, she actually turned in the other direction.

At about this time the body of a woman, later identified as Elizabeth Stride, was discovered in a yard off Berner Street, Whitechapel. It was the first murder in what would become known as the 'double event'.

At about 1.30am James Blenkinsop, a nightwatchman minding roadworks in St James's Place near Mitre Square, was asked by 'a respectably dressed man' whether he had seen a man and woman go through the passage. Mr Blenkinsop replied that he "didn't take any notice. I have seen some people pass."[2]

There is no record that the City of London Police took this witness seriously, but there remains a possibility that Blenkinsop might well have seen Catherine Eddowes with her killer, as this matches the timeline with the couple being seen by other witnesses a few minutes later.

At 1.35am, Joseph Lawende, Joseph Levy and Harry Harris left the Imperial Club on Duke Street, less than ten yards from Church Passage, which led to Mitre Square, and saw a man and a woman in conversation standing at the entrance to the passage.[3]

Five minutes after the trio had passed the couple, PC James Harvey walked the portion of his beat which took him down Church Passage to the edge of Mitre Square and back again, but saw nor heard anything suspicious.[4]

Four or five minutes after Harvey exited Church Passage, PC Edward Watkins walked into Mitre Square from Mitre Street and almost immediately discovered the body of Catherine Eddowes in the south west corner of the Square.

At the inquest, Watkins would describe what happened next:

> The woman was on her back, with her feet towards the square. Her clothes were thrown up. I saw her throat was cut and the stomach

---

2   *The Star*, 1st October 1888. Philip Sugden, in his book *The Complete History of Jack the Ripper*, suggests that Blenkinsop may have misjudged the time of the incident and it may have actually occurred after the murder of Eddowes, with the man asking whether he had seen a couple passing through the passage being a detective.

3   *Evening News*, 9th October 1888.

4   Inquest testimony of City Constable James Harvey.

ripped open. She was lying in a pool of blood. I did not touch the body. I ran across to Kearley and Long's [sic] warehouse. The door was ajar, and I pushed it open, and called on the watchman Morris, who was inside. He came out. I remained with the body until the arrival of Police-constable Holland. No one else was there before that but myself. Holland was followed by Dr Sequeira. Inspector Collard arrived about two o'clock, and also Dr Brown, surgeon to the police force.[5]

The alarm had been raised by George Morris, the Kearley and Tonge nightwatchman, who, after shining his light on the body, ran up Mitre Street towards Aldgate blowing his whistle.

He soon met PC Harvey and told him of the discovery, and the constable, together with City PC Holland, ran to the square. Holland then left to fetch Dr George Sequeira from his surgery at 34 Jewry Street, in the City.

At 1.55am Inspector Edward Collard at Bishopsgate Police Station received news of the murder, and sent a constable to fetch the City Police's surgeon, Dr Frederick Brown, from his home at 17 Finsbury Circus.[6]

PC Holland arrived at the scene with Dr Sequeira at 1.55am,[7] and at the same time Detectives Daniel Halse, Robert Outram and Edward Marriott, on plain-clothes patrol in the area near St Botolph's church, heard news of the murder and at once headed for Mitre Square.

Dr Frederick Gordon Brown arrived at 2.18am, and began to examine the body of Catherine Eddowes as she lay on the pavement. While he was doing this, Superintendent Alfred Foster and Detective Inspector James McWilliam arrived at Mitre Square.

Superintendent Foster's son Frederick, the City Surveyor, was called to Mitre Square to draw plans of the scene and surrounding area. He would also record the wounds to Catherine's body at the

---

5   Inquest testimony of City Constable Edward Watkins
6   Coroner's Inquest (L) 1888, No. 135, Catherine Eddowes's Inquest 1888 at London Metropolitan Archives.
7   Ibid.

Golden Lane mortuary, where she was taken at 2.35am.[8]

Inspector Izzard and Sergeants Phelps and Dudman arrived at Mitre Square to protect the area from the public.

At 2.55am, just over an hour after Catherine Eddowes was found by PC Watkins, the Metropolitan Police's PC Alfred Long found a bloodstained portion of an apron in the entrance to 108-119 Wentworth Dwellings on Goulston Street, with a chalked message written on the wall above.

At half past two the following afternoon, the post mortem of Catherine Eddowes was completed by Drs Brown, Sequeira and Sedgwick Saunders.

The body was finally identified by John Kelly, Catherine's partner, who had read of the murder and presented himself to the police. He was taken from Bishopsgate Police Station to Golden Lane Mortuary by Sergeant Miles.[9]

Finally, there was a name for the murdered woman who had been killed within the boundaries of the City of London.

The Metropolitan Police ruling regarding those found drunk in the streets meant that they would be kept in the cells all night, whether they had sobered up or not. The City of London Police ruling was different; once a person was deemed sober they were then released.

This is what happened to Catherine Eddowes - she was released when deemed sober enough, and within 45 minutes was found dead in Mitre Square. She was inches away from the Metropolitan Police boundary when she was picked up and taken to Bishopsgate Police Station, and therefore inches away from being picked up by a Met officer, taken to a different police station and detained all night. She would have been safe, she would have survived... and we probably would never have heard of her.

---

8   *Daily News*, 2nd October 1888.

9   Her death must have hit her John Kelly hard as he sadly passed away from laryngitis on 29th November 1888, just a month after Catherine was murdered, in the Whitechapel Workhouse Infirmary.

PART THREE

THE POLICEMEN'S LIVES

CHAPTER NINE

Making an Impression
of a Fire Engine?

PC Louis Frederick Robinson and PC George Simmons

Louis Robinson

PC Louis Robinson was only 23-years-old when he became entangled in the greatest mystery the Victorians had ever known. He had no idea when he started his beat on the night of 29th September 1888 that his meeting with a woman along Aldgate High Street would have such dramatic consequences.

Had he turned into Aldgate High Street a few seconds earlier, or later, than he did, she may have managed to walk a few more steps into Metropolitan Police territory. She would have been nowhere near Mitre Square at half past one the following morning and her life would not have ended in the way it did.

Sadly, this did not happen...

Born on 13th August 1865 to Edward Robinson and Ellen Tott, who married in Reed on 9th July 1849,[1] Louis Frederick Robinson was the sixth child born to the family.

1   Records of St Mary's church, Therfield.

The family, completed by siblings Annie,[2] Emma,[3] Allen,[4] Henrietta,[5] Edwin,[6] Clara[7] and Reginald,[8] lived in the small village of Therfield, near Royston in Hertfordshire,[9] predominantly a farming village. All the Robinson children were baptised at St Mary's church, including Louis on 24th September 1865.

By 1871, the Robinson family lived at 72 Groom's Cottage, which ironically stood near a street called Police Row. Joining the Robinsons in this small farmer's cottage was one William Tott, recorded as Edward Robinson's stepson.[10] This has led to a suggestion that Louis's mother, Ellen, had been married before, but as her maiden name was Tott it is likely that she had given birth to William outside of wedlock.

Edward Robinson worked as a gardener at this time, with eldest son Allen working as a farmer. All the other children were in school, including 5-year-old Louis.

By September 1880, at the age of fourteen, Louis was living in London and working as a porter and delivery driver for Messrs Copestake, Hughes, Crampton & Co.[11]

---

2   Born 25th November 1850. Annie would later marry George Kennett.

3   Born 21st January 1853. Emma ended her days in Arlesey Lunatic Asylum, Bedfordshire, built to replace Bedford Lunatic Asylum which had been built in 1812. It had the longest corridor in Britain at about half-a mile long.

4   Born 18th October 1856, Allen later married Annie Bolton.

5   Born 28th January 1859, Henrietta was also confined to an asylum, although where is not known.

6   Born 19th November 1861, Edwin later went on to marry Lizzie Preston on his 26th birthday in 1887. At the time he was working at Copestakes, where his younger brother Louis once did.

7   Born 3rd December 1867. Clara died aged 15.

8   Born 6th May 1869, Reginald also died young, at just 16-years-old.

9   Records of St Mary's church, Therfield.

10   1871 census.

11   Messrs Copestake, Hughes, Crampton and Co. began trading in 1825 as Copestake and Co. They were originally a wholesaler dealing in lace, operating from a small room above a shop at 7 Cheapside. By the time Louis Robinson started working for them, the company was making a wide variety of items including artificial flowers, bed linen, shawls and umbrellas, and had premises not just in London but also Manchester, Glasgow, Paris and New York. Records of Therfield held in the Church of St Mary's.

In the 1881 census Louis was recorded as 'Lewis', a porter residing at 32 Goswell Road, St Luke's, an area dotted with all different kinds of businesses from jewellers to tobacconists. The head of the household was listed as a packer and foreman to Messrs Copestake, Hughes, Crampton and Co,[12] and the fact that the company held business meetings at the address indicates that Louis was given accommodation at his place of work.[13]

Louis completed his application form to become a police officer in the City of London Police Force on 18th October 1886, witnessed by Chief Inspector Robert A. Sillcock.[14] Louis had to provide three references to his good character, and these were provided by Mr J. Calvert, a warehouseman working for the same company at which Louis had been employed for six years before joining the force, William Edward Tinker, a fellow coachman of the same company and who had lived with Louis at 32 Goswell Road in 1881 but now was living at 7 Mortimer Road, Kingsland, and James Sill, another porter.[15]

These references were checked and cleared by Sergeant James Egan.[16] It wasn't until 9th December 1886 that Louis officially joined the City of London Police, at the same time as George Vinden Parton (warrant number 5920).[17]

Louis was recorded as being 5ft 9in tall, with hazel eyes, a dark complexion with dark brown hair and with a birthmark on his hip and back.[18]

He was given collar number 931[19] and warrant number 5921. He was sent to the police surgeon to be certified fit for police service

---

12 1881 census.

13 *Good Templar's Watchword Volume II.*

14 At the time of the 1881 census Robert Sillcock was living at Snow Hill Police Station with his wife Susannah and their children Ellen, Alice, Robert Jr, Ernest and Harry.

15 Louis Robinson's application form to join the City of London Police, CLA/048/AD/01.

16 According to the 1881 census, Sergeant James Egan was living at Bishopsgate Police Station.

17 City of London Police Record file held at Bishopsgate Police Station.

18 Louis Robinson's application form, CLA/048/AD/01.

on 4th February 1887, passing without any problems. Louis was now earning 25s a week. However, something happened within the first three months of his service - perhaps a combination of the long hours, bad weather and work conditions proved a shock to his system, as it did for many young officers - and he was sent again to the police surgeon on 10th May 1887, with the result that Louis was signed off work sick for 21 days.[20]

Louis seems to have relaxed in his new career as a policeman and possibly thought he could push his luck a little. This failed on 15th January 1888, when he was caught drinking in the doorway of a public house. The punishment came directly from the Commissioner, with three days deducted from his fortnightly leave. Compared to some other City of London Police officers, Louis Robinson's service record is relatively quiet, possibly the strong punishment of losing three days holiday shocking him enough to abide by the rules.[21]

This may explain why he did not go easy on Catherine Eddowes when he met her at 8:30pm on 29th September 1888 outside 29 Aldgate High Street.[22] He could have been lenient and just given a stern warning - after all, there were worse crimes a person could commit. However, the rules stated that a warning could be issued only if Catherine had not been unruly enough to draw a crowd, and she had, which meant that PC Louis Robinson had only one course of action open to him, going strictly by the rules, and that was to take her to the nearest police station, in this case Bishopsgate, and have her placed in the cells to sober up.[23]

Louis' career bloomed after his brush with the Whitechapel murders case. On 17th January 1889 he was promoted to second-

---

19 Robinson's collar number would change over the years to 1150, 903 and 303C.

20 Louis Robinson's service record, CLA/048/AD/01.

21 Louis Robinson's misconduct record, CLA/048/AD/01.

22 The address '29 Aldgate High Street' is a mystery in its own right, because officially it did not exist in any records of 1888. According to census returns between 1871 and 1901, the numbering on Aldgate High Street went from 28 to 30. Research in recent years suggests that No. 28 was a furniture warehouse which could have spread over into a space next door, making that No. 29.

23 Order Book for Division Six (Bishopsgate) held at the City of London Police Museum.

class constable, receiving a pay rise. A year and a half later his salary was further increased to 32s 2d,[24] a reasonable sum of money and, with his address at this time being Bishopsgate Police Station, you can imagine that with not much rent to be paid and no travel costs to get to work, he would have been quite comfortable. Life must have seemed very different from his childhood, and the thought of having to work hard on the farmlands was long gone from his mind. In 1891 he was still single and living at Bishopsgate Police Station.[25]

At this time there were over 30 officers living at the station, including Inspector Edward Collard and his family.[26]

On 19th August 1892 Louis was again awarded 21 days' sick leave, approved by Commissioner Sir Henry Smith himself. We do not know why Louis required this leave, but it is interesting that while he could have received confirmation of his sick leave from quite a few people lower down on the ladder in the force, he actually received it from the highest possible person.[27]

Due to a change in regulations Louis found himself technically ranked as a third-class constable, but on 19th January 1893 was 'promoted' to second-class constable and awarded an increase in his weekly wage to 34s, and just a year later, on 25th January 1894, was promoted to first-class police constable, earning a weekly wage of 36s 3d.[28]

After all the good work, Louis let himself down somewhat on 1st September 1894, when he was caught 'idling and gossiping with PC 954' for roughly ten minutes. Possibly because of his previous good service, Louis received just a stern talking to - it could have been a lot worse.[29]

There are no blemishes on his record for the next five years. Louis is still unmarried living at Bishopsgate Police Station, a first-class

---

24 Louis Robinson's pay record, CLA/048/AD/01.
25 1891 census.
26 Ibid.
27 Louis Robinson's service record, CLA/048/AD/01.
28 Louis Robinson's pay record, CLA/048/AD/01.
29 Louis Robinson's misconduct record, CLA/048/AD/01.

constable earning a more than comfortable wage. But on 26th August 1899, thirteen days after his 34th birthday, he was caught drunk at muster before going out on duty, a serious offence. The result was a demotion to second-class constable, and a decrease in pay.[30]

It took Louis a year of good behaviour to return to his first-class position, and the associated salary. A few months later, on 15th November 1900, he received a further increase in wages, so that he was receiving 40s per week.[31]

In the 1901 census, Louis Robinson was recorded as still living within Bishopsgate Police Station with all the new recruits to the City of London Police force, who were also unmarried. This would have meant that Louis had been living in the same police station for 20 years.

At some point between 1901 and 1910, he met architect's daughter Edith Mary Taperell, and the couple married on 4th October 1910 at St Mary's Parish Church in Stoke Newington,[32] where by coincidence the churchwarden was Wynne Baxter, the coroner at the inquests of Whitechapel murder victims Annie Millwood, Martha Tabram, Mary Ann Nichols, Annie Chapman, Elizabeth Stride and Frances Coles.

A year later, in the 1911 census, Louis was living with his wife at 85 Aden Grove North, Stoke Newington, a small residence with three rooms.[33] He was now 45-years-old. Perhaps a combination of a long career and the fact that he was now a married man had resulted in his attitude to policing changing, but within a year Louis decided to retire from the City of London Police force.

On 1st February 1912 he walked into Bishopsgate Police Station and handed over the uniform he had known for almost 26 years to PC Meads, who then handed it to Inspector Bracknell, the station's storekeeper. As with all policemen who left the force, his description was recorded, revealing that his dark hair had by this time turned

---

30 Louis Robinson's misconduct record, CLA/048/AD/01.

31 Louis Robinson's pay records, CLA/048/AD/01.

32 Louis Robinson's marriage certificate held within his City of London Police file, CLA/048/AD/01.

33 1911 census.

grey.[34] Louis was awarded his 25 year pension, which amounted to £62 12s 3d per year.[35]

This was not the last the City of London Police was to hear of Louis Robinson, however. On 4th January 1916 they received a letter from a Mr F C McQuown, secretary of the County of London Electric Supply Company, asking for Louis's service record because he had applied for the role of Slot Meter Collector.[36] It seems as if Louis, who was now 51-years-old, could not rest in his retirement. The Commissioner replied with what we can only assume was a good reference, and Louis started working again. However, sadly this new working life was not to last and Louis died within a year, on 30th December 1916.[37]

Thirteen years later, rules had changed yet again and police widows were now entitled to claim on a fund set up to help them. So on 14th December 1929, at the age of 55, Edith could have been entitled to claim on that fund. However, we have to assume she was not informed of this and it was not until 1956, at the age of 82, that she wrote to her local police headquarters in Kent[38] asking whether she could receive the Police Widow's pension. Her letter was sent to the City of London Police, who asked for proof of her marriage to Louis. After Edith sent a copy of her own wedding certificate, her request was granted and from 15th October 1956 she received a weekly allowance of 22s 8d.[39]

George Simmons

On the night of 29th September 1888, at just after eight thirty, PC George Simmons walked along Aldgate High Street, as his beat book instructed, when he was summoned by PC Robinson to help with a woman who was quite obviously drunk. The pair helped the inebriate

34 Louis Robinson's service record, CLA/048/AD/01.
35 Ibid.
36 Ibid.
37 Death register.
38 She was at this time living in Whitstable, Kent.
39 Louis Robinson's service record, CLA/048/AD/01.

to her feet, and marched her to Bishopsgate Police Station.

George Simmons was born in the same year the City of London Police force was created, 1839, to Arthur and Mary Simmons in Cuckfield, Sussex. He was the third of six children, with Arthur Jr (b.1833), Susan (b.1835) preceding him, and Elizabeth (b.1844), Mary (b.1847) and Caroline (b.1851) following.[40] At the time of the 1841 census, when George was two years of age, the Simmons family were living at Mackerel's, Newick in Sussex, a small village which in 1831 had a population of just 724.

By 1851 George had left school and was working as an errand boy for a local business within the village. He was now the oldest child still living at home, with younger sisters Elizabeth, Mary and Caroline. George's father was recorded in that year's census as a house servant and groom.[41]

Ten years later, at the time of the census on 7th April 1861, George had moved out of the family home, living in the neighbouring village of Chailey and working as domestic gardener for one of the manor houses.[42]

However, just four months later it seems that George had decided life as a gardener did not suit him, for it was at this time that he joined the City of London Police with the collar number 959 and warrant number 3224.[43] He finally started his new duties on 15th August 1861 after completing his training, on the same day as six other new police officers, John Allen, George Chish, William Green, Charles Mercer, Charles Searle and William Read.[44] George was 22-years-old and was sent to Division Six, Bishopsgate.[45]

In 1863, George met Mary Ann Holmes and returned to his home

---

40 Simmons family tree.
41 1851 census.
42 1861 census.
43 City of London Police File held at Bishopsgate Police Station.
44 From 1840, this was done at 26 Old Jewry.
45 City of London Police File held at Bishopsgate Police Station.

county of Sussex to marry her in the parish of Worthing.[46]

Two years later, the couple had set up home at 3 Gracechurch Street in the City. Their first son, named Arthur George after the child's grandfather and father, was born in 1866.[47] Another boy, William, was born in 1871.[48]

By 1881 George had spent over fifteen years in the force, and the family had grown. Now, the Simmons family also included Edmund[49] and Mary, both born within the City of London. George was now 42-years-old and still a beat constable.[50]

Seven years later, on 29th September 1888, George was walking his beat along Aldgate High Street when he saw fellow City of London Police Constable Louis Robinson struggling with a crowd surrounding the drunken Catherine Eddowes, and helped his colleague take her to Bishopsgate Police Station.

On 8th January 1890, sixteen months later, George retired from the force aged 51. He had served more than 28 years, and was awarded a pension of £54 40d.[51]

George, his wife and their younger children - Edmund, Mary[52] and young Herbert, born in 1884 - moved to Roseberry Cottages on Heatherside Road in Epsom, Surrey. Not just a retired policeman, in the 1891 census George was recorded as a Local County Court Bailiff.[53]

Ten years later, in 1901, George was 62-years-old and retired; wife

---

46 1863 marriage records.

47 1866 birth records.

48 1871 census.

49 Edmund married in 1894 and spent the remainder of his life in Epsom, passing away in 1927.

50 1881 census.

51 George Simmons' complete service record is missing at the time of writing, as so many of the files are. Information used in this chapter is from files held at Bishopsgate police station.

52 Mary married Alfred Ernest Lacey in Epsom in 1899, going on to have three children: Ernest (b.1902), Gladys (b.1905) and Herbert (b.1907). Alfred Lacey worked at the City of London Asylum as its Head Attendant.

53 1891 census.

Mary Ann was 57. Now that the children had finally left home the couple probably hoped for a quiet life. Sadly, it would not be for long.

The *Police Review* of 27th October 1905 reported that there had been an accident involving ex-City of London Constable George Simmons, aged 67, causing 'total paralysis from the shoulders downwards'. It was reported that George regularly travelled on his cart to East Preston, Sussex, and on the day of the accident had been standing on the cart taking some hedge trimming being passed to him by a colleague when he slipped, falling to his eventual death.[54]

His widow, Mary Ann Simmons, continued to live in Epsom,[55] claiming from the City of London Police Widow's fund.

George Simmons' role in the hours preceding Catherine Eddowes' murder may seem minimal, but considering he had met her while she was still alive and carried her the eight minutes or so to Bishopsgate Police Station on the night before she died, we cannot deny that he would have been in a state of shock when news of her murder broke.

---

54 *Police Review*, 27th October 1905.

55 At 177 Hook Road, according to the 1911 census.

CHAPTER TEN

Pull The Door To

PC George Hutt and Sergeant James Byfield

George Henry Hutt

The part played by PC George Hutt in the last hours of Catherine Eddowes' life was quite significant.

Everything that George did for her, the way he spoke to her and her responses, must have all been in a day's work for him. But when news of her murder broke, did his mind turn back to their conversation, and did he feel some sense of guilt that it had been he who had released her onto the streets to meet her fate?

George Henry Hutt was born in Hackney in the latter part of 1853, the first child born to George and Jane Hutt.[1] Two years earlier, the family had been recorded in the census as living at 4 Mayfield Road, Myrtle Place, with George Sr working as a clerk at the Rock Life Assurance Office.[2]

By the 1861 census, the Hutt family had grown again, with Clement

---

1 Birth Record.
2 1851 census. According to the *London Gazette* for 1830, the company was first formed in 1806 and held offices at 14 New Bridge Street, Blackfriars.

(b.1855), Ada (b.1856) and Mabel (b.1859). Also living with the family at this time was George Jr's cousin Mary Hutt. It appears that the Hutt family was relatively comfortable financially, as they also employed a domestic servant, Fanny Gray.[3]

Ten years later the family moved a 30 minute walk away to Church Crescent, South Hackney. George Sr was working as an accountant for an insurance company, with George Jr listed as 'clerk to an underwriter'. Clement was working as a clerk to a metal merchant, Ada had left home and all the other children were in school. Another child, Maud, had been born, and the Hutt family employed a new young domestic servant, Elizabeth Jones.[4]

Perhaps initially planning to follow in his father's footsteps and work in an office, George Jr soon decided on a change of career and enlisted into the 88th Regiment of Foot, known as the Devil's Own, on 27th May 1871.[5]

The Regiment had not long returned from a long stay in India during the Mutiny, and would later fight in the Kaffir and Zulu wars, but during George's time with them was engaged in home service.[6]

On 20th June 1871 George was in Portsmouth, and a year later travelled to Aldershot. He was promoted Corporal on 8th March 1873 and sent to Colchester that September, at which point things began to go wrong.

On 27th September 1873 George was recorded in the Regimental Defaulters list for the first time.[7] He was court-martialled and sent to prison at Colchester from 4th to 31st October 1873. He was released and reduced to the rank of Private.

On 8th December 1875 he was sent from Colchester to Preston, then in April 1876 to Armagh, and on 16th August the same year transferred to Athlone. On 27th September George was promoted

---

3   1861 census.

4   1871 census.

5   Army Forces records at the National Archives: WO/12/9080.

6   Ibid.

7   Hutt would appear on the Defaulters list a total of seven times.

to Sergeant.[8]

In early 1877 he married local girl Delia Cunniffe,[9] and was sent to Galway in April. The following month George complained of pain due to a varicocele of his left testicle, and was discharge as 'unfit for service' on 25th May 1877. On 2nd July he applied successfully for an army pension.[10]

George and Delia left Ireland for London, and Hutt began working at the warehouse of the Great Northern Railway Company on 29th July, employed as policeman and porter.[11]

At this time George and Delia were living at 32 Delhi Street,[12] a short walk along Regent's Canal to his place of work. Delhi Street was a row of residences designed to house people who worked on the railways in one way or another, and the 1871 and 1881 census returns show an engineer, a signalman and a ticket collector all living on Delhi Street.

After almost 18 months working for the Great Northern Railway Company George decided it was time for another change, and on 23rd January 1879 applied to join the City of London Police. One of his references was Major Sir Edward Hopton of his old regiment.[13]

A change of career meant that the Hutts lost their home. They are missing from the 1881 and 1891 census returns - it is possible they were given a home within the police force, somewhere within the City, such as Rose Alley, which was and still is very close to Bishopsgate Police Station and was home to many families of City policemen.

On his application form George is described as being 5ft 10½in tall, with blue eyes, brown hair and a fair complexion.[14]

On 1st August 1880, after serving 18 months as a policeman,

8   Army Forces records at the National Archives: WO/12/9080.
9   Marriage Record.
10 Army Forces records at the National Archives: WO/12/9080.
11 George Henry Hutt's application form for the City of London Police, CLA/048/ AD/01/364.
12 Ibid.
13 Ibid.

George had one day's leave taken away from him because he did not pass on information that he had received about a crime. This was a serious offence, but George seems not to have learned from the punishment because less than three months later, on 19th October 1880, he had his pay reduced to third class because he was found away from his beat and subsequently 'telling a falsehood'.[15]

On 27th July 1883 George was found drunk on duty and another leave day was again deducted, and on 3rd April 1885 he was found drunk, and although this time he was off duty and wearing plain clothes, because he was near Bishopsgate Police Station he still received a punishment of a reduction of his weekly pay to that of a third-class constable.[16]

Thankfully, the rest of George's police career was more positive.

On 24th January 1886, 'when snow lay in three or four inches' on the ground,[17] George was walking his beat along Broad Street near Bishopsgate churchyard when he saw the ground rise up in front of him. When the snow had fallen away, he realised that it was a flap to the cellar of a jeweller's shop opening and closing. He signalled to another policeman who was standing guard within the churchyard[18] and they both moved towards the shop, finding a man inside with over 80 watches and more than 200 rings in his pockets. George and the other officer took the man to the headquarters of the City of London Police, Old Jewry.[19]

On 2nd January 1887, PC Hutt is mentioned, if only briefly, in *Lloyd's Weekly Newspaper*. PC Pegram was walking his beat near

---

14 George Henry Hutt's application form, CLA/048/AD/01/364.

15 George Henry Hutt's misconduct record, CLA/048/AD/01/364.

16 Ibid..

17 *From Constable to Commissioner, The Story of Sixty Years Most of Them Misspent* by Lieut–Col Sir Henry Smith K.C.B.

18 Although in '*From Constable to Commissioner...*' by Sir Henry Smith, he stated that PC Hutt 'whistled for other policeman at the Churchyard,' this could not have happened as City of London Police beat constables did not have whistles until 1889. However it is worth noting that this book was written by using memories so some elements of it may not always be correct.

19 This is mentioned in '*From Constable to Commissioner...*' by Sir Henry Smith, although it does seem a little odd for two beat constables to take a thief to the headquarters of

Fleet Street at 1:45am when he saw a horsedrawn cab moving very slowly. On investigating, the constable found the driver, John Cox, drunk with a fare in his cab. PC Pegram stopped the cab and decided to take the driver to the cells to sober up. It was at this point that the passenger, Mr Thomas Lovell, an actor known for playing a clown on stage, became annoyed with the situation and being held up by this policeman, complaining that Mr Cox needed to finish the journey before being taken to the station. When PC Pegram tried to explain that this could not happen, Mr Lovell used abusive language, acting like 'a madman'. Mr Lovell called out to PC Hutt who, Lovell believed, knew him as an honourable gentleman. PC George Hutt's reply was that 'he was sorry to see [Mr Lovell] in this state'. Thomas Lovell was fined 20s for stopping the policeman doing his job, and John Cox was remanded for a short time.[20]

At this point, George Hutt was classed as being a Police Constable, and we know that a year later he was Bishopsgate Police Station's Gaoler. He must have been living somewhere in this area in 1887, perhaps even in Bishopsgate Police Station itself, and may simply have been away from home on the day the census enumerator called.

George Henry Hutt was a man of letters, strangely for a policeman at the time. He wrote constantly to the newspapers offering his opinions about life within the City. He even wrote poetry on certain subjects, becoming known as 'PC Poet', but this was to come later.

In 1888, writing under the initials 'G.H.H.', George wrote a letter to the *Evening News* which was published on 11th September 1888. George described that when he walked through the streets of Whitechapel he often overheard locals insulting the Jewish people who lived there. This was enhanced by the thought that Leather Apron, the unknown man linked to the Whitechapel Murders, was supposed to have a Jewish appearance. George asked the newspaper to print his letter because, 'being a pure Christian', he believed that

the City of London Police. As Sir Henry later mentions that Detective Robert Sagar was called in to investigate, one wonders if the thief was more important than just an every day street thief.

20 *Lloyd's Weekly Newspaper*, 2nd January 1887.

this hatred would get worse, perhaps even resulting in the murder of innocent persons if people did not calm down.[21] Hauntingly, this worry about how the public reacted to the Jewish community was highlighted only 19 days after the letter was published, with the discovery of a chalked message on the wall in Goulston Street, supposedly pointing a finger at the Jews.

What is also interesting about George's letter is that he gave his address as 48 and 49 Bishopsgate Without. In 1887, 48 and 49 Bishopsgate Without was a wine and beer distillery and a public house, one of many within the area. Both buildings were owned by William Barker. The public house was called The Old Jerusalem in the early part of 1880s, but after hearing the local story of a man who owned a warehouse near the public house, a man said to have been the inspiration for Charles Dickens' Miss Havisham, the pub's name was changed to 'Dirty Dicks', which it is still called today.[22]

George giving the address of a public house has led to the suggestion that he deliberately gave a fake address, as his employers may not have been happy with him writing to the newspapers on such a matter.

On the night of 29th September 1888, George walked into Bishopsgate Police Station at approximately 9:30pm, as according to regulations he had to turn up for his shift fifteen minutes before he was due to start. After being informed of what had happened in the previous shift, and possibly having a quick cup of coffee, his first duty was to visit the cells to check that any prisoners were safe and not causing themselves harm.[23]

He checked on the woman brought in just forty minutes earlier by PCs Robinson and Simmons, at 9:55pm.[24] He may have opened the small window of the cell door and looked through, seeing the sleeping woman lying under vast amounts of clothing, still smelling

21 *Evening News*, 11th September 1888.

22 Business Records: London Metropolitan Archives.

23 Inquest testimony of City Constable 968 George Henry Hutt, Coroner's Inquest (L) 1888, No. 135, Catherine Eddowes's Inquest 1888 at London Metropolitan Archives.

24 Inquest testimony of George Henry Hutt.

of drink, and closed the door window and thought nothing more about her.

George repeated his round a number of times over the hours which followed, until at 12:15am when he noticed that the woman was now sitting up and fully awake, singing quietly to herself.[25]

Fifteen minutes later, the policeman heard the woman calling out, and went to see what she wanted. Asked when she would be released, George replied: "When you are capable of taking care of yourself." He ignored her claims of being able to do so already, and left her for a further thirty minutes, before being told to fetch her by Station Sergeant Byfield, who, after speaking with the woman, judged her to be sober enough to be released and ordered George Hutt to escort her out of the station, sadly to her eventual doom.[26]

On 6th November 1889, just a year after he appeared at the inquest of Catherine Eddowes, George Henry Hutt resigned from the City of London Police. In his resignation letter, George asked Major Henry Smith, Commissioner of the City of London Police, for a 'Parchment Certificate of Discharge', a document used as a form of good reference to the next employer because, as George stated, he had only been reprimanded twice in the last six years of his service, referring to the two occasions he had been found drunk.[27]

We can only wonder what was going through George's mind while he waited to see if he would indeed get that all-important 'Parchment of Certificate', as this was rather an odd situation for him to be in because something rather significant had happened on 2nd September 1889, two months earlier, something which quite possibly ended George's career as an officer in the City of London Police force.

He had assaulted a prisoner in Moor Lane Police Station, while the prisoner was in the dock. George's service record doesn't go into detail about this - it would be very odd if it had done so, because to

25 Inquest testimony of George Henry Hutt.

26 Ibid.

27 Resignation letter held in George Henry Hutt's City of London Police record, CLA/048/AD/01/364.

advertise wrongdoings was unheard of.

His punishment was to have his pay reduced to that of a third-class constable, to receive no payment while on suspension and to have no increase in payment for the next three years.[28]

Although the force was not officially stating it, they were trying to pressure George Hutt into leaving on his own accord. Knowing he would be on a third-class constable's pay for the next three years, no matter how well he behaved from then on, must have been the reason why George chose to find other work.

It is difficult to understand why he neglected to mention this incident on his letter of resignation. The response from Commissioner Henry Smith was perhaps predictable, and it is possible that Smith was waiting for Hutt's letter of resignation to appear on his desk. He agreed to George's release from his role as a policeman, stating 'this Constable may be struck off the strength... at once'.[29]

A note written in red ink on George's letter of resignation states that the offence was so serious that he cannot have a Parchment, and these comments meant George Hutt would surely have known that he wouldn't receive one.

By the time of his departure from the office, George had already found employment as a constable at the London Central Meat and Poultry Markets in Smithfield's, London.[30]

In 1901, at the age of 47, George Hutt was working as a toll clerk and collector for the Corporation City of London, and living with wife Delia at 2 Canonbury Grove.[31]

He carried on working at Smithfield Market for a further five years before retiring, claiming his pension of 27s a week from the City of London Police force.[32]

In 1913, 24 years after he had left the City of London Police, the

28 George Henry Hutt's misconduct record, CLA/048/AD/01/364.

29 George Henry Hutt's service record, CLA/048/AD/01/364.

30 Resignation letter. George Henry Hutt's City of London Police record, CLA/048/AD/01/364.

31 1901 census.

force received a letter regarding George Hutt from British Canteens Limited who wanted a reference, preferably a good one, for George, who at the age of 60, had applied for the position of Canteen Manager.[33]

There could be a number of reasons why George felt the need to find work again. Maybe he had simply realised that retirement wasn't for him, or perhaps he and Delia were struggling to live on his 27s pension.

This is another odd situation. George must have put the City of London Police as a reference for the British Canteens company to contact - there really would not have been anyone else for him to use - but he must have felt nervous about the force's response, given the reaction to his earlier request for a Parchment. As it turned out, George did in fact have nothing to worry about because on 1st December 1914 the British Canteens Limited received a letter from the City of London Police, giving George a respectable reference.[34]

Sadly, George Henry Hutt died on 15th November 1918 of a heart attack brought on from heart disease.[35] He was buried on 25th November 1918 at Islington Cemetery.[36]

In a sense, simply writing that George died from a heart attack is misleading. An article in the *Islington Daily Gazette* revealed the full sad story.

PC 221J Sidney Garrett had to break into the Hutts' home after a neighbour, Mrs Hart, contacted the police when the Hutt's dog had been barking constantly and no one had answered the door. PC Garrett found George lying over the sink, where he had tried to get a glass of water, but had passed away in mid task.

Delia was found in the same room, on her knees, within yards of her husband, and she too had died. It was suggested by the famous

32 George Henry Hutt's service record, CLA/048/AD/01/364; 1911 census.
33 George Henry Hutt's service record, CLA/048/AD/01/364.
34 Ibid.
35 Death certificate.
36 Grave reference M/20754 Number 97976.

pathologist Dr Bernard Spilsbury, who worked on both their post mortems, that after seeing her husband pass away so quickly, Delia - who suffered from a heart condition - had a heart attack herself, and that sadly both had died within moments of each other.[37]

George Henry Hutt seems to be a man of two characters, and there is a temptation to describe him as a Jekyll and Hyde character. He seems to have cared about the way animals should be treated,[38] and used his talent with words to express this. He cared about religions other than his own and the treatment of those who followed them, as his published letters to the newspaper show.

However, his recorded serious assault on a prisoner within his care reveals a different side. But was it really bad behaviour? It was the Victorian era, when policemen were meant to be something to fear for the criminals. Perhaps on occasion they had to be a little rough in their approach and George took it too far. He was an ex 'army man' after all.

In truth, we will never understand why he did what he did, or his own thoughts on the matter. However, the naturally curious among us may wonder if Catherine Eddowes ever popped into his mind on occasion...

Station Sergeant James George Byfield

On the night of 29th September 1888, at about 8.45pm, two police constables struggled into Bishopsgate Police Station, where James Byfield was on duty as Desk Sergeant. He must have looked up at the commotion as PCs Robinson and Simmons brought in Catherine Eddowes.

James was one out of a few people that actually spoke to her in the last hours of her life, but whether he actually cared what her reply to him was – giving her name as 'Nothing' - can only be guessed at. In

---

37 *Islington Daily Gazette*, 19th November 1918.

38 In a previous letter titled 'A HORSE'S LETTER to Ex-Police Constable 365 John Pegg', Hutt gives his opinion on how horses should be treated. John Pegg was another policeman who seemed to care about the treatment of horses, as shown in an article in the *Illustrated Police News* of 23rd September 1882.

all likelihood, to him she was just another drunk to be added to the system, recording her details and then locking her up until she was sober.

James George Byfield was born in 1849 to James Sr,[39] a teacher of music and Emma, a dressmaker.[40] In 1851 the family was living in Lewisham, Kent, at 14 Charlotte Street.[41] James had gained a sister, Mary Ann, born earlier that year.[42]

Ten years later, at the time of the 1861 census, although the Byfield family was still living at the same address it had grown with the addition of two more children, Edward (b.1858) and Alice Rose (b.1860), and James was recorded as a scholar.[43]

The nearest school to where the Byfields were living was Plumstead Central School, which was a seventeen minute walk away. Built in 1856 on what was classed as 'waste land of the Manor of Plumstead',[44] James would have been one of the earliest pupils at this school, which was designed to help the education of the labouring and poorer classes.

The school could hold 165 boys, 118 girls and 147 infants at the time James would have attended, but as the number of pupils seeking places grew, the School Board of London decided to charge a fee to attend. So by 1877, the highest grade of children were paying 6d per month and the lowest 2d.[45]

In 1868 James headed into the world of work, taking perhaps an unconventional step by joining the police rather than the Royal Artillery at nearby Woolwich. At the age of 19 James became a

---

39 Born in 1827.

40 Also born in 1827.

41 Now called Perrott Street. All the homes along this street was later demolished to make way for a business block called Maynard House.

42 1851 census.

43 1861 census.

44 St Margaret's Church of England School records.

45 Ibid.

Constable in the City of London Police force, with the collar number 330 and warrant number 4171.[46] He was soon living in a police home at 13 West Smithfield.[47]

Numbers 24 to 30 West Smithfield have long disappeared to make way for an early 1970s-style building, however numbers 1 to 13 survive and show the Victorian brickwork that James would have seen.[48]

13 West Smithfield was situated opposite St Bart's Hospital[49] and to the left of Smithfield Market, and within two years of James moving there the market was greatly expanded on its west side, with the Jones' Poultry Market being built.[50] On a more personal note, James married Ellen Mary Grover in 1870, close to his hometown of Woolwich.[51]

On 16th October 1874, James was involved in a case of a theft of a purse, containing £2 3s and a railway ticket belonging to Ada Moxon. She had been waiting for her train at Ludgate Hill Station at 5:45pm, and when it arrived a man named John Lewis rushed at her and she felt his hand inside her pocket. He then ran off, with Ada shouting "Stop that man, he has my purse." Two men attempted to stop the thief but he got past them, only to be stopped by the station stairs by another man, and the purse was handed back to a grateful Ada. PC James Byfield was called to the scene at 5:50pm and took John Lewis to the nearest police station, Snow Hill, where he searched the criminal and found 14s 3d and a railway ticket from Ludgate Hill to Borough Road. At the Old Bailey, John Lewis, alias

---

46 James's City of London Police service record is missing from the London Metropolitan Archives and details are limited within the Bishopsgate Police Station record. However, a few details were unearthed by the author such as the collar number and warrant number he had at the start of his career.

47 1871 census.

48 Smithfield Conservation Area Character Summary and Management Strategy Supplementary Planning Documents, City of London Cooperation.

49 St Bart's allowed the police force to rent land from them to house the police home.

50 Smithfield Conservation Area Character Summary and Management Strategy Supplementary Planning Documents, City of London Cooperation.

51 In later census returns Ellen Mary was listed as Mary Ellen; this is a common mistake.

John Anderson, received seven years penal servitude, the strong punishment reflecting a previous conviction for theft in 1868.[52]

The Byfields' first child, Ellen Alice, was born in 1876 in the City of London, and a son, George Henry, was born in Shoreditch in 1880,[53] the family's address at this time being 123 Gladstone Buildings, Willow Road in Shoreditch.[54] This larger home was required to house the growing family, because not only did they already have two children, but Ellen would soon give birth to another son, Charles.[55]

Gladstone Buildings was a 23 minute walk from James's previous police home, but more importantly it was only a 13 minute walk away from Bishopsgate Police Station, where he had been appointed Station Sergeant.

Two tragedies then struck the Byfield family. First, at the beginning of 1886, daughter Ellen died at the age of ten,[56] and just over a year later, in late 1887, James's wife Ellen Mary also passed away.[57]

So when we meet Station Sergeant James Byfield[58] on the night of 29th September 1888, he was suffering from the grief of losing his own wife and daughter in a space of a year, and was now a single father of two growing boys, one aged eight and the other seven.

Three years later, in the 1891 census, James was recorded as a widower but had become a Station Inspector of the City of London Police force. He, Charles and George – both listed as scholars - had moved to Godwin Road, West Ham,[59] and one wonders if he kept in touch with former colleague James Harvey, who now lived less than

---

52 Old Bailey records.

53 Birth record.

54 Gladstone Buildings no longer exists. Built in the late 1860s and demolished in the 1970s, Gladstone Buildings was situated on the south side of Willow Street.

55 Charles Edward Byfield was born in 1881, although again on the census forms, his first name and middle name are reversed.

56 1886 death record.

57 1887 death record.

58 By now James had the collar number 44. Collar numbers did change over the period in which an officer would be in the force and one can presume that James's collar number changed when he was promoted from PC to Station Sergeant.

59 1891 census.

20 minutes away in Tower Hamlets Road, West Ham.

Then, in 1892, James finally enjoyed some happiness when he married for the second time, to Frances Sarah Harper in Lambeth.[60]

On 2nd April 1894, Station Inspector James Byfield was called to the Old Bailey to be a witness in a case of manslaughter. John Daniels was driving a pony and cart at high speed along Grave Lane, near Houndsditch, on 17th March when he knocked over a young boy called Israel Rosenberg. The boy was hit by the pony's chest, and fell back into the road and was sent to London Hospital.[61]

The incident was witnessed by Police Sergeant James Fuller, who was checking on the beat constables at the time. He ran over to the driver and discovered that not only was he was drunk and not in a fit state to drive, but he was also carrying another man in his barrow who was also drunk. Daniels was taken to Bishopsgate while PC Webber came back from the hospital with the news that Israel Rosenberg might die from his injuries, so Sergeant Fuller charged the driver of causing the death of the boy.[62]

At the station the driver claimed he was not drunk, at which point James Byfield got involved as the Station's Inspector, and stated to Daniels: "You are drunk", receiving the reply: "The boy ran from behind the van". This excuse was cut short by Sergeant Fuller, who stated there were no other vehicles in the road. However, at the Old Bailey John Daniels was found not guilty of manslaughter, it being decided that although the cart had caused the death of the child, it could not be proven whether the driver was actually drunk, or just appeared to be so.[63]

James retired from the City of London Police in 1895, and on the 1901 census he was recorded living at 34 Jasper Road, Lambeth, with wife Frances and his niece Alice Steed, the daughter of his

60 1901 census.

61 Old Bailey records. 'Grave Lane' is possibly a misspelling of Gravel Lane.

62 Old Bailey records.

63 Ibid.

64 Ladywell Cemetery death record.

sister Mary, who had passed away on 25th May 1900.[64] Also at the address was a servant named Ellen Ardley.[65]

James's son Charles Byfield was in 1901 living and working at 431 Norwood Road, Lambeth, as a Grocer's Assistant. Ten years later he was recorded at 41 High Street, Colchester, a Manager of a provision store.[66]

James's other son, George Henry Byfield, disappears from all census and workhouse records between 1901 and his death in Lambeth in 1927.[67] One possible answer for this could be found in the military service records for the First World War, which contain a Private 46230 in the Royal Defence Corps named George H Byfield. Whether the 'H' stands for Henry we do not know, but it would explain the missing years for George.[68]

In the 1911 census James described himself a Pensioner of the Police force, and was still living at 34 Jasper Road, Lambeth with his second wife Frances and his niece Alice, now employed by him as a domestic servant alongside Ellen Ardley.[69]

James died in the last quarter of 1927 in Lambeth at the age of 79,[70] at the same time and place as his son George Henry Byfield. Records cannot be found of their graves but one wonders if they were buried together.

We can never know the impact that the death of Catherine Eddowes had on James Byfield, at a time in which he was already dealing with so much grief in his own life. Was he racked with guilt at his decision to release Catherine?

---

65 1901 census.

66 1911 census. Charles later married a Daisy G Bloice in 1914 at Colchester, and died in Norfolk in 1944.

67 Death record.

68 Private George H Byfield, W0372/3, (National Archives).

69 1911 census.

70 Death record.

CHAPTER ELEVEN
'I Saw No-One'[1]

PC James Harvey

At 9.45pm on the night of 29th September 1888, PC James Harvey left Bishopsgate Police Station to begin his patrol of the Houndsditch area. It was a beat he had done before, and there were no expectations that this night would be different from any other. However, it took but one moment on James's beat, one decision, which changed James Harvey's life forever, perhaps spending the rest of his life filled with regrets and 'what ifs'...

Given his possible later regrets, it is an unhappy coincidence that James's beginnings were also not good. He was born on 4th February 1855 to mother Emily Mancer and father Thomas Harvey.[2] Any illusion that this was a normal family occasion was far from the truth; there is no record of a marriage between the couple, and in fact Thomas was already married with children of his own,[3] despite

---

1   Inquest testimony of City Constable 964 James Harvey, Coroner's Inquest (L) 1888. No. 135 Catherine Eddowes's Inquest 1888 held at the London Metropolitan Archives.

2   James Harvey's birth certificate.

3   1841 census.

Emily stating that she was married on the boy's certificate. However, the fact that Thomas Harvey is named as James's father on the birth certificate hints at an element of affection between he and Emily, as if had he wanted nothing to do with either her or his son it would be likely that the father would be unrecorded.

Thomas Harvey was a bricklayer living in the same town where James was born.[4] On the 1851 census, four years before James was born, we find Thomas Harvey, a bricklayer, living in a house called Pigknowel in Ashburnham, near Battle in Sussex. He was listed as head of the household, aged 38, with his wife Carroline Harvey aged 34 and their children Carroline (b.1839), William (b.1840), Hannah (b.1845) and Mary (b.1850).[5]

Thomas is also listed at the same address in the 1841 census, indicating that he had lived there for quite some time.

What happened to Emily Mancer is unknown, for she seems to disappear from all records after James' birth. However, we can pick up James again on the 1861 census. He was a six-year-old boy living with the Cramp family as a lodger, but a lodger that the Cramps had allowed to go to school rather than to work with the family of farmers.[6]

Interestingly, the Cramp family and James are recorded as living in a house called 'Pignoll' in Ashburnham. Although the spelling is slightly different, we can be fairly certain it is the same house in which James's father lived for at least twenty years. Now, in 1861, a new family had moved in and the Harvey family seems to have left James behind - a sign of the father's illicit union with Emily Mancer perhaps? One wonders if the Cramp family were being paid to look after James, as an extra mouth to feed would have certainly been a strain on a family which was already quite large, and yet the Cramp

4   James Harvey's birth certificate.

5   1851 census.

6   On the 1861 census, the Cramp family consisted of Charles Cramp, Agricultural Labourer, (b.1816), Clarissa, wife, (b.1819) and children, James (b.1843), Charles (b.1847), Harriett (b.1849), Horace (b.1852), William (b.1857), Mary (b.1859) and Elizabeth (b.1861).

7   1861 census.

family were able to send him to school.[7]

By the time James was 16 he had moved to Tarrett's Farm in Wartling, Hailsham in Sussex, living with the Morris family (who claim that James is their nephew), and working as a miller's apprentice.[8]

A look at Samuel Morris's family shows that he was the only child of John Morris and Maria Brazier,[9] which mean that James cannot be his nephew. So let us turn instead to Ann Morris, Samuel's wife, and all becomes clear, as her maiden name was Mancer.[10]

Ann was the sister of Emily Mancer, James' mother, and the reason why she and Samuel Morris took in James. However, they must have treated James well, for he remembered them years later when his own first son was born, naming him James Samuel Morris Harvey. Coincidentally, James Harvey and Samuel Morris shared the same birthday of 4th February.

At some point between 1871 and 1874, James gave up being a miller's apprentice and worked for a Mr David Shaw in his grocer's shop at 193 Eastern Road, Brighton.[11]

By April 1875, James left his aunt and uncle in Wartling and left his employment in Brighton to travel westwards to Southsea, Portsmouth. He found work at the warehouse of Herbert, Reeves and Company on Greenham Street,[12] spending eighteen months there before making another big move, this time to London, where in October 1876 he completed his application form for the City of London Police force.

James gave his address as Two Temple Lane, London, which fulfilled the requirement that constables live within the City boundary.

---

8   On the 1871 census, the Morris family consisted of Samuel Morris, a shoe maker (b.1821), Ann Morris, his wife (b.1828) and their son William Vitler (b.1853). William later married Mary Ann Ballard and they had twelve children together. William died on 29th June 1908 in Utah.

9   Born on 4th February 1821.

10 Ann Mancer (born 24th June 1827) and Samuel Morris married in 1849.

11 James Harvey's application form for the City of London Police held at the London Metropolitan Archives.

12 James Harvey's application form for the City of London Police. (CLA/048/AD/01/306).

On 15th November 1876, his prospective new employers wrote to the constabularies in which James's two previous places of work were based. The Borough of Brighton Police was contacted with a view to confirming that the reference of Mr Shaw the grocer was indeed correct and genuine. The Brighton police replied on 18th November confirming everything was above board.[13]

The Portsmouth Police received a letter asking whether the reference from Herbert, Reeves and Company was authentic, and they replied on 18th November that James Harvey had 'conducted himself with satisfaction,' and that 'Mr Reeves's signature is authentic.'[14]

Being a single man, James was housed within a police station, like many single officers, in his case at Bishopsgate.

On the morning of 10th January 1880 James was involved in a case of the attempted murder of two priests. He was called to the Italian Church in Hatton Garden at 10:30am, where he found a man named Alexander Scoseha standing by the altar. He had apparently entered the church at 9:45am, while a service was being performed. He sat down at the front of the church, and as one of the priests turned his back Scoseha stood up and shouted for everyone to leave, firing a revolver. He had fired at the priests and missed by only a few inches, the bullet travelling just past one of the priest's ears.

A man named James O'Donnell tried to tackle the shooter as he began smashing items around the altar, which included some lighted candles, and a fire was started. When PC James Harvey entered the church, he 'saw the prisoner near the altar, going towards the centre of the church. He went to the side of the church so as to get out of the way of the police. A gentleman accorded him, when it was found that he had a pistol in one hand and a dagger in the other.'[15]

Scoseha then attempted to stab both Jameses – Harvey and O'Donnell – as the latter grabbed the revolver out of the shooter's

13 James Harvey's service record, CLA/048/AD/01/306.
14 Ibid.
15 PC James Harvey's testimony as reported in the *Nottingham Evening Post*, 12th January 1880.

hand, and the constable succeeded in taking the dagger from the other hand. PC Harvey brought the prisoner outside, with Scoseha admitting: "I intended to kill the priest". He was taken Clerkenwell Police Court.[16]

James was still living in Bishopsgate Police Station at the time of the 1881 census with a number of other constables. In the same month in which the enumerator visited, Harvey was called to the home of Michael Taylor at 28 Duke Street, Houndsditch. Taylor's daughter Ellen, who lived with her father, had returned home drunk, and violently attacked her father, who called the police. Ellen was so violent that she turned her attentions on PCs Lees and Harvey when they arrived at the scene, and scratched James's face as he tried to take control of the situation.

Although she was examined, it was assumed that Ellen was of sound mind. Her father asked for protection from his daughter's violent ways, but she herself claimed that she was the injured party. Her final moment in court came when she was being taken down from the dock having been sentenced to one month's hard labour. Threatening that on her release she would "mark her father and the constables for what they had done to her," she was handed another two months on top of her sentence for her threat.[17]

In 1885 James married Clara Adelaide Craddock in West Ham,[18] suggesting James shortly afterwards moved out of the police station and to the address where he lived by the time of the 1891 census, 60 Tower Hamlets Road, West Ham.

His first born son, James Samuel Morris Harvey, was born in 1886 and was registered in Aldgate. This might seem to indicate that the family was still in Bishopsgate, but it could be the case that James simply registered the birth on his way to or from work. The family had certainly moved out of the City by 1889, when eldest daughter Alice was born, for she was registered in Stratford.[19]

16 *The Nottingham Evening Post*, 12th January 1880.
17 *Reynolds's Newspaper*, 17th April 1881.
18 Marriage record.
19 James and Clara's second son, William, was registered in Forest Gate.

It is unknown whether James was promoted or had any incidents to reduce his pay during his time with the City of London Police as his surviving service record is incomplete, but in 1888 he was a police constable with twelve years' service under his belt.

On the night of 29th September 1888 he started his beat at 9:45pm. Leaving Bishopsgate Police Station, he headed towards Bevis Marks, where his beat began, roughly from where No. 14 is today. Above him would have been, as it is today, an ornate plaque commemorating in Hebrew the oldest Jewish Synagogue in London.[20]

PC James Harvey carried on walking straight along the main road where Bevis Marks turns into Duke Street, now Duke's Place, he then turned sharply to the left before walking along the short road of Little Duke Street,[21] checking all the locks of the businesses along the way until he reached Houndsditch. He then crossed Little Duke Street and headed back towards Duke Street on the opposite side, checking the locks of this side too.

On re-entering Duke Street, James turned left and crossed over the road to walk along the small alleyway called Church Passage,[22] which led into Mitre Square.

James would have known not to have entered the square itself, as this was outside of his beat, so he turned back on himself, walking back up Church Passage and joining Duke Street once again, this time turning right towards Aldgate, walking along this road as far as Mitre Street then crossing the road in order to walk back along Aldgate towards Aldgate High Street. One wonders whether he took a moment to take a glance at the Aldgate Pump, to check all was unharmed or whether people were being a nuisance around it.[23]

---

20 Bevis Marks Synagogue, or Qahal Kadosh Sha'ar ha-Shamayim, was built in 1701. The Hebrew wording on the plaque which PC James Harvey would have seen, reads 'Holy Congregation Gate of Heaven'. The Synagogue was built for the Spanish and Portuguese communities, and is now a Grade I listed building. *Jewish Encyclopedia: 1901–1906.*

21 This is now called Creechurch Lane.

22 Now called St James's Passage, this is much larger than it would have been in James's time.

23 Aldgate Pump, which PCs James Harvey and Edward Watkins would have seen on their beats, was placed on the junction of Fenchurch Street and Leadenhall Street in 1876.

James then walked back past Duke Street and crossed Aldgate near the point where it became Aldgate High Street,[24] checking that all the businesses windows and doors were secure.[25] He then turned left into Houndsditch, passing St Botolph Aldgate church.[26]

While walking along Houndsditch, James had a few business premises to check, such as the recently closed hardware merchants at No. 22.[27] Turning left off Houndsditch into Little Duke Street, then back into Houndsditch, he turned left along Goring Street to head back towards Bevis Marks to complete his beat, before starting once again.

PC James Harvey would testify that:

> At twenty to two on Sunday morning I went down Duke Street and down Church Passage as far as Mitre Square. I saw no one. I heard no cry or noise. When I got to Aldgate, returning to Duke Street I heard a whistle blown and saw the witness Morris with a lamp.[28]

This meant that in the time it took James to leave the edge of Mitre Square, head along Duke Street to Aldgate, walk to the entrance of Mitre Street and be on his return to Houndsditch, Jack the Ripper had already met Catherine Eddowes, had taken her into Mitre Square, had killed and mutilated her, had escaped, and the body had been found and the alarm raised. This happened in not much time at all. Taking timings into account, it is very likely that as James was walking along Church Passage towards Mitre Square, Jack was killing Catherine Eddowes in the shadows, unseen by PC Harvey.

How must James have felt when he realised this was the case? That if he had perhaps broken the rules and had entered further into the square he might have caught the most famous serial killer

---

24 From this position James would have seen, at least, numbers 79 to 82 Aldgate High Street, part of what was known as 'Butcher's Row'.

25 Inquest testimony of City Constable 964 James Harvey.

26 Apparently known as the 'prostitutes' church', although there has been recent discussion that this is a relatively recent invention as there is no evidence that in 1888 the church was called this.

27 *The London Gazette*, 19th December 1890.

28 Inquest testimony of City Constable 964 James Harvey.

of his time red-handed, or could possibly even have saved a life? Did he wonder if the light from his Bullseye lamp signalled his approach to the killer, allowing him to hide himself?

This is all, of course, assuming that James Harvey was keeping time on his beat. He would never state otherwise as being late was against the rules, but we know from weather records that rain had fallen quite heavily from 9:45 that evening, and according to the testimony of the witnesses who had seen Catherine Eddowes with a man moments before she had died, they had sheltered from the rain after leaving the club.

Had PC Harvey done the same? Could he have sheltered from the rain, allowing the worst to pass before setting off again? If this was indeed the case, he would have had to make up the time on his beat – did he miss out the short walk into Church Passage at that fatal moment?

We have no information as to why James Harvey was dismissed from the City of London Police force less than a year later, on 1st July 1889. While colleagues would retain their jobs despite being caught going with a girl while on his beat[29] or assaulting a prisoner,[30] it does make one wonder exactly what James Harvey did, and when. Did he really not venture down Church Passage, and his slip was discovered? Or did the regret of not catching the Ripper prompt him to do something considered to be extremely bad, more so than the other misdemeanours already mentioned?

Incredibly, James Harvey has been suggested as a suspect in the Whitechapel murders. Did James go with a girl on his beat? Did something go wrong and he had to silence her, covering his tracks by killing her in the same fashion as 'Jack'? As ludicrous as this sounds, with so many holes in his surviving service record the answers to these questions will probably never be answered.

On leaving the force James was recorded as being 34 years and 4 months old, 5ft 11in tall, with grey eyes, brown hair and a fair

---

29 PC Edward Watkins.
30 PC George Hutt.

complexion.[31]

Two years later, in the 1891 census, James was living with wife Clara and children James Jr, Alice and newborn William. James had found work similar to what he had undertaken before he joined the police, and was employed as a warehouseman.[32]

Ten years later the Harvey family had moved to 74 Pearcroft Road in Leytonstone,[33] and James was now working as a foreman dustman. All the children were still at home, with the new addition of Clara Amelia Rose Harvey, born in 1899.

James Harvey died at the age of 48 from pneumonia in the Union Workhouse in Leytonstone on 21st April 1903.[34] However, it was not until 18th September that year that he was buried, at West Ham Cemetery. The five month wait could be a sign that the Harvey family were trying to come up with the money for a private grave, but the fact that James was finally buried in a pauper's grave which to this day has sixteen other people in it[35] indicates that the family was unable to raise the funds. There is no headstone to commemorate him.[36]

Thankfully, his family carried on with their lives. Clara was still living at 74 Pearcroft Road on the 1911 census, with her daughter Clara Jr,[37] who was now twelve-years-old and in school.[38]

Also living with his family was James Jr, even though he had married Esther Mary Lloyd the previous year in West Ham. They already had a son, Cyril J Lloyd Harvey,[39] and Esther was heavily

---

31 James Harvey's service record, CLA/048/AD/01/306.

32 1891 census.

33 1901 census.

34 Death certificate.

35 Cemetery record.

36 It is possible that there was originally a headstone, as sadly a pile of broken headstones lie in a ditch to the right of James Harvey's grave.

37 Clara Amelia Rose married William A Hartley in 1923 at West Ham. She died in 1991 at the age of 102. One wonders if she ever picked up a Jack the Ripper book, and if so what did she think about her father being mentioned in it?

38 1911 census.

39 Ibid.

pregnant with their second child, James H Harvey. Sadly, the child would not survive long.[40]

The location of James Harvey's grave, registration number 86276 in the G Plot, is hard to distinguish. Although the plot is somewhat small compared to the size of West Ham Cemetery in its entirety, it is a rather calming plot positioned on top of a hill. In the middle is a grave marked out but without a headstone; one wonders if this is the final resting place of the man who may have been the closest person to have caught Jack the Ripper in the only way a Victorian policeman could, red-handed.[41]

---

40 Birth and death records. James and Esther went on to have two further children, Alice (b.1912) and William A D Harvey (b.1915).

41 West Ham Cemetery records.

CHAPTER TWELVE

I Saw Everything

PC Edward Watkins

On the cold, wet morning of 30th September 1888, PC Edward Watkins was still walking the same beat he had begun the night before, but now the night had turned into the next morning and Edward was now probably thinking of having a warm breakfast inside him and being away from this bad weather. All he needed to do was to complete his beat, checking various locks belonging to businesses he passed along his way. All was well and thoughts of a breakfast was drawing nearer, when he turned from Mitre Street into Mitre Square to check the coal hole that was situated in the bottom right-hand corner as he entered the square was secure.

Mitre Square was dark, darker than it would normally be as some lights within the square were not working correctly that morning, and perhaps PC Edward Watkins unclipped his Bullseye lamp from his belt to angle the light in order to see the coal hole. We can imagine that it was very far from his mind that he would encounter the sight that he saw, lying on top of coal hole...

Born in 1842 in St Pancras, north London,[1] Edward was the youngest child of three born to John and Elizabeth Watkins, his elder siblings being Mary (b.1836) and Thomas (b.1840). When he was nine years old, the whole family was living at 15 New Street in Kensington, London,[2] a fairly well to do area judging by Henry Mayhew's comments on neighbouring Silver Street.[3] In the 1851 census John Watkins was listed as being as a butler, and all three of his children were at school.

Edward might have walked the eleven minutes from his family home to the nearest school in the area at that time, the Charity School in Kensington High Street. The school building, on the northern side of the street, was known for its unique architecture, which included a shallow bell-tower designed by Nicholas Hawksmoor between 1711 and 1712.[4] The charity school grew in size due to the increasing numbers of children in the area, and teachers promising to teach freely to the poorer classes. A new girls' school was added in 1804,[5] so by the time Edward probably attended school it must have seemed to be an enormous place for the little boy of nine-years-old.

In the 1861 census, the whole of the Watkins family disappears off any record. They were not recorded at any workhouse or asylum. The fact that the whole family are missing suggests that they had moved out of 15 New Street and, knowing that the western side of New Street was demolished in 1862, probably resulting in the families on that side being evicted the year before, research had to be undertaken to see if no. 15 existed on the 1861 census. It did not.[6] We therefore have a probable reason for the Watkins family not appearing in the census of that year, although it is still unknown where they moved to, or if they simply was not in their new home

1   Birth record.

2   New Street changed its name in 1912 to Newcombe Street.

3   Now called Kensington Church Road. *The Shops and Companies of London* by Henry Mayhew, 1865. pp.152-3.

4   Nicholas Hawksmoor made himself known as a Clerk of Works at Kensington Palace at the same time he designed the bell for the Charity School. The statue of a girl and boy by Thomas Eustace which was situated at the entrance of school now stands in the grounds of St Mary Abbots School.

5   Charity School minutes, 8th March - 3rd July 1804.

6   On the 1861 census, New Street starts at Number 18.

when the enumerator called.[7]

Wherever Edward Watkins was living, he was most likely not that far from New Street as he could well have been courting a certain Elizabeth Pryke at that time, a 19-year-old domestic servant living in 1861 at her workplace at 5 St Mary Terrace, Paddington.[8]

The couple married in 1863 at Kensington,[9] and the newlyweds would move to 2 Walmer Road, Bramley Street, Kensington,[10] next door to his parents.

In the 1871 census it stated that one 'Mary Watkins', daughter of Elizabeth Watkins, was born in 1864 and that another daughter, 'Sophia Watkins', was born in 1866. There seem to be a few mistakes in this entry, as ten years later 'Mary' becomes 'Emily Watkins' with the birth year of 1867, and 'Sophia' was listed as 'Sophy', born in 1870. Further research showed that there was an Emily Mary Watkins born in 1866 in the right area, and a Sophia Watkins born in the correct area in 1870, which corrects the errors found in the 1871 census.

With a new wife and two young daughters, it seems that Edward decided he ought to change jobs for a more secure career, so he joined the police... the Metropolitan Police force!

Aged 29, Edward Watkins joined the Metropolitan Police on 31st October 1870, being given warrant number 53299 and collar number 84 of the Lambeth Division.[11]

He would not last long in this new career, in fact just seven months. On leaving he was awarded Leavers Register Conduct Cert 4. This could mean one of two things; either there is no record of any good or bad service for Edward, or that he left on a 'latterly good' record. This was not always the best way to leave the Metropolitan Police force, as Leavers Register Conduct Cert 1 means 'Exemplary', Cert 2

---

7   The 1861 census was taken on 7th April 1861.

8   1861 census.

9   Marriage record.

10 The 1871 census, and Edward's application form for the City of London Police.

11 Edward Watkins' file held at the Historical Collection of The Met Collection, Summary of Police Service at the Heritage Centre.

means 'Very Good', Cert 3 means 'Good', and Cert 4 means 'Latterly good'.

'Latterly' is an interesting word; it could mean 'recently', 'currently' or even 'in recent times'. Considering this is the lowest number you can leave the force without actually being dismissed, this seems to suggest that something went wrong 'recently'. Edward had a good record, but it begs the question of when did he not have one?

Edward left the Metropolitan Police on 15th May 1871. What had happened to cause this? He joined the City of London Police on 25th May 1871, and sheet of paper held in his service file contains a note dated 22nd May by City Sergeant J. Marshall that 'no report against him' had been made - does this hint at some incident or other involving Edward Watkins from his Metropolitan Police days?

On his application form to join the City Police force Edward claimed that he was living with his wife and family at 2 Walmer Road, Bramley Street, Kensington. However, on the census taken just seven weeks earlier, Edward was recorded as a boarder at 2 Great Charlotte Street[12] in Southwark, residing above a coffee shop run by Edwin Griggs and his wife Anne, along with children Henry, Anna and Emily.[13]

This has led in recent years to a suggestion that Edward had separated from his wife for some reason but did not want to admit it to his new employer. However, the simple answer to this conundrum is that on 2nd April, when the 1871 census was taken, Edward was still working for the Metropolitan Police force in Lambeth Division, and despite being a married officer and therefore able to live outside of the police section houses, would have required to be close by should he be needed. The address at Great Charlotte Street was within Lambeth Division, just an 18-minute walk from Kennington Police Station. His enforced living apart from his family could well explain why he only spent seven months in that force.

Then Edward applied to join the City of London Police, who not

---

12 Now called Union Street.

13 Although this property is now an estate agent, you can still see the Victorian windows above the shop which Edward no doubt looked out of in 1871.

only paid more money than the Met[14] but also allowed him to live with his family, and another factor in his decision to leave the Met was that his wife was pregnant with a third child - Howard Vincent's *Police Code* stating clearly that '...no candidate must be over thirty five years of age, *or have more than two children depending upon him for support.*'

A third daughter, Julia Ann Watkins, was born in the City of London in late 1871.[15]

On his application to the City Police Edward is described as being 5ft 9in tall, with brown hair, grey eyes and a dark complexion.[16] After his introduction training[17] he was certified fit for service on 20th July 1871, starting his working life for the City of London Police as a Police Constable of the third class, with a rate of pay of 21s per week.[18] He began his new career with no problems and was soon promoted to Police Constable Second Class, with a pay rise of an extra 3s a week.[19]

Perhaps Edward felt a little too comfortable within the City of London Police force, or maybe the time spent apart from his family created a small fracture in his previous strong relationship with his wife Elizabeth. For whatever reason, Edward made a serious mistake.

On 25th August 1872, PC Edward Watkins was called before Acting Commissioner Henry Smith and given a dressing down. Despite having committed an offence which might well have seen

---

14 Something which was used to encourage capable young men to join the City Force rather than the Met Force, this carried on for many years as in 1901 the basic wage was for Met constables was 25s 6d, whereas the equivalent for a City PC was 33s 6d.

15 In the 1881 census, Edward's third child was listed as Annie, born 1872 in Bishopsgate, but ten years later she is called Julia, born 1872 in Bishopsgate. Surprisingly, there is a simple answer to this. There was only one Julia Ann Watkins born in the latter quarter of 1871 in the City of London, and as Julia Ann Meek nee Watkins was buried with Edward, we can be sure this is the answer to the name problem on the census.

16 Edward's application form for the City of London Police force, CLA/048/AD/01/770.

17 From 1840, this was done at 26 Old Jewry.

18 Edward's service record for the City of London Police force, CLA/048/AD/01/770.

19 Ibid.

him lose his job, Edward was lucky to escape with the punishment of the loss of 2s 6d, a sign perhaps of how well he was received in the City force before this incident. Edward had been seen having sexual intercourse with an unknown woman while on his beat.[20]

Perhaps Edward breathed a sigh of relief at not losing his job, but this may have been the beginning of the end for Edward's marriage to Elizabeth.

In the same year, the wage of a second class constable was raised to 28s. Edward did indeed receive this welcome increase in salary although only for a short time, for yet again he failed in his duties. On 1st January 1873, New Year's Day, Edward was found drinking heavily in a public house, the name of which is not recorded in his disciplinary file.[21] The Commissioner of the City of London Police, Sir James Fraser, was a little harsher than his Acting Commissioner had been four months earlier, and demoted Edward to third class and an associated loss of pay. He was also fined following an incident on 12th February when he had failed to notice a key left in the lock of a business premises while on his beat.[22]

We can only assume that Edward's mind wasn't entirely on his work. Was it a sign of a breakdown in the marriage?

A year later, Edward seems to have pulled himself together, and was promoted Police Constable second class on 2nd February 1874, his salary increasing to 28s per week.[23]

A further two and a half years on, on 8th June 1876, he was again promoted to Police Constable first class, with the high rate of pay of 31s per week.[24]

At this point, did Edward think to himself that he was now comfortable and as a result became slack? For this promotion lasted but a few weeks, when he was caught yet again drinking on duty on

---

20 Edward's Disciplinary record for the City of London Police, CLA/048/AD/01/770.

21 Ibid.

22 Ibid.

23 Edward's service record for the City of London Police, CLA/048/AD/01/770.

24 Ibid.

the night of 1st July 1876.[25] Although it would take his superiors a month to demote him back to second class wages for a period of three months, another punishment which seems somewhat lenient. On 5th October 1876, Edward received his first class pay back again,[26] this time managing to stay out of trouble.

By 1881 Edward had certainly separated with his wife, as she is no longer with the family. Elizabeth Watkins seems to disappear completely - she is in no workhouse, asylum or even death record. Edward continues to claim he is married until his dying day, with no record of another marriage to someone else, suggesting no divorce from Elizabeth.

Along with Edward's three children, the 1881 census lists a housekeeper named Augusta Fowler, who in one form or another would spend 32 years with Edward Watkins, including claiming to be his wife in the 1891 census.

She was born Augusta Ann Fowler in 1843 in Hull, Yorkshire, to James Augustus Fowler and his wife Ann. Although Augusta was baptised in Hull's Holy Trinity church on 14th August 1843, something her parents no doubt were wishing to give her the best start in life, research into her parents' life suggests that all did not go well.

In the census before Augusta was born, 1841, James Augustus Fowler was listed as a servant to the Lundy family in a large manor house in Whitefriargate with three other servants, William Hall, Ann Alkinson and Ann Glenn.[27] The last 'Ann' is of interest, because in the 1851 census Augusta Fowler (now aged eight) was listed as a visitor at the household of the Glenn family at 4 Union Place, St Mary's, Chatham in Kent.[28] Was Ann Glenn her mother, and Augusta was visiting her mother's side of the family?[29] If so, we have two servants of the Lundy household having a child together at a time

---

25 Edward's Disciplinary record for the City of London Police. CLA/048/AD/01/770.

26 Edward's service record for the City of London Police. CLA/048/AD/01/770.

27 1841 census.

28 In the 1851 census, Augusta was recorded as being a visitor at the home of James Glenn and his wife Ann, and their children Louisa, Charles, James and Julia.

when it might not have been socially accepted.

Interestingly, ten years later Augusta was 17-years-old and working at 148 York Street, Manchester, as a servant to a certain Jane Lundy, the youngest daughter in the Lundy household who were the employers of both parents in 1841.[30]

In 1871, Augusta had moved back down to Kent to be a servant for Jessie Cooke, who was actually much younger than Augusta at the age of 19. It may be for this reason that Augusta started to lie about her age, because although her age had changed with every census to that point,[31] it had only been a few years' difference. But from 1871, large discrepancies were recorded in her age, as she told the enumerator that she was 24 despite really almost turning thirty.

Ten years later, when she joined the Watkins household in rooms at 6 Eldon Street, not that far away from Bishopsgate Police Station, she said she had been born in 1850, a whole seven years later than she actually was.[32]

The family had moved away from Eldon Street by 1886, when Edward's father John Watkins sadly passed away. He was buried on 14th October 1886,[33] and his last abode was 23 Hamilton Buildings, Great Eastern Street. This was the address to which Edward and his family moved to after Eldon Street.

At the beginning of that year, on 11th January, Edward appeared at the Old Bailey as a witness in a case of theft. He had been called

---

29 The most likely member of the Glenn family to have a connection to Augusta's mother would have been the head of the household, James, as he was the only member to be born in Yorkshire. His job as a shipwright quite possibly resulted in him moving down to Chatham in Kent.

30 1861 census.

31 Augusta was born and baptised in 1843, but in the 1861 census she was apparently born in 1844.

32 In 1891, Augusta moved with Edward and his daughters Emily and Julia to Hamilton Buildings, Great Eastern Street. She claimed to have been born in 1846 and was recorded as Edward's wife, although there is no marriage record. This could be a mistake by the census taker. In 1901, Augusta reverted to her maiden name of Fowler, but she still claimed to be married, and said she was born in 1847 (rather than 1843). She died in Romford in 1922.

33 Death record of John Watkins.

to the Hercules public house near the Royal Exchange at about 10.45pm on 23rd December 1885, where he saw Thomas Knoling Edwards and Clara Turner engaged in a fierce argument. Edwards told PC Watkins that the 23-year-old Clara had stolen some money out of his trouser pocket, to which Clara replied that she had not. PC Watkins asked Mr Edwards, 'Do you charge her?' receiving the reply that if Clara returned him his money he would not charge her.

Clara still claimed she had nothing belonging to Thomas Edwards, so Edward asked again: 'Will you charge her?' Thomas again stated no, because he was a married man. At this point Edward decided there was nothing more he could do and left the scene. He probably thought that would be the end of it, but was not to know that the scene carried on, with fellow City Policeman Thomas Overton 914 arriving and taking Clara to Bishopsgate Police Station, an eight minute walk away. Here, she was searched and five sovereigns, a sixpence, a comb and a pencil case were found on her person. The case was taken to the Old Bailey, where Clara pleaded guilty and was sentenced to ten months hard labour.[34]

Now we turn to another case and to the year 1888, specifically the night of Saturday, 29th September. Edward left his quiet home in Great Eastern Street at approximately 9:15pm, closing the door and entering the street. Noises from the nearby Red Lion public house, which was now behind him as he turned in the direction of Bishopsgate Police Station, might have seemed dull to Edward's accustomed ears. He may have kept one eye on the weather all day, seeing the dark clouds building over the City and sensing it would be another night where he would get soaked through while on his beat.[35]

Entering Bishopsgate Police Station less than fifteen minutes later,

34 Old Bailey records (t18860111-223).

35 Weather records for the night of 29th September 1888 state that it started to rain heavily from 9:45pm.

during muster he was informed of everything that had occurred on the day's previous shifts and told that he would be walking his beat left-handed that night, as previously mentioned the switch designed to confuse any criminals who may have been observing a constable's beat.[36]

Edward might have made doubly sure that he had enough oil in his Bullseye lamp; it was going to be a dark night, with cloud coverage at 100% and the moon only 39% illuminated.[37]

We will never know if Edward wondered who was in the Bishopsgate Police Station's cells that night, but as he was getting ready for the number eight beat which he had been given,[38] the woman that he would soon discover horribly murdered was probably sleeping off her drunkenness in the cells a few levels below him.

By the time Edward left the station, at roughly 9:45pm, to start his beat at 10:00pm, the heavens had indeed opened. Nevertheless, he turned to the left and walked the short distance along Bishopsgate itself, turning left again towards Duke's Street. He turned right onto Heneage Lane, a small, short lane full of dwellings and shops to bring him out through a part of Bury Street, and with a turn to the right Edward was in Creechurch Lane and walking towards Leadenhall Street.

On reaching this main artery of the City, Edward turned left and walked along the road that was lined with tall buildings whose brickwork was similar in colour to that of the Bank of England.

He turned left again onto Mitre Street, and next, right into Mitre Square.

PC Watkins walked around the square in an anti-clockwise direction. He checked the back of Mr Taylor's picture framing business, whose frontage was in Mitre Street. Perhaps he raised his lamp from his belt, to check that the windows had been closed

---

36 See 'As Far as Mitre Square' by Jake Luukanen and Neil Bell, *Ripperologist* 71, September 2006.

37 Weather record and lunar phases for the night of 29th September 1888.

38 City of London Police Order Books for sixth division (Bishopsgate) 1889-1891.

and secured, and that all shutters were connected and locked. Possibly he hit his hand or kicked his foot against the wooden fence of Heydemann and Company's warehouse, to check whether it was locked. Edward also had to check on the coal hole that was situated on the ground at the entrance of Heydemann's warehouse, to make sure that the cover was firmly placed over the hole and secure. This coal hole would be important on a later round of his beat, but for the moment all was well.

On reaching the south-eastern corner of the square he turned left to walk north alongside the tall warehouse of Horner and Co., checking once again all the windows, locks and doors.

He then reached another of the entrances into the square, Church Passage. As this passage was part of PC James Harvey's beat, perhaps Edward briefly stood underneath the gas lamp at the end of the passage and shone his lamp up towards Houndsditch, knowing that Church Passage was under the patrol of another constable.

After seeing nothing unusual, Edward turned to his left and strolled alongside the warehouse belonging to Kearley and Tonge. One wonders if he would have seen the door to this warehouse slightly ajar at this time, perhaps even seeing a dimly light through the gap,[39] but Edward would have known not to have been concerned as Kearley and Tonge hired a nightwatchman, who he may have had a quiet conversation and perhaps even shared a cup of coffee with from time to time.

Edward then turned left again, past St James's Passage, coming to the second warehouse owned by Kearley and Tonge in Mitre Square. Now, he was facing back into the square as he walked along the side of this warehouse. One wonders if Edward could see the other dwellings within the square from the weak light of his Bullseye lamp, including number 3 Mitre Square, the home of PC Richard

---

39 Although in *The Curse Upon Mitre Square: A.D. 1530-1888* by John Francis Brewer, written just a few months after the murder of Catherine Eddowes, it is stated that 'A large tea house in the square hires a private watchman, and he was on duty last night, with lights blazing from five windows.' Although this book is a wonderful read if you like to know how people were feeling at the time of the murders, whether it is technically factual is another matter.

Pearce, who was off duty at this time and amazingly at home with his family.[40]

Leaving the square, Edward turned right back into Mitre Street, and then into King Street[41] where he might have spent a few seconds to tune his ears in the direction of the Old Jewellery Mart public house to see whether he could hear more than the normal brawls and loud voices. If he worked number eight beat regularly over the years, Edward would have known this public house, and it could have been where he had been caught drinking while on duty.

Edward then walked through to St James's Place, a square of considerable size.[42] There would have been a gas lamp in the centre with a wooden fire station, which at the time was being updated and no doubt caused some 'roadworks'.[43]

Edward would then have walked back into Duke Street, his beat taking twelve to fourteen minutes to complete if there was nothing amiss in all his security checks and he walked at the regulation pace.

Edward repeated the route a few times in his shift,[44] and started another such circuit at about 1:30am on the morning of 30th September.

Back along the familiar streets he walked, until arriving on Mitre Street at about 1:42am. No doubt he wished that one of the coffee rooms which were situated at 6 and 7 Mitre Street were open.

As he entered Mitre Square he slid the shield of his Bullseye lamp over to give him full access to the light, for the two lamps within Mitre Square - the lamp at the bottom of Church Passage and the light attached to the Kearley and Tonge factory - were not working

---

40 PC Richard Pearce was later to claim that he had heard nothing unusual the whole night and early morning.

41 Now the extended Creechurch Lane.

42 Henry Mayhew wrote that St James's Place was 'a large square yard, with the iron gates of a synagogue in one corner.' It is interesting to note that in the 1881 census it is stated that a policeman lived at this synagogue, perhaps as protection for the Jewish community.

43 James Blenkinsop was the nightwatchman for these roadworks. See 'As Far as Mitre Square' by Jake Luukanen and Neil Bell, *Ripperologist* 71, September 2006.

44 About thirteen circuits in total.

correctly that night, and with the poor weather the square would have been very dark.

As Edward passed Mr Taylor's picture framing shop he no doubt shone his lamp onto the spot on the ground where he expected to see the coal hole, but this time, oddly, he could not see it, something was blocking his view.

It was the body of Catherine Eddowes.

Edward must have been in a state of shock - he had passed this spot no more than fifteen minutes earlier, and all had been safe and well. At some point since PC Watkins' last visit, the killer had walked here with his victim, killed her in the most brutal fashion and left her for Edward to find. Edward would later say that the woman's 'stomach was ripped up and that she was lying in a pool of blood',[45] but however shocked the constable was, his policeman's instincts must have kicked in and perhaps his knowledge of the *Police Code* came to mind.

Sir Howard Vincent's *Police Code* stated in relation to murder that 'when a dead body or part of a dead body, is found, whereof the cause of death was evidently due to foul means, the constable whose attention is first called thereto should on no account move it or anything surrounding it; or allow any other person to do so; or in any way confuse footmarks in its vicinity until the arrival of an Inspector or other superior officer, for whom, and for a Surgeon, a message should be sent...'[46]

Edward therefore knew that he had to raise the alarm for a message to be sent for an Inspector at the nearest police station, in this case Bishopsgate, and another message needed to be sent to the nearest doctor. Edward Watkins had no whistle as a part of his City of London Police uniform[47] to raise the alarm, but he knew someone who did and although it would mean that he would have to leave the scene, it would only be for a few seconds and he would not be

---

45 Inquest testimony of City Constable 881 Edward Watkins.

46 *Sir Howard Vincent's Police Code, 1889* by Neil R A Bell and Adam Wood (2015).

47 The City of London Police did not issue whistles until 1889.

leaving the square.

He decided to run across the square, to where he had seen a door slightly open at the Kearley and Tonge warehouse on an earlier beat. Once he reached it he pushed open the door and saw the nightwatchman George Morris[48] still sweeping the stairs. Edward shouted to the man 'For God's sake mate, come to my assistance!'[49] Perhaps seeing a combination of disbelief and horror in Edward's face, Mr Morris did not question him further and instantly shouted back, 'Stop! Till I get my lamp!'[50]

While he waited for Mr Morris to fetch his own lamp, Edward noted the time as 1:45am. Once they were both outside the warehouse, Mr Morris asked Edward what was the matter, to which Edward replied 'There's another woman cut to pieces!'

On arriving back at the body Morris was able to see for himself the horrendous state the woman was in and he began blowing his own whistle, heading towards Aldgate via Mitre Street to fetch help, leaving PC Edward Watkins with the body.

Edward continued to follow the *Police Code*, which advised that he must make 'a careful examination of the area, for any footmarks about the body, which should be modelled or covered over before fresh imprints are made by the surgeon or police.'[51]

Edward knew he had to make note 'of the position of the body and of the condition of its clothing.'[52] He did in fact note the bloodied fingermarks, almost certainly the killer's, which were on the victim's chemise, and her other soiled clothing which had been ripped and torn in many places, the rest pushed up around her waist. Edward noted that she was on her back, her stomach had been ripped opened with her bowels protruding. One wonders what unpleasant odours he must have smelt as he was making his notes.

---

48 Ex-Metropolitan Police officer George Morris served in that force between 1856 and 1863 and also 1864-1882.

49 Inquest testimony of George Morris.

50 Ibid.

51 *Sir Howard Vincent's Police Code, 1889* by Neil R A Bell and Adam Wood (2015).

52 Ibid.

George Morris then returned with City constables James Harvey and Frederick Holland, and because it was Edward Watkins who had found the body, it was he who took control. He sent PC Holland to fetch the nearest doctor, Dr George Sequeira at 34 Jewry Street. Edward stayed with the body until the doctors and Inspector Collard turned up at the scene.

How Edward coped with what he saw on the morning of 30th September 1888 we will never be certain, for he was later quoted as saying that 'A more dreadful sight I never saw; it quite knocked me over.'[53]

Picking up his career after the Jack the Ripper atrocities, Edward Watkins would be in trouble for one more misdemeanor, when just over a year later, on 14th October 1889, he was caught drinking while on duty yet again. This time, he was reprimanded and 'pointedly cautioned', which leads one to consider that this was enough for Edward to break his bad habits, for he never again needed to be called into his superior's office for bad behaviour.

In 1890 Edward was given a 15% pay rise, bringing his wage to 36s and 3d per week. The family were living in a smaller abode at 3 Potters Cottages, Rush Green near Romford, due to the reduction of family members. John Watkins, Edward's father, had died on 9th October 1886,[54] and Sophy, Edward's second daughter, had left the family unit and moved completely out of London.

In the 1891 census she was listed at a convent in Truro, Cornwall,[55] working as a laundry servant and classed as a 'pennant'. Whether this meant she was paying for her sins, whatever they might have been, or training to become a nun, we will never know. It is interesting to note that in some cases, women who become nuns either changed their name completely or developed a name with

---

53 *The Echo*, 30th September 1888.

54 John Watkins was buried on 14th October 1886 in Manor Park Cemetery.

55 This convent is no more and has now been turned into a hotel.

a mixture of their old name, a religious name and their mother's name. This may explain why after 1891 'Sophy Watkins' disappears, but in the records of Brompton Cemetery, near her place of birth, a 'Sophia Maria Elizabeth Watkins' was listed as having been buried on 12th September 1928.[56]

She had her first name spelt in this way on the 1871 census; 'Maria' can be classed as a religious name, and Elizabeth was her mother's name. Could this have been the reason for her mother's disappearance from all records in 1881? Did daughter follow mother into a convent? Did mother change her name completely? And does that finally explain why Edward claims to be married for the rest of his life, despite not living with his wife?

In 1891, Edward still had his other two daughters with him. His eldest, Emily Mary Watkins, was still working within the confectionery business and Edward's youngest, Julia Ann Watkins, was also working, as a boot trimmer.

Five years later, on 25th May 1896, Edward resigned from the City of London Police force after serving his 25 years of service, handing back his uniform and other items.[57] On 28th May 1896, he was described as being 52 years of age, 5ft 9in tall, with grey eyes and a flesh complexion.[58] He was awarded a pension of £56 14s 1d, a nice sum for Edward as his two daughters would shortly leave the family home and he would be left with the housemaid, Augusta. Commissioner Sir Henry Smith stated that Edward's overall conduct in the force was 'good', which as a testimonial, considering Edward's past misdemeanors, could have been a lot worse.

Just one year later, Edward became the father of the bride when Julia Ann, aged 25, married one Charles Meek, going on to have four children with him.[59]

For the first time since the 1870s, Edward was without any children

---

56 Brompton Cemetery records.
57 Edward Watkins's leaving record for the City of London Police.
58 Ibid. His description was made by Sergeant George Hills.
59 Marriage records.

at home in 1901. Oddly, in this census, Augusta Ann Fowler claimed her name to be Jessie Ann.[60] It was the name of her former employer, but that is the only known connection she had to that name. She also claimed to be married, despite there being no marriage record, and to have been born a year later than she was. The last two statements could be passed off as mistakes on behalf of the enumerator, but the mistake in the name is a little more puzzling.

Ten years later, in 1911, Edward and Augusta had moved again - the final time for Edward - to 1 Low Shoe Lane, Collier Row. According to the census return, the house had four rooms. This census was filled in by Edward himself, and he gave correct information on Augusta: she was single, her name was Augusta Ann Fowler, and although he was technically wrong with her age, it was only by two years.[61]

Edward Watkins died two years later. Although it has been suggested that his date of death was 10th November 1913, his cemetery record states that he was buried on 19th March 1913 in Romford Cemetery.[62] What is humbling is the fact that Edward is buried with one other person. Not Augusta Fowler, who spent 32 years with him, although she is buried within the same cemetery. Edward Watkins is actually buried with his youngest daughter, Julia Ann Meek, who died in 1931. Is this a final sign of a good father?

Watkins the Ripper?

The suggestion that Edward Watkins was Jack the Ripper or, at the very least, the killer of Catherine Eddowes, originates from a post on JTRforums.com.[63] Whatever you believe on this idea, it is now 'out there' as part of the myths of the case and does need to be at least discussed for a serious final note to ponder on.

The suggestion of a policeman being Jack the Ripper is nothing new.

---

60 1901 census.

61 1911 census.

62 Cemetery records. He is buried over the grave reference 69BB.

63 JTRforums.com: 'pc edward watkins (881-city police) was he the ripper, poss new evidence.'

The post on JTRforums.com states that a box had been found in the 1940s underneath some damaged floorboards in a bombed house off Brick Lane. Supposedly inside the box were two knives and a truncheon; one knife has been described as a 'butcher's knife' with a wooden handle, and the other more like a dagger. The truncheon was of plain dark wood, about eighteen inches long, with lead at one end and the words 'PC 881 CITY POLICE' and 'EDWARD WATKINS'.

The find was shared with others looking around the damaged houses for anything of use. The truncheon was apparently kept for many years, until the owner saw a Ripper film and connected the name 'Watkins' to the case. The truncheon was sent to the Museum of London, who forwarded it to a 'London Police Museum' who claimed it was not a police truncheon. After some confusion over the name of the victim, where she was found and how close Edward was living to Brick Lane, it was this account that set the ball rolling.[64]

Since then, PC Edward Watkins's supposed police whistle, handcuffs, truncheon (with the same scratch marks as the account) and notebook came to auction and were bought by the owner of the Jack the Ripper Museum on Cable Street. Questions about these items have arisen, such as the handcuffs not being correct for the time, and the notebook actually being empty but with its cover bearing Watkins's details. Had there been notes within the pad, handwriting comparisons could have been made against Edward's known writing in his service file and the 1911 census.

As for the truncheon and whistle, there are a few problems. The whistle can be seen at the Museum, and photographs can be taken. On its side can be clearly seen the words 'Metropolitan Patent, Metropolitan Police', which would not make it more likely to be Edward's because normally a City of London beat constable would not be carrying a whistle as a part of their uniform until 1889. Could the whistle be a relic from Edward's short career in the Metropolitan Police? No, because the Met did not supply whistles to their beat

---

64 JTRforums.com: 'pc edward watkins (881-city police) was he the ripper, poss new evidence.'

constables until the mid 1880s, by which point Edward had already left that force.[65]

Then there is the wooden truncheon. Even after considering all the possibilities of Edward having made the scratches, the fact remains that his City of London Police service files proves that he returned everything, uniform and all other items, back to the force following his resignation. There is no note to suggest that anything was missing or scratched upon, it was all registered normally.

However, we cannot dismiss the suggestion of Edward Watkins as being a killer on the basis of this flimsy provenance. He does, after all, have a recorded history of having sexual relations with a woman while on his beat.

We have a policeman who would have known his colleagues' beats. A policeman who had already entered Mitre Square many times that night, who would therefore have known that the gas lamps were not working properly, resulting in more shadows for him to hide in. Compared to some theories, these are intriguing possibilities.

However, a question of why arises. Why did Edward kill Catherine? Did he go with another prostitute? His wife had left, and the relationship with his housemaid, Augusta Fowler, is ambiguous.

Did he and Catherine agree a fee, only for something to go wrong and Edward had to silence her? Even if this was the case, why destroy her in the way she was? Did he think that he could cover his tracks by making it look like a 'Jack the Ripper' killing?

---

65 Police Order, 10th February 1885.

The author at the
City of London Police Museum

St Botolph without Aldgate church
© Amanda Harvey Purse

Left: Bishopsgate Police Station in the 1860s
Above: 'Big Chap'
© City of London Police Museum

Top:
Bishopsgate Police Station cells,
date unknown

Right:
Bishopsgate Police Station 1910
© City of London Police Museum

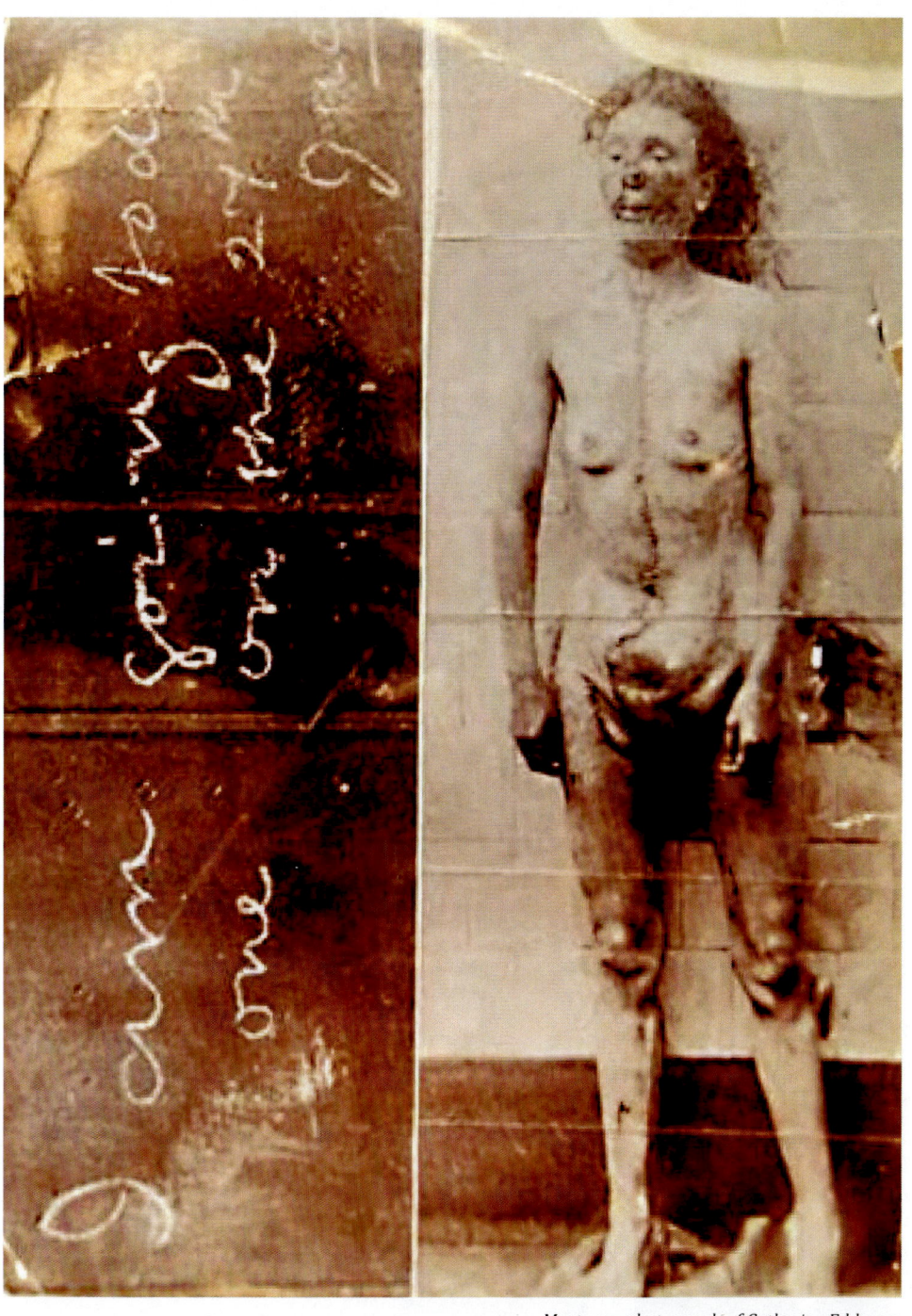

Mortuary photograph of Catherine Eddowes,
with a contemporary photograph of Ripper-related wall writing

Top:
Artist's impression of Catherine in life
© Alan M Clark

Left:
Marker showing her final resting place
at the City of London Cemetery
© Amanda Harvey Purse

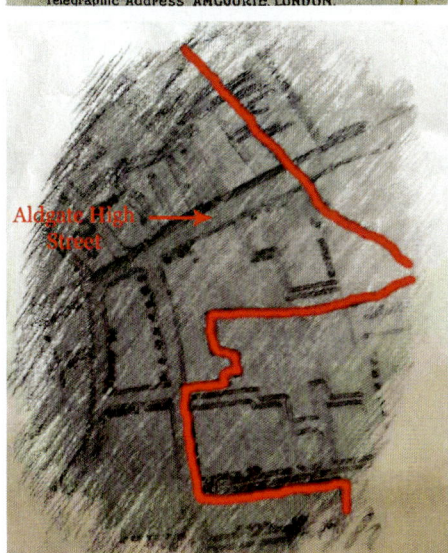

Left: Map showing boundary of City of London Police jurisdiction, indicating how close
Catherine Eddowes was to Metropolitan Police territory at the time she was taken into custody
© Amanda Harvey Purse

Right: The author at the spot where Catherine was killed in Mitre Square
© Amanda Harvey Purse

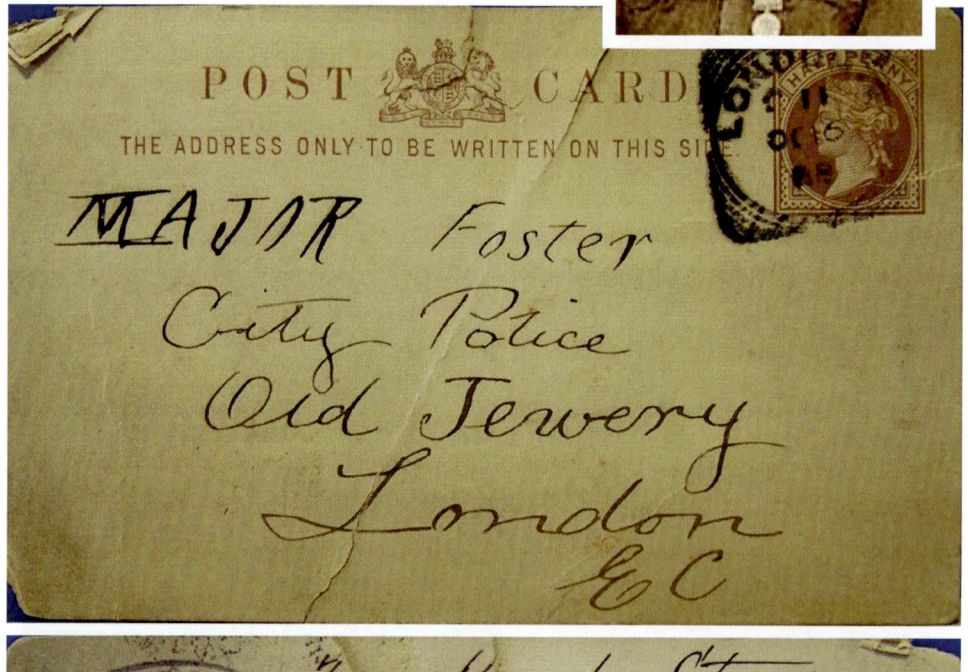

Right: Superintendent Alfred Foster
Below: Postcard sent to Foster
© City of London Police Museum

POST CARD

THE ADDRESS ONLY TO BE WRITTEN ON THIS SIDE

MAJOR Foster
City Police
Old Jewery
London
EC

CITY POLICE OFFICE
OCT 1888
LONDON

3 ...lbych Street
Strand
Oct 16/88
Dear Major
Has it not occurred
to you that your men
are unable to find
"Jack" because he
"Mitre Square'd" them
Yours   J. N. K.

Map of Mitre Square drawn by Frederick Foster, on display to the public
© London Hospital Museum / photograph Adam Wood

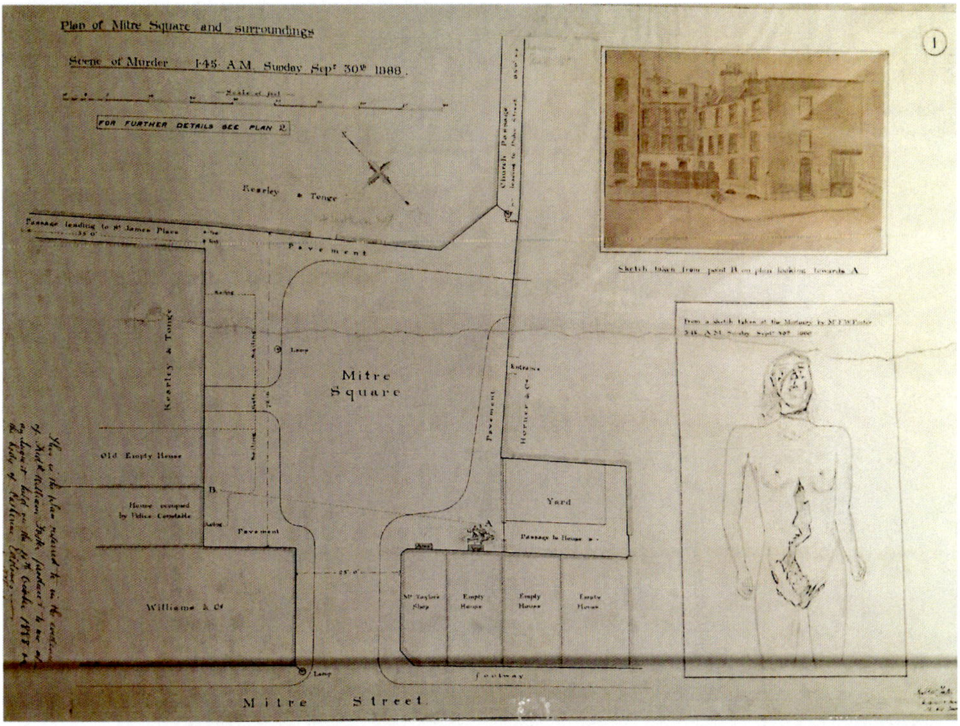

Map drawn by Frederick Foster, not on display to the public
© London Hospital Museum / photograph Amanda Harvey Purse

Right: Station Sergeant James Byfield
© City of London Police Museum

Below: West Smithfield Police Headquarters,
where James Byfield lived
© Amanda Harvey Purse

Clockwise from top: PC George Hutt
© City of London Police Museum

Hutt's place of work prior to joining the City Police
The house in which he and his wife died
The area in which George Hutt is buried
All © Amanda Harvey Purse

Right: 6 Eldon Street,
home to PC Edward Watkins

Below:
Plot at Romford Cemetery
where Watkins is buried
All © Amanda Harvey Purse

PC F WATKIN.

PC James Harvey
© City of London Police Museum

Below:
Area in West Ham Cemetery where
Harvey is buried
© Amanda Harvey Purse

Above: Dr Frederick Gordon Brown
Right: Dr William Sedgwick Saunders
Below: His final resting place

Top:
The author at the doorway of Happy Days restaurant on Goulston Street, formerly the entrance to Wentworth Model Dwellings

Left: The headstone on Detective Daniel Halse's grave

© Amanda Harvey Purse

Top: Tug of War shield held at the City of London Police Museum

Bottom: James Izzard (left of shield) as part of the Bishopsgate Station tug of war team, 1899

© City of London Police Museum / photograph Amanda Harvey Purse

CHAPTER THIRTEEN

Called To The Scene

Inspector Edward Collard, Dr Frederick Gordon Brown,
Dr George William Sequeira, Dr William Sedgwick Saunders
and Assistant Commissioner Sir Henry Smith

Inspector Edward Collard:
He knew the location very well[1]

The Bishopsgate Police Station's Inspector on the morning of 30th
September 1888 was Inspector Edward Collard, and at 1:55am
he received the information that there had been a murder in Mitre
Square. His first action was to communicate this to the Headquarters
of the City of London Police at Old Jewry, and next he called for the
force's surgeon, Doctor Frederick Gordon Brown, to attend the scene
of the crime, while Inspector Collard himself left Bishopsgate to arrive
at Mitre Square for three minutes past two in the morning. One can
imagine that Edward was not quite expecting the sight which awaited
him...

---

1   In 1881 Edward Collard and his family lived at 41 Mitre Street, a location that was
    within minutes of the spot where Catherine Eddowes was found in Mitre Square.

Born in 1846 in Clifton, Gloucestershire to John and Jane Collard,[2] Edward's upbringing was a rough one almost from the start of his life, as at the age of five he was in Compton Bishop Workhouse in Somerset, listed as a 'pauper'.[3]

Why Edward was in the workhouse at such a young age is not known. In the same census his father was working as a servant within Brislington House Lunatic Asylum in Somerset,[4] but Jane, Edward's mother, is nowhere to be found. With no record of a death, one presumption could be that there may have been something wrong with her and perhaps Jane was a patient at the asylum in which John worked and he wanted to be near her,[5] or perhaps they could not afford to house the child, Edward not being allowed to live with his father in Brislington House.

Whatever the reason, Edward did not stay in the workhouse for long, for in 1861 he was back living with his mother and father at 86 Ware's Gardens, St Paul, in Bristol. By this time his father was 47 and still working as a labourer at the asylum, his mother 48 and Edward 15.[6]

Edward Collard's service file is missing from the London Metropolitan Archives, however in the file held at Bishopsgate Police Station,[7] it states that he joined the City Police on 6th March 1868, with the warrant number 4157.

A year after joining the force, Edward was involved in an unusual case which was reported in *Lloyd's Weekly Newspaper* of 11th April 1869.

On 24th February that year, one James Cook found himself in Guy's Hospital with appalling injuries. His right eye had been pushed

---

2   Birth record.

3   1851 census. John Collard was born in 1815 at Henbury in Gloucestershire, Jane in 1813 in Salisbury.

4   1851 census.

5   Most records bear have the initials of the patients, so a 'J.C.' could mean anyone.

6   1861 census.

7   The author was granted special permission to view this file. With thanks to Sabine Thornton and Richard Thomas.

in, and his other eye was bruised. It transpired that his wife Ellen had caused the injuries that morning, after the couple had become intimate and she had tied him to the bed, only to take a knife to her husband's torso and attempt to gouge out his eyes. She had learned that her husband had brought prostitutes into the house, and wanted to 'put a stop to it'. PC Edward Collard arrived and took the wife into custody, where she admitted to everything apart from trying to kill her husband, saying she just wanted to wound him. She revealed that her husband had ten children by another woman, and five children with her, and although they had been married for eighteen years he still used ladies of the night. Nevertheless, she was sentenced to fifteen years' imprisonment.

Edward was unmarried at this time, and was probably living at the City Police's section house at Great Tower Street, All Hallows, where he was recorded in the 1871 census.[8]

On 8th September 1873, Edward married Amelia Ann Sayer[9] in Greenwich, Kent.[10] Their daughter Amelia Ann Collard was born the following year,[11] being followed by Esther Jane,[12] Elizabeth Ellen,[13] Edward John[14] and Emma Sarah.[15]

A search for the Collard family in the 1881 census draws a blank, but a little tweaking of the spelling of the surname in our search and we find the family recorded as 'Collen', the head of the household being one Edward Collen, who was a City Police Sergeant. Interestingly, the family are recorded as living at 41 Mitre Street.[16]

More children followed: William John in 1883, Alice in 1885 and Albert in 1887.

---

8   1871 census.
9   According to the 1881 census, born in 1850 in Hackney.
10 Marriage record.
11 1881 census.
12 Born 1875.
13 Born 1877.
14 Born 1879.
15 Born 1881.
16 1881 census.

1888 began in busy fashion for Inspector Collard, with the officer being involved in a case which resulted in an inquest held at the City Mortuary on Golden Lane on 24th January.

The incidents which led to this were reported in the *Echo* of the same date:

> On the previous Friday morning, City Policeman Charles Webber was walking his beat which took him past 15 Hutchinson Street in Houndsditch at about ten minutes past three in the afternoon. When he saw the beginnings of a fire through the parlour windows at the back of what was a shop, the policeman instantly rattled his rattle for help as he did so he heard a voice from within the shop shouting 'Police, Police, Murder, Murder!'

Seeing that the smoke would have been too much to cope with, he ran for the Fire Brigade. When PC Webber returned, he saw through the smoke someone on the first floor in the act of jumping out of the window. He attempted to catch this person, but was knocked to the ground on impact and found himself in the City Hospital.

By the time the Fire Brigade arrived from Bishopsgate a few minutes later the house was ablaze, covering most of the building in a deep, dark smoke. Witnesses stated they had seen two people fall from the second floor window and one person from the first floor window, but as the smoke was so dense they were unable to see where these people were.

The fire had started from under the stairs, where the owner kept coke which had caught alight, and sadly four people died. These were Rosetta Boginsky, Judith Salzedo (who was aged 75 and bedbound), her daughter Sophia Salzedo, aged 39, and Sophia's son Mordecai, who was only three and was deaf.

At the inquest held by Coroner Samuel Langham, with Inspector Collard and Superintendent Foster attending on behalf of the City Police force, the verdict was that this was a terrible accident, but the mystery of the cries of 'Murder' which PC Charles Webber had heard was never solved.[17]

---

17 'A Protective Policeman' by Amanda Harvey Purse. *The Whitechapel Society Journal* Issue 55, April 2014.

On 30th September 1888, at 1:55am, Edward had heard the terrible news of a murdered woman being found shortly before within the City's boundary in Mitre Square.[18] He was Bishopsgate Police Station's Inspector, and knowing that his family was living at this station in the 1891 census, we can assume that they had moved into the station by 1888, if not sooner.

Edward's first task on hearing of the murder was to inform the headquarters of the City Police, so he sent a telegram to the station at the Old Jewry. He then sent for the City of London Police's Surgeon to appear at the murder scene at Mitre Square. Once these two tasks were done, Edward himself left Bishopsgate Police Station and travelled the short distance to Mitre Square, arriving there at three minutes past two o'clock.[19]

On arrival, he noticed that Dr George Sequeira was examining the body of the woman and that he had already pronounced her dead. Inspector Collard told the doctor that he had ordered the City of London Police's Surgeon, Dr Gordon Brown, to attend, and Dr Sequeira halted his examination, as Edward Collard later told the inquest:

> The body was not touched until the arrival shortly afterwards of Dr Brown. The medical gentlemen examined the body, and in my presence Sergeant Jones picked up from the foot way by the left side of the deceased three small black buttons, such as are generally used for boots, a small metal button, a common metal thimble, and a small penny mustard tin containing two pawn-tickets. They were handed to me. The doctors remained until the arrival of the ambulance, and saw the body placed in the conveyance. It was then taken to the mortuary, and stripped by Mr Davis, the mortuary keeper, in presence of the two doctors and myself. I have a list of articles of clothing more or less stained with blood and cut.[20]

Edward continued:

> No money whatever was found. A piece of cloth was found in Goulston-street, corresponding with the apron worn by the deceased. When I

18 Inquest testimony of Inspector Edward Collard.

19 Ibid.

20 *Daily Telegraph*, 5th October 1888.

got to the square I took immediate steps to have the neighbourhood searched for the person who committed the murder. Mr M'Williams, chief of the Detective Department, on arriving shortly afterwards sent men to search in all directions in Spitalfields, both in streets and lodging-houses. Several men were stopped and searched in the streets, without any good result. I have had a house-to-house inquiry made in the vicinity of Mitre-square as to any noises or whether persons were seen in the place; but I have not been able to find any beyond the witnesses who saw a man and woman talking together.

I made a careful inspection of the ground all round. There was no trace whatever of any struggle. There was nothing in the appearance of the woman, or of the clothes, to lead to the idea that there had been any struggle. From the fact that the blood was in a liquid state I conjectured that the murder had not been long previously committed. In my opinion the body had not been there more than a quarter of an hour. I endeavoured to trace footsteps, but could find no trace whatever. The backs of the empty houses adjoining were searched, but nothing was found.[21]

Edward had ordered house-to-house searches of the nearby area, which resulted in the discovery of the three witnesses Joseph Hyam Levy, Joseph Lawende and Harry Harris.[22]

Continuing with his career after the murder of Catherine Eddowes, the following year Edward was involved in a case of attempted stealing by Thomas Perry, aged 62, and John Cox, aged 50. On 21st August 1889, these two men were being watched in Liverpool Street, and later in the day in New Broad Street by City PC Whitehead. Perry and Cox were observed several times attempting to steal items from ladies' pockets. Although they appeared to have their hands in their own coat pockets, there were in fact holes inside the jackets. On being arrested and taken to Bishopsgate Police Station, one of the prisoners, Thomas Perry, assaulted PC Whitehead and was charged for that too.

At the station Edward Collard checked the pockets of both prisoners and was unable to find a hole, but City of London Detective

21 Inquest testimony of Inspector Edward Collard.
22 *Daily Telegraph*, 5th October 1888.

Shephard searched the pockets again and was able to find a slit in the lining. At court Edward demonstrated how the thefts had been carried out through the hole in the jackets. Thomas Perry was found guilty of both attempted stealing and also assaulting PC Whitehead and was sentenced to a month's imprisonment, while John Cox was also found guilty, but because of a previous conviction he was sentenced to three months hard labour.[23]

At the time of the 1891 census, the Collard family were still living at Bishopsgate Police Station, but sadly Edward died just a year later, on 4th June 1892, after spending some time as a patient in Bishopsgate Police Hospital.[24]

His widow Amelia moved out of the Police Station into 69 Brighton Road, Stoke Newington, Hackney, and on the 1901 census was there living with all her children as well as her cousin, Alice Sayer.[25]

Amelia Collard died in 1912.[26] She is actually buried within the same cemetery as Detective Daniel Halse: Abney Cemetery in Stoke Newington. To add more woe to the Collard family, Amelia's final resting place also contains the remains of Ronald Albert Collard, who died in February 1917. Ronald was her grandson, his parents being Amelia's son Albert E Collard and Elsie Harrow.[27] Ronald was sadly only six-months-old when he died.[28]

Doctor Frederick Gordon Brown:
The Doctor, the Tour Guide and the Would-Be Detective

Doctor Frederick Gordon Brown was the City of London Police's Surgeon at the time of Catherine Eddowes' murder. He was called to the scene of Jack's latest crime by Inspector Edward Collard, and left

23 *The Wandsworth and Battersea District Times*, 24th August 1889.

24 As noted in a file held at Bishopsgate Police Station, which the author was granted kind permission to access.

25 Born in 1880 in Essex.

26 Death record.

27 The couple married in 1909 at Hackney.

28 Information supplied by the staff at Abney Cemetery. The author wishes to thank Haydn of Abney Cemetery staff, who has always gone above and beyond to help with my research.

his home in Finsbury Circus to travel the eleven minute walk to the Mitre Square. Whether the sight before him shocked him we do not know, however Frederick should be mentioned within this book for his detailed description of how Catherine was left by the unknown fiend...

Born on 10th March 1842[29] to Thomas[30] and Mary Brown,[31] Frederick was baptised on 22nd April 1842 in St Botolph's, in the City,[32] ironically very close to the murder scene of Catherine Eddowes 46 years later.

In the 1851 census, Frederick, aged nine, was living with his parents and older brother Thomas Edwin Benton Brown[33] at St Mary Axe, St Botolph, Aldgate.

With his father being a General Practitioner of Medicine with a practice in Wormwood Street, and an older brother working as an Apprentice to Medicine at this time, it really isn't any wonder that at a young age Frederick was a scholar at the private school of Merchant Taylors in the parish of St Lawrence Pountney, in the City of London. When he was old enough to leave that school, at the age of eighteen, Frederick went to train at St Thomas's Hospital as a medical student.[34]

By the 1861 census Frederick had turned nineteen years of age and was living with his family, who had moved to 16 Finsbury Circus. By this time the family had grown, with Frances (b.1835) and Charles (b.1837) already born by the time Frederick came along, with Henry (b.1852), Mary (b.1855) and Emmaline (b.1861) following.[35]

29 *Ipswich Journal*, 30th January 1869.

30 Thomas was born in 1803.

31 Born in 1823 in Islington, north London.

32 Baptism record.

33 Born in 1833.

34 Frederick's obituary published in the *British Medical Journal*, 21st January 1928. While at St Thomas's, Frederick was noted for his prize-winning paper on Diphtheria – Medical and Physical Society of St Thomas's Hospital (held at King's College Hospital London Archives).

35 1861 census.

While studying at St Thomas's Hospital, Frederick gained a Surgical Practice Admission card, dating from 1859 until 1861. This meant that Frederick could be a part of a surgical team at hospitals such as St Thomas's and Guy's.[36] In 1863 he received his diplomas L.S.A, M.R.C.S and L.M.[37]

On 21st January 1869, Frederick married Emily Appleford at St Peter in Chains church in Colchester, Essex. She was the sister of his practice partner Stephen Appleford, and the couple were married by another brother, Rev. William Appleford, him being assisted by Rev. W.J. Dampier and also Frederick's brother, Rev. W.H. Brown.[38]

By the 1871 census, the couple had moved to St Mary Axe in the City of London, with their own servant, 37-year-old Elizabeth Muskill. Frederick was described as a local GP and had his father-in-law, William Appleford, and brother-in-law Bithiah visiting.[39]

Frederick's life as a Freemason had begun when he became a member of the St Paul's Lodge, London, on 21st January 1868, and by 1874 he was a Master of this Lodge, leaving a year later. At this time he was also Secretary of the Hunterian Society,[40] of which he would later become President.[41] Frederick joined the Grand Master Lodge Number One on 9th February 1878.[42]

On 28th October 1885 Frederick became the Surgeon for the City of London Police force, with a salary of £300 per year. The job description required him to 'examine surgically all applicants for the force, to report any medical and bodily aliments of members of the force that need a discharge.' He had to 'attend daily from one to three pm at the police hospital', and while there he had to be 'responsible for the good order and sanitary conditions of all the wards within the police station.' Finally, Frederick had to send an

---

36 Admission Cards from 1800 to 1900: H1/ST/MS/G10 held at the London Metropolitan Archives.

37 Frederick's obituary in the *British Medical Journal*, 21st January 1928.

38 *Ipswich Journal*, 30th January 1869.

39 1871 census.

40 *The British Medical Journal*, 1876.

41 Frederick's obituary in the *British Medical Journal*, 21st January 1928.

42 Library and Archives of Freemasonry.

annual report to the Commissioner of the City of London Police, providing information of the health of its policemen.[43] Frederick was offered no security for this role.[44]

On 6th April 1886, Frederick joined the Royal Arch in the Grand Lodge Number One in London, and served as its Grand Steward from 1887 to 1888.[45]

On the morning of 30th September 1888 he was called from his bed at almost two o'clock, the message, as stated previously, coming from Inspector Collard at Bishopsgate Police Station. He arrived at Mitre Square at eighteen minutes past two, to be informed that Dr Sequeira, who had arrived at the scene before him, had already pronounced the woman dead. One can imagine this was an easy task considering her injuries.

Lloyd's Weekly Newspaper reported what happened next:

> They [Drs. Sequeira and Brown] made a minute examination of the body, Dr Gordon Brown taking a pencil sketch of the exact position in which it was found. This he most kindly showed to the representative of *Lloyd's*, when subsequently explaining the frightful injuries inflicted upon the body of the deceased. The throat had been cut from the left side, the knife severing the carotid artery and other parts of the neck. The weapon had then apparently been stabbed into the upper part of the abdomen, and cut completely down. Besides the fearful wound on the face the tops of both of the thighs were cut across. The intestines, which had been torn from the body, were found twisted into the gaping wound on the right side of the murdered woman's neck.[46]

At half past two in the afternoon that day, Frederick arrived at Golden Lane Mortuary, where the body of Catherine Eddowes had been taken, and proceeded to record the injuries inflicted:

> The body was on its back, the head turned to left shoulder. The arms by the side of the body as if they had fallen there. Both palms

---

43 1908 Tax Returns for the City of London Police Force held at the London Metropolitan Archives.

44 Unlike Dr Childs, who had personal security.

45 Library and Archives of Freemasonry.

46 *Lloyd's Weekly Newspaper*, 30th September 1888.

upwards, the fingers slightly bent... Left leg extended in a line with the body, the abdomen was exposed. Right leg bent at the thigh and knee. The throat cut across...

The intestines were drawn out to a large extent and placed over the right shoulder - they were smeared over with some feculent matter. A piece of about two feet was quite detached from the body and placed between the body and the left arm, apparently by design. The lobe and auricle of the right ear was cut obliquely through.

There was a quantity of clotted blood on the pavement on the left side of the neck round the shoulder and upper part of arm, and fluid blood-coloured serum which had flowed under the neck to the right shoulder, the pavement sloping in that direction.

Body was quite warm. No death stiffening had taken place. She must have been dead most likely within the half hour. We looked for superficial bruises and saw none. No blood on the skin of the abdomen or secretion of any kind on the thighs. No spurting of blood on the bricks or pavement around. No marks of blood below the middle of the body. Several buttons were found in the clotted blood after the body was removed. There was no blood on the front of the clothes. There were no traces of recent connection. When the body arrived at Golden Lane some of the blood was dispersed through the removal of the body to the mortuary. The clothes were taken off carefully from the body. A piece of deceased's ear dropped from the clothing.

I made a post mortem examination at half past two on Sunday afternoon. Rigor mortis was well marked; body not quite cold. Green discoloration over the abdomen.

After washing the left hand carefully, a bruise the size of a sixpence, recent and red, was discovered on the back of the left hand between the thumb and first finger. A few small bruises on right shin of older date. The hands and arms were bronzed. No bruises on the scalp, the back of the body or the elbows.

The face was very much mutilated. There was a cut about a quarter of an inch through the lower left eyelid, dividing the structures completely through. The upper eyelid on that side, there was a scratch through the skin on the left upper eyelid, near to the angle of the nose. The right eyelid was cut through to about half an inch.

There was a deep cut over the bridge of the nose, extending from the left border of the nasal bone down near to the angle of the jaw on the right side of the cheek. This cut went into the bone and divided all the structures of the cheek except the mucous membrane of the mouth.

The tip of the nose was quite detached from the nose by an oblique cut from the bottom of the nasal bone to where the wings of the nose join on to the face. A cut from this divided the upper lip and extended through the substance of the gum over the right upper lateral incisor tooth. About half an inch from the top of the nose was another oblique cut. There was a cut on the right angle of the mouth as if the cut of a point of a knife. The cut extended an inch and a half, parallel with lower lip.

There was on each side of cheek a cut which peeled up the skin, forming a triangular flap about an inch and a half. On the left cheek there were two abrasions of the epithelium... under the left ear.

The throat was cut across to the extent of about six or seven inches. A superficial cut commenced about an inch and a half below the lobe below (and about two and a half inches below and behind) the left ear, and extended across the throat to about three inches below the lobe of right ear. The big muscle across the throat was divided through on the left side. The large vessels on the left side of the neck were severed. The larynx was severed below the vocal cord. All the deep structures were severed to the bone, the knife marking intervertebral cartilages. The sheath of the vessels on the right side was just opened. The carotid artery had a fine hole opening. The internal jugular vein was opened an inch and a half - not divided.

The blood vessels contained clot. All these injuries were performed by a sharp instrument like a knife, and pointed.

The cause of death was haemorrhage from the left common carotid artery. The death was immediate and the mutilations were inflicted after death.

We examined the abdomen. The front walls were laid open from the breast bone to the pubes. The cut commenced opposite the enciform cartilage. The incision went upwards, not penetrating the skin that was over the sternum. It then divided the enciform cartilage. The knife must have cut obliquely at the expense of the front surface of that cartilage. Behind this, the liver was stabbed as if by the point of a sharp instrument.

Below this was another incision into the liver of about two and a half inches, and below this the left lobe of the liver was slit through by a vertical cut. Two cuts were shewn by a jagging of the skin on the left side.

The abdominal walls were divided in the middle line to within a quarter of an inch of the navel. The cut then took a horizontal course for two inches and a half towards right side. It then divided round the navel on the left side, and made a parallel incision to the former horizontal incision, leaving the navel on a tongue of skin. Attached to the navel was two and a half inches of the lower part of the rectus muscle on the left side of the abdomen. The incision then took an oblique direction to the right and was shelving. The incision went down the right side of the vagina and rectum for half an inch behind the rectum.

There was a stab of about an inch on the left groin. This was done by a pointed instrument. Below this was a cut of three inches going through all tissues making a wound of the peritoneum [sc. perineum] about the same extent.

An inch below the crease of the thigh was a cut extending from the anterior spine of the ilium obliquely down the inner side of the left thigh and separating the left labium, forming a flap of skin up to the groin. The left rectus muscle was not detached.

There was a flap of skin formed from the right thigh, attaching the right labium, and extending up to the spine of the ilium. The muscles on the right side inserted into the frontal ligaments were cut through.

The skin was retracted through the whole of the cut in the abdomen, but the vessels were not clotted. Nor had there been any appreciable bleeding from the vessels. I draw the conclusion that the cut was made after death, and there would not be much blood on the murderer. The cut was made by someone on right side of body, kneeling below the middle of the body.

I removed the content of the stomach and placed it in a jar for further examination. There seemed very little in it in the way of food or fluid, but from the cut end partly digested farinaceous food escaped.

The intestines had been detached to a large extent from the mesentery. About two feet of the colon was cut away. The sigmoid flexure was invigilated into the rectum very tightly. Right kidney pale, bloodless, with slight congestion of the base of the pyramids.

There was a cut from the upper part of the slit on the under surface of the liver to the left side, and another cut at right angles to this, which were about an inch and a half deep and two and a half inches long. Liver itself was healthy.

The gall bladder contained bile. The pancreas was cut, but not through, on the left side of the spinal column. Three and a half inches of the lower border of the spleen by half an inch was attached only to the peritoneum. The peritoneal lining was cut through on the left side and the left kidney carefully taken out and removed. The left renal artery was cut through. I should say that someone who knew the position of the kidney must have done it.

The lining membrane over the uterus was cut through. The womb was cut through horizontally, leaving a stump of three quarters of an inch. The rest of the womb had been taken away with some of the ligaments. The vagina and cervix of the womb was uninjured.

The bladder was healthy and uninjured, and contained three or four ounces of water. There was a tongue-like cut through the anterior wall of the abdominal aorta. The other organs were healthy. There were no indications of connexion. I believe the wound in the throat was first inflicted. I believe she must have been lying on the ground.

The wounds on the face and abdomen prove that they were inflicted by a sharp pointed knife, and that in the abdomen by one six inches long.

I believe the perpetrator of the act must have had considerable knowledge of the positions of the organs in the abdominal cavity and the way of removing them. The parts removed would be of no use for any professional purpose. It required a great deal of medical knowledge to have removed the kidney and to know where it was placed. Such a knowledge might be possessed by someone in the habit of cutting up animals. I think the perpetrator of this act had sufficient time, or he would not have nicked the lower eyelids. It would take at least five minutes.

I cannot assign any reason for the parts being taken away. I feel sure there was no struggle. I believe it was the act of one person. The throat had been so instantly severed that no noise could have been emitted. I should not expect much blood to have been found on the person who had inflicted these wounds. The wounds could not have been self-inflicted.

My attention was called to the apron. It was the corner of the apron, with a string attached. The blood spots were of recent origin. I have seen the portion of an apron produced by Dr Phillips and stated to have been found in Goulston Street. It is impossible to say it is human blood. I fitted the piece of apron which had a new piece of material on it which had evidently been sewn on to the piece I have, the seams of the borders of the two actually corresponding. Some blood and, apparently, faecal matter was found on the portion found in Goulston Street. I believe the wounds on the face to have been done to disfigure the corpse.[47]

47 A handwritten copy made by Coroner Langham is held at the London Metropolitan Archives.

On 4th October 1888 Frederick appeared at Catherine Eddowes' inquest, where he deposed:

I am surgeon to the City of London Police. I was called shortly after two o'clock on Sunday morning, and reached the place of the murder about twenty minutes past two. My attention was directed to the body of the deceased. It was lying in the position described by Watkins, on its back, the head turned to the left shoulder, the arms by the side of the body, as if they had fallen there. Both palms were upwards, the fingers slightly bent. A thimble was lying near. The clothes were thrown up. The bonnet was at the back of the head. There was great disfigurement of the face. The throat was cut across. Below the cut was a neckerchief. The upper part of the dress had been torn open. The body had been mutilated, and was quite warm - no rigor mortis. The crime must have been committed within half an hour, or certainly within forty minutes from the time when I saw the body. There were no stains of blood on the bricks or pavement around.

Before we removed the body Dr Phillips was sent for, as I wished him to see the wounds, he having been engaged in a case of a similar kind previously. He saw the body at the mortuary. The clothes were removed from the deceased carefully. I made a post-mortem examination on Sunday afternoon. There was a bruise on the back of the left hand, and one on the right shin, but this had nothing to do with the crime. There were no bruises on the elbows or the back of the head. The face was very much mutilated, the eyelids, the nose, the jaw, the cheeks, the lips, and the mouth all bore cuts. There were abrasions under the left ear. The throat was cut across to the extent of six or seven inches.

The cause of death was haemorrhage from the throat. Death must have been immediate. The uterus was cut away with the exception of a small portion, and the left kidney was also cut out. Both these organs were absent, and have not been found. In my opinion the woman must have been lying down [when asked what position Catherine was in when she was killed]. The way in which the kidney was cut out showed that it was done by somebody who knew what he was about. It must have been a sharp-pointed knife, and I should say at least 6 in. long [when asked what weapon might have been used to kill Catherine]. He must have had a good deal of knowledge as to the position of the abdominal organs, and the way to remove them, [when talking about the possible killer] It might be done in five minutes. It might take him longer; but that is the least time it could be done in.[48]

This was not the only time that Frederick was involved in the Ripper crimes, as he was also called to 13 Miller's Court, Dorset Street, on the morning of 9th November 1888 after the remains of Mary Jane Kelly were found, and assisted Dr Phillips in the post mortem.[49] Frederick also made an appearance in testimony following the murder of Alice McKenzie in Castle Alley in 1889, as Dr Phillips mentioned at her inquest that Dr Brown had agreed with his findings.[50]

Frederick was also there when Dr Phillips examined the Pinchin Street torso found on 10th September 1889.[51]

It is interesting that Frederick was at the post mortem of other murder victims who had been killed outside of the City of London, for whom he worked. This could mean a number of things. Firstly, it is of course another example of the two police forces actually working together, which goes against the grain of what we are meant to believe. Or was he in attendance 'unofficially', and this was confirmation that Dr Brown had an interest in police work? Thirdly, it has been mentioned a few times that Metropolitan Police surgeon Dr Phillips listened to Frederick's view on the other murders - does this suggest that Frederick Brown was respected in his field? There is nothing to suggest otherwise, but when looking at Frederick as a man rather than simply his role within the Catherine Eddowes murder investigation, which is what we are trying to do, it is

---

48 Frederick Gordon Brown's inquest testimony.

49 *The Times*, 12th November 1888.

50 It was at 12.50am on 17th July 1889 that Metropolitan PC Walter Andrews, who was new to the job, was walking his beat by Castle Alley, which at the time was a dark and narrow thoroughfare off Whitechapel High Street. He spotted a woman lying on the ground. When he looked closer he noticed a gash of about two inches on the left side of her neck but the body was quite warm and although he had heard someone running away from the scene, he did not follow as per the rules if the body showed signs of life, he had to stay with the body. Something he no doubt regretted later. It has been debatable whether Alice was one of the Ripper victims or not, even today.

51 Dr Phillips talking at the inquest of the Pinchin Street torso. *The Times*, 12th September 1889.

interesting to learn how other people felt about him.

However, this still leaves us with the question of how a City Surgeon was allowed to have any involvement in crimes that were not in his district.

One clue could be in an article in the *British Medical Journal* dated 10th November 1888, the day after Mary Jane Kelly was found murdered at 13 Miller's Court. It states:

> The first annual meeting of the recently formed Association of Police Surgeons was held on Wednesday afternoon [7th November], followed by a dinner under the presidency of Mr McKellar [sic], chief surgeon of the Metropolitan Police Force. The President was supported by Sir Charles Warren (Commissioner of Police), Mr Ernest Hart, Dr Gordon Brown (Surgeon to the City Police), Mr Phillips (Treasurer), Sir Thomas Crawford (Director-General AMD), Mr T. Holmes (late Chief Surgeon), Dr R. McDonald, MP, Mr Nelson Hardy, and Dr Waters (Honorary Secretaries). The vice-chairs were occupied by the Vice-Presidents, Mr Bond and Mr Buckle.

> A large number of divisional surgeons from all parts of the metropolis were present. Mr McKellar [sic] dwelt on the great advantages which had already resulted in the medical charge of the police, and in the humane and efficient performance of the duties of the divisional surgeon from the opportunities of conference which the formation of this Association had afforded. Among other matters he referred to the improvements which had been effected in the direction of preventing the use of public vehicles for infectious cases, and the substitution of ambulances: the better means of obtaining isolation for contagious cases occurring among the police force, and the improved sanitation and general care for the health of the men of the force. He paid warm tribute to the uniform kindness and consideration with which every suggestion put before Sir Charles Warren had been met, and the readiness with which, whenever possible, such suggestions for the benefit of the men or persons charged had been carried out. Sir Charles Warren, in reply, expressed his great satisfaction at the formation of this Association; every suggestion, whether general or referring to individual cases, which the divisional surgeons felt in necessary to make should have the most prompt and favourable consideration, and he assured the Association from his experience as an army officer that the medical department of such a force was, perhaps, more powerful than any other for securing the carrying out of their recommendations and the personal welfare of the force to which they were attached.

The subsequent toasts included the "Health of the President" and of "The Guests;" other toasts having duly honoured, the dinner was brought to a close amid general congratulations at the satisfactory progress of this young Association, and the excellent prospects for scientific discussion and administrative efficiency which this new organisation afforded.[52]

This shows that in the midst of the Whitechapel murders, surgeons from all areas of the capital were called to give their opinions of a subject that must have been at the foremost of their minds. The fact that Frederick Gordon Brown was invited shows us that his opinions were thought important enough to be at least listened to.

In 1889, Frederick became Master of the Grand Lodge Number One in London.[53] It is also interesting to note in the 1889 Building Proposals records that Frederick was listed as owning 26 Eldon Street in the City, where his surgery was based. That in itself may not sound that interesting to those who are researching the policemen involved in catching the Ripper, however the record then goes on to state: 'Number 26, previously number 6 North Buildings, Eldon Street...' We have heard of 6 North Buildings, Eldon Street, earlier in this book, for it was the address of PC Edward Watkins, who found the body of Catherine Eddowes.

A year later, in 1890, Frederick's wage from the City of London Police went up to £400 pounds a year.[54] In 1891 the Brown family were still living in Finsbury Circus, but had moved to number 16.[55] Recorded as living with Frederick and his wife are Emily's sisters Ellen[56] and Fanny,[57] and her brother Stephen,[58] who was also a surgeon and Frederick's practice partner. Also at the address were

---

52 *British Medical Journal*, 10th November 1888.

53 Library and Archives of Freemasonry.

54 1908 Tax Returns for the City of London Police Force held at the London Metropolitan Archives.

55 1891 census.

56 Born 1845.

57 Born 1851.

58 Born 1852.

Frederick's sister Fanny Brown,[59] and four servants, Susan Weyman (aged 36), Jane Swain (aged 28), Alice Forth (aged 20) and John Clayson, aged only fourteen.[60]

In 1892 Frederick became the President of the Hunterian Society,[61] and in 1894 a Founder Member of the Train-bands Masonic Lodge in London.[62]

In 1895 his pay from the City of London Police force was raised again to £500 a year, and he also became a Master of his Freemason Lodge again as well as its First Principal. A year later Frederick became the Assistant Grand Director of Ceremonies and Past Grand Standard Bearer of the Royal Arch for the same lodge, and also a Senior Past Master of the Society of Apothecaries of London.[63]

Frederick received a mention in *The Times* of 29th July 1898 because of the journalist George Ward, who was reporting in Egypt when he became painfully ill with rheumatic fever. The pain was apparently so bad that Ward had returned home to London in June 1898. However, George did not get better and the pain was too much for him to handle. He committed suicide by jumping onto the train track at Moorgate Underground Station. Dr Brown was called in to examine the body. An open bottle found near the body was labelled 'poison' but in fact contained morphia, which Frederick thought George Ward had taken before he jumped so that he felt no pain. The incident was later declared a case of suicide while temporarily insane.[64]

In 1900, Frederick's wage from the City of London Police force went up again to £600 per year.[65]

A year later, by the 1901 census, the Brown family were still living

---

59 Born 1835.

60 1891 census.

61 *British Medical Journal*, 20th February 1892.

62 Library and Archives of Freemasonry.

63 Ibid.

64 *The Times*, 29th July 1898.

65 1908 Tax Returns for the City of London Police Force held at the London Metropolitan Archives.

in Finsbury Circus[66] but the household was getting larger, for living with Frederick and his wife were still his wife's two sisters, but also three cousins of Frederick's named Agnes Louisa Greenall,[67] Annie Ethel Gibbons[68] and Florence Minnie Gibbons,[69] along with four servants, Clara Amelia Rider,[70] Flora Rose Hills,[71] Annie Louisa Clark[72] and Bernard Harley.[73]

Frederick made another appearance in *The Times*, this time on 9th November 1904, sixteen years to the day that he was called to 13 Miller's Court to see the body of Mary Kelly. In a case similar to the Sherlock Holmes story *The Man with the Twisted Lip*,[74] one Cecil Brown-Smith was caught begging in the area of Bishopsgate, looking very pitiful with his 'head hanging on one side, his foot dragging behind him and his limbs shaking.'[75] However, by the end of the day he was seen to be moving much better, going up and down the underground stations on his way home. Dr Brown was called in to examine the prisoner, who told him that he had received the injuries when falling from a horse trap three years earlier. However, Frederick's view was that there was 'no instance of paralysis on record consistent with his symptoms', and Brown-Smith received a sentence of three months hard labour.[76]

By the April of 1905, it may have been seventeen years since the murder of Catherine Eddowes and the murders attributed to the unknown fiend known as 'Jack the Ripper', but Frederick Gordon

---

66 1901 census.

67 Born in 1854.

68 Born in 1874.

69 Born in 1878.

70 Aged 39.

71 Aged 19.

72 Aged 19.

73 Aged 14.

74 Written by Sir Arthur Conan Doyle and first published in December 1891, *The Man With The Twisted Lip* is a story in which the respectable Neville St Clair made himself up to look as pitiful as possible in order to beg on the streets of London.

75 *The Times*, 9th November 1904.

76 Ibid.

Brown had not forgotten them as, in a sense, he became the first of a kind in that year. Today, Ripper tours seem normal to us, with several guides showing the murder sites to thousands of still interested members of public, but in 1905 it was a new idea. It was Frederick, who we have already mentioned seems to have had a love of all things crime related, to take some very famous people around the places where the murders had happened, giving a running commentary of his own views and opinions.

This trip was recorded in *The Life and Memoirs of John Churton Collins*, first published in 1912:

> Yesterday, Wednesday, April [1905], I went round all the scenes and sites of the Whitechapel Murders (the nine, as well as where the trunk was found) with Conan Doyle, Laurie, Ingleby Oddie, & Dr Crosse of Norwich. Dr Gordon Browne [sic] was our escort and two detectives also escorted us. In addition to these sites we visited Petticoat Lane, the Jews' fowl-slaughtering houses, a Dosshouse, and the like places. Dr Gordon Browne, [sic] who was concerned in all of them, seeing most of the corpses just after they were murdered, conducting post-mortems, etc. He told me these particulars: He was inclined to think that he (the murderer) was or had been a medical student, as he undoubtedly had a knowledge of human anatomy, but that he was also a butcher, as the mutilations slashing the nose, etc., were butchers' cuts.[77]

As with every good tour guide, Frederick left the members of his group with a mysterious twist to think about at the end of his tour:

> There was absolutely no foundation, in his opinion, for the theory that he was a homicidal maniac doctor, whose body was found in the Thames, tho' that is the theory at Scotland Yard, because (1) the last murder, possibly the last two murders, were committed after the body was found, he was strongly of opinion that the last two were Ripper murders; (2) the murderer was never seen near enough for any trustworthy identification, and Dr G. Browne [sic] was absolutely of opinion that they still remain an unsolved mystery. He thought the murderer suffered from a sort of homicidal satyriasis - that it was sexual perversion. The trunk found in Finsbury St. in September 1889 which he inspected, had the same incision as was characteristic of the Ripper murders, but it may have been an imitation, and it may

---

77 *The Life and Memoirs of John Churton Collins*, 1912.

have been one of the dynasty of murders he could not say.[78]

It is worth noting that the first motorised ambulances brought in for the use of the City of London Police by Commissioner Nott-Bower in 1907 have a connection to Frederick Gordon Brown. On 26th October 1907, he was part of a group comprising the Commissioner, the President of the Royal College of Surgeons, a Mr Henry Morris, and the company of Harrison and Dixon of the Home Office, demonstrated these ambulances for the first time at the Headquarters of the City of London Police Force, at Old Jewry.[79]

By 1911, after the death of his wife Emily, Frederick had moved out to 'Tailours' in Chigwell, Essex.[80] He was still living with his wife's two sisters, Ellen and Fanny, but now had two nieces, Hilda Lett[81] and Beatrice Benton Brown[82] with him, and three servants, Emily Anne Scott,[83] Louisa Mary Ann Nook[84] and Sophia Augusta Carter.[85] Frederick himself was described on the 1911 census as 'a Surgeon for the City of London Police'.

When the Great War broke out in September 1914 Frederick decided to leave the payroll of the City of London Police and perform medical duties for the army, whereby he could release younger men for the war service.[86]

Frederick sadly died on 15th January 1928 at his home in Chigwell at the age 85.[87] Five days later, on 20th January, a memorial service was held at St. Andrew Undershaft Church in Leadenhall Street,[88] not that far from Mitre Square, where he was called to on the morning

---

78 *The Life and Memoirs of John Churton Collins*, 1912.

79 *British Medical Journal*, 26th October 1907.

80 1911 census.

81 Born in 1885, a Personal Violinist (1911 census).

82 Born in 1893, a student at Newnham College (1911 census).

83 Aged 30.

84 Aged 29.

85 Aged 47.

86 Frederick's obituary in the *British Medical Journal*, 21st January 1928.

87 Ibid.

88 *The Times*, 21st January 1928.

of 30th September 1888. What would follow from him would be certainly one of the most detailed descriptions of the injuries suffered by a victim of Jack the Ripper.

Doctor George William Sequeira: First Doctor to the Scene

Doctor George William Sequeira was at his surgery, at 34 Jewry Street, when at 1:55 in the morning of 30th September 1888 PC Holland of the City of London Police was at his door with a message which no doubt caused a little shock to the doctor, for it seemed as if 'Jack the Ripper' had left his normal killing ground and murdered within the City of London boundary, and in a place not that far away from him. Of the three doctors who would be called to the scene, George was the first to arrive at Mitre Square...

George was the second child to be born to Henry Little Sequeira[89] and Amelia Brook,[90] who had married in 1853 in Clerkenwell, London.[91] Henry was a surgeon[92] at the time of George's birth in the first quarter of 1859.[93] With George's grandfather James[94] being a chemist,[95] is it any wonder that George would in time become a surgeon himself?

His older sibling was a sister, Amelia Louisa Sequeira, who had been born in London in 1856.[96] She went on to marry Henry Halford in 1881,[97] having five children with him before sadly passing away

89 Born 1828 in Whitechapel.
90 Born 1830 in Surrey.
91 Marriage record.
92 1861 census.
93 Birth record.
94 Born 1796 in Middlesex (1841 census).
95 1841 census.
96 Birth record.
97 Marriage record.

in Croydon in 1915.[98]

George's younger siblings were John Bailey Sequeira, born in 1867,[99] who became a Distiller's Agent[100] and married Alice Sadler in 1896,[101] with whom he had three children before passing away in 1921 in Lancashire.[102] George had a second brother named Alfred Edmund Sequeira, who was born in 1870,[103] but who sadly died at the age of four in 1874.[104] His youngest sibling, Septimus Willie Sequeira,[105] also worked in the medical field, being a Medical Dispenser.[106] He married Jessie Wardley in 1898,[107] and had four children with her.

The 1871 census shows that George, his parents and siblings were living at 34 Jewry Street with two servants[108] and an assistant for George's father's surgery.[109]

It is interesting to note that the surgery at 34 Jewry Street still belonged to George's father until quite possibly his death in 1888,[110] given that Henry still worked and lived there on the 1881 census, when he was recorded as living with his wife, son Septimus[111] and a new assistant named William E Goodwill, who was born in 1862 in Scarborough, Yorkshire. Henry also employed one servant, 27-year-old Maria Oliver.[112]

---

98 Death record.

99 Birth record.

100 1881 census.

101 Marriage record.

102 Death record.

103 Birth record.

104 Death record.

105 Born in 1873.

106 1891 census.

107 Marriage record.

108 Mary Sophia Millard (born in 1843 in Middlesex) and Elizabeth Simons Mary Ann Read (born in 1850 in Surrey) - 1871 census.

109 Charles Hard Hall, who was 28-years-old at the time.

110 Death record.

111 An eight-year-old scholar at the time.

112 1871 census.

It is interesting to consider that George Sequeira may have only just taken ownership of the surgery at 34 Jewry Street and was probably still grieving over his father's death when PC Holland knocked on his door, asking him to attend a murder scene at Mitre Square.

In 1881 George was not living with his parents. Given that in 1886 he gained his L.S.A. diploma from the London Hospital, it seems likely that five years earlier he was away training or just working at the hospital when the census man called.

George married Georgina Peachey in the fourth quarter of 1886, and the couple moved to Arlington Villas, Fairlop Road, in West Ham, East London.[113] They had their first child, Horace, in 1888,[114] and a second son, Edmund, quickly followed in 1889.[115] At the time of Catherine Eddowes' murder and George being called to that scene, therefore, he was dealing with the death of his father, the gaining of the surgery, his first born child and the fact that his wife was probably pregnant again. These facts do seem to make George more real and human to us than just mentioning that he was the first doctor to the scene at Mitre Square.

So, at five minutes to two in the morning of 30th September 1888, the door to 34 Jewry Street opened to a policeman wearing the City of London police uniform. The pair then travelled the short distance to Mitre Square, getting there at two o'clock.[116]

Once at the scene, in the light of the policeman's lamp George was able to see, in detail, what had been done to the victim. He pronounced that the woman lying on the cold, wet pavement, with her blood clotting before him, was dead, and that she had died, in his opinion, no more than fifteen minutes before his arrival.[117]

After the arrival of Inspector Collard, Dr Sequeira was told to stand down pending the examination of Dr Frederick Gordon Brown. We do know that George stayed at the scene to watch Dr Brown take his

---

113 1891 census.

114 Ibid.

115 Ibid.

116 Coroner's Inquest (L) 1888, No. 135, Catherine Eddowes's Inquest.

117 Ibid.

notes, and he would reappear later at two in the afternoon at Golden Lane Mortuary to watch the post mortem being performed.

George stated at the inquest held on 11th October 1888:

> Where the murder was committed was probably the darkest part of the square, but there was sufficient light to enable the miscreant to perpetrate the deed. I think that the murderer had no design on any particular organ of the body. He was not possessed of any great anatomical skill.[118]

He mentioned that, owing to the cut to the windpipe and blood vessels, the death of the woman would have occurred instantly and that her murderer may not have actually had any blood on him that could be easily seen. Although he generally agreed with Dr Brown's opinions on the case, George did not actually think that the murderer had any anatomical knowledge.[119]

In 1891, George and his wife were still living in Arlington Villas in West Ham, but with a new edition, daughter Ida Sequeira having been born that year.[120] Also living with the family were two servants, Ellen Edmonds aged 21 and Minnie Simpson aged 18.[121]

Two years later George's second daughter Marion Sequeira was born, but a further two years on, his son Edmund died at only six-years-old. A year later, in 1896, the Sequeira family welcomed a third daughter, Bertha Sequeira.

By the 1901 census the Sequeira family had moved to Oakleigh, 66 Wellington Road, in Edmonton, North London. George was 42 by this time and still a surgeon.[122]

George Sequeira died on 14th October 1926, his final address being 72 Wellington Road, Bush Hill Park in Enfield.[123] His effects totalled £3,854 6s 2d.[124]

---

118 Inquest report in the *Daily Telegraph*, 12th October 1888.

119 Ibid.

120 Ida Sequeira married Norman Frost in 1922.

121 1891 census.

122 1901 census.

123 Probate records of 1926.

124 Ibid.

His wife Georgina passed away in 1949 in Winchmore Hill, London.[125] Son Horace, who painted the well-known portrait of Dr George Sequeira holding a pipe in his later years, died in 1973 in Oxford.[126] Marion Sequeira died in 1961 in Hatfield, and Bertha Sequeira passed away in 1980 in Dorset.[127]

George's role in the investigation into the death of Catherine Eddowes was a relatively small one, but he was the first doctor to Mitre Square, and he pronounced her death.

We now know that at the time of Catherine's death George himself was coping with the loss of his father and gaining the family's surgery, as well as having a newborn and his wife being pregnant again.

One wonders if PC Holland woke up the whole household when he knocked on the doctor's door with the message of the murder in Mitre Square, and if George left his home with the sound of a newborn crying in the distance that morning?

William Sedgwick Saunders: There was Not the Faintest Trace...[128]

Being the City of London's Medical Officer of Health and Public Analyst, William was at the post-mortem of Catherine Eddowes in the afternoon of 30th September 1888. He was with Dr Frederick Gordon Brown and Dr Sequeira. William's role was that he analysed the contents of Catherine's stomach looking for poisons...

Born on 10th September 1824 in Compton Giffard, near Tavistock in Devon, William Sedgwick Saunders was baptised the same year

125 Death record.

126 Ibid.

127 Ibid.

128 *St James's Gazette*, 12th October 1888: a quote from William Sedgwick Saunders given at the post mortem of Catherine Eddowes.

at St Andrew's Church in Plymouth.[129] His parents were James Sedgwick Saunders, a schoolmaster, and his wife Harriet Todd.[130]

William's schooling was at King's College, and by 1843 he had begun his medical training at St Thomas's Hospital. Three years later he had his own practice,[131] as well as gaining a position as Assistant Surgeon in the Royal Fusiliers. This took him to places such as the West Indies and North Africa.[132]

By 1850, William was back on British soil and in Brighton, Sussex, where he married Charlotte Skerrett Abrahams[133] on 9th September 1850.[134] The two witnesses were William's father, James, and Charlotte's father, William.[135]

That same year, William Sedgwick Saunders changed positions and became a Medical Officer for the military prison Fort Clarence in Rochester, presumably why on the 1851 census he and Charlotte were living at 15 Maidstone Road, Rochester in Kent.[136] They lived there with Charlotte's older sister Louisa,[137] as well as two servants named Elizabeth Pickard, aged 26, and Jane Murrell, aged 18.[138]

Later in 1851 William was posted overseas in his role as a medical man in the Kaffir War. However, he fell ill and was unable to travel on HMS *Birkenhead* as planned.[139]

This might have seemed unlucky to a man who wanted to serve his country, but it turned out to be a lucky escape because as the ship was travelling to Gansbaai it collided with a rock and sank. As the

---

129 Baptism record from South West Heritage Trust.

130 Ibid.

131 *The City of London Cemetery and Crematorium Newspaper.* Issue Number 9 of the Crematorium Centenary.

132 Ibid.

133 Born in 1821 in Taunton, Somerset.

134 Marriage record.

135 Ibid.

136 1851 census.

137 Born 1820 in Taunton, Somerset.

138 1851 census.

139 First relaunched as HMS *Birkenhead* on 30th December 1845, it was previously known as HMS *Vulcan*. It was reclassified for the Army in 1851.

women and children were placed in lifeboats, the soldiers stood in rank and went down with the ship, resulting in over three hundred deaths.

William Sedgwick Saunders did recover from his illness, but did not return to army life. From 1852 to 1874 he seemed to prefer a quieter life with his practice in the City.[140] However, he had still an active interest in the City of London, and became a Common Councilman around this time. It was recorded that "to him mainly is due the Guildhall Library and as Chairman of the Library Committee, it fell to his lot to lay the foundation stone."[141] In an odd coincidence, today the Guildhall Library hosts the City of London Police Museum, which in turn stages a display on the death of Catherine Eddowes, a case in which William had his own part to play, and the reason we are mentioning him within this book.

However, life between 1852 and 1888 was not an easy one for William.

In 1853, Charlotte bore William his first child, who they named Eliza.[142] Sadly, in the first quarter of 1861, when Eliza was just eight-years-old, Charlotte died in the City of London.[143] William remarried just a year later, on 15th January 1862, aged 37, to Lydia Volekman in Stockwell, Surrey.[144] Maybe the possible reason for a quick marriage was that William thought that his daughter Eliza needed a motherly figure in her life at such a young age?

In 1864 William wrote his book, *On the Nature of Cholera as a Guide to Treatment*,[145] in which he suggested for the first time that cholera could be a nervous disorder rather than a blood disorder when comparing it to perforation and traumatic peritonitis.[146]

---

140 *The City of London Cemetery and Crematorium Newspaper*. Issue Number 9 of the Crematorium Centenary.

141 Obituary in the *British Medical Journal*, 26th January 1901.

142 1881 census.

143 Death record.

144 Marriage record.

145 *The Lancet*, 1864.

William became Medical Officer of Health and the Public Analyst for the Commissioner of Sewers in 1874.[147] This was at a time when the medical officers of the City were becoming worried about the overall death rate in the capital due to unsanitary conditions. In fact Dr Henry Letheby,[148] the President of the Society of Medical Officers of Health, had noticed that death rates had remained constant in London for over three decades, indicating that sanitary conditions needed improving in order for mortality levels to decrease.[149]

William's role did not always make him popular. On 21st October 1874 there was a meeting of the City Commissioners of Sewers at which William's actions were called into question.[150] William had tested one hundred and fifty chests of re-dried teas belonging to Messrs J.C. Sillar which had accidently sunk in the Thames. William's analysis indicated that the tea was fine, and it was resold on 29th September that year. It was advised in the auction catalogue that these teas had been 'analysed by William Sedgwick Saunders, M.D., public analyst for the City of London and pronounced by him fit for sale.'[151]

This also meant that the Customs Department could receive duty on the teas, which was suggested by a Mr Davis as the reason why William had passed the teas as fit for consumption. Mr Davis wanted William to account for his actions, but when the meeting was called he was too ill to speak, having inhaled gas from sewers a few days before.[152]

A year later, in 1875, William and his second wife had their first son together. He was named Godfrey and was born in Chislehurst, Kent.[153] This could suggest that William had moved out of London

---

146 *Medical Times and Gazette*, 8th September 1866.

147 *The City of London Cemetery and Crematorium Newspaper*. Issue Number 9 of the Crematorium Centenary.

148 Dr Henry Letheby took over this role in 1855 from John Simon.

149 Sanitary Record Number One 1874, pp 305-8.

150 *Iron News*, 24th October 1874.

151 Ibid.

152 Ibid.

153 1881 census.

by then, as by 1881 we know from the census that the family were living at Bromley in Kent.

In 1878, the port of London was teeming with poisoned flour, tainted by the presence of gypsum.[154] By the January of 1879, William had discovered where the flour had come from and tried to bring the fact that gypsum was a public health hazard to court, because before that tampering with food was considered only a fraud.[155]

The Sanitary Record of 1879 commented on the event by stating:

> Dr Sedgwick Saunders, medical officer of health for the City, applied to the Lord Mayor for an order for the condemnation of seventy-nine sacks of flour which was unfit for human food. Dr Saunders said the application was made under the 2nd section of the Nuisances Removal Act 1863 that the Lord Mayor would give an order preventing the consumption as human food of seventy-nine bags of stuff which was called flour, and which had been imported as meal, and had been sold as such. This meal he had ascertained by analysis consisted of seventy-nine per cent, of sulphurate of lime or plaster of Paris.

> As far back as September last the sanitary inspector of the district received information that 100 sacks of this meal had been imported by a member of what was called the Long Firm who had been endeavouring, by giving sampling orders and otherwise, to sell the stuff as meal or flour. At that time he (Dr Saunders) was unable to get a sampling order, as he was unable to find the consignees, Jackson and Co. The flour came by the Baron Osy from Antwerp, in August last, and, failing to get the sampling order, he made application for the condemnation of the stuff, but he was advised that unless he positively obtained a sample and analysed it the authority he required could not be obtained. The thing, therefore, remained in abeyance until Mr Alexander, manager of the Belgian Bank, Lombard Street, applied to him privately to analyse some of this very flour, upon which he had advanced £30. Through Mr Alexander he obtained a sampling order in connection with eighty sacks of flour described as meal.

> The Lord Mayor: Why does Mr Alexander not prosecute?

> Dr Saunders: That is not a question for me.

> The Lord Mayor: But it is a very pertinent one for me to consider.

154 A soft white or grey mineral consisting of hydrated calcium sulphate.
155 *The Sanitary Record*, 1879.

Dr Saunders: I am acting simply as the guardian of the public health. In the meantime, and while the ulterior proceedings are pending, this stuff may be sold; in fact, I am informed that it has already been sold to a French baker. I would ask your lordship to put your veto, and say it shall not be removed.

The Lord Mayor: No; I cannot put my veto on it at all. The first step is for the person who has been taken in to proceed by summons or warrant against those who have taken him in, for obtaining advances by false pretences. I must see if I cannot punish the party for importing such stuff. Besides, I have no proof that this was sold as flour. The party may come here and say that he has not offered it as flour, and that he does not intend to sell it as such.

Dr Saunders said he had already seized the stuff.

The Lord Mayor: Then let the party who has been deceived come forward and prosecute.

Dr Saunders: I have no power to deal with the stuff until your lordship condemns it. It is not fit for human food.

The Lord Mayor: I do not know that it has been offered as food.

Dr Saunders: That is the difficulty.

The Lord Mayor: With all due respect to the position you hold, Dr Saunders, I am bound to protect the public here. The first step is to bring forward evidence of the party disposing of the flour.

Dr Saunders: With all respect I submit that I have nothing to do with Mr Alexander or anyone else.

The Lord Mayor: I have nothing further to say. That is my decision.[156]

These cases brought William to the public's attention. There was even a sketch of him in his position as the City of London's Medical Officer in the *Illustrated London News*, showing a determined-looking man, with his eyes focused and staring off to his right.[157]

William was in the news again that year in conjunction with another case. This time it was not flour making the headlines, but whisky. It was suggested that Banagher Whisky, made in Ireland, was 'odd, old, dry and digestible.'[158] William analysed a sample but

156 *The Sanitary Record*, 1879.

157 *Illustrated London News*, 18th July 1874

158 *New Zealand Herald*, 7th June 1879.

wanted a second opinion, so had it sent to Mr T. Redwood, the Public Analyst of the County of Middlesex, who finally gave the accepted answer that it was fine.[159]

In 1881 William was living with his wife and two children at Elmstead Wood, Elmstead Lane, Bromley in Kent. He had four servants living with him, those being Margaret Warner (aged 27), Eliza Stockley (also 27) and her sister Mary Stockley (17), with Harriot Friswell (24).[160] By now, William was 56 years of age and describing himself as Dr L.C.O.P.[161]

By 1888, the Saunders family had moved back to London, living at 13 Queen's Street, Cheapside.[162] On the afternoon of 30th September William travelled the short distance from his home to Golden Lane Mortuary, arriving at 2:30pm. He was there to observe and assist with the post mortem of Catherine Eddowes.[163]

William analysed the contents of Catherine's stomach to see if there had been any poisons used, but that was negative: "There was not the faintest trace of these, (narcotic) or any other poisons."[164]

The post mortem stated that the victim was

> 5'-3", about 45 years old Rigor mortis well marked; Green discoloration over abdomen; Body not quite cold; No traces of recent connection; Recent bruise, size of a sixpence, on left hand between thumb and first finger; Left eyelid cut; Deep cut on bridge of nose; Cut on right cheek; Tip of nose detached; 2 abrasions on left cheek under left ear; Throat cut nearly ear-to-ear, dividing all tissues down to the bone; Frontal abdominal walls cut open from the pubic area to the breast bone; Liver was stabbed; Left of the groin, a stab wound; Cuts made between the thighs and labium on both sides; Stomach contained very little food or fluid; Intestines had been detached; Right kidney bloodless and pale; Gall bladder had bile; Pancreas was cut; Left kidney removed; Uterus lining was cut; Womb was cut through leaving ¾" of a stump; Womb was removed; Bladder was

159 *New Zealand Herald*, 7th June 1879.
160 1881 census.
161 Ibid.
162 The *Echo*, 11th October 1888.
163 Coroner's Inquest (L) 1888, No. 135.
164 *St. James's Gazette*, 12th October 1888.

healthy.[165]

William believed that the killer had 'no great amount of anatomical skill',[166] and that the murderer 'had no desire to obtain any particular organ.'[167]

He did not see the portion of kidney which was sent to Mr George Lusk, but was quoted in the *Liverpool Daily Post* as to his opinion on whether the 'Lusk kidney' was human or not, and perhaps slyly mentioned his own thoughts on other doctors for having done so:

> It is a pity some people have not got the courage to say they don't know. You may take it that there is no difference whatever between the male and female kidney. As for those in animals, they are similar, the cortical substance is the same, and the structure only differs in shape. I think it would be quite possible to mistake it for a pig's.[168]

In 1891, William and his family were recorded as living at 58 Onslow Gardens, Kensington, with visitors Kate and Frances Noddall, in addition to servants Emily Jones, Esther Cassidy, Alice Oliver and Eliza Bedford.[169]

In June 1895, a letter from Mr Walter Hazell of Leicester to the President of the Local Government Board highlighted that 'large quantities of unwholesome meat' were on sale within the City of London.[170]

William had written in March that meat condemned as unfit by the inspectors could still go on to be sold in Holborn, where there were not as many qualified inspectors as other areas. Mr Hazell wondered if William would use his 'influence' to stop this from happening,[171] but the reply was in the negative, as Mr Shaw Lefevre of the Local Government Board stated:

---

165 Coroner's Inquest (L) 1888, No. 135.

166 *St. James's Gazette*, 12th October 1888.

167 Ibid.

168 *Liverpool Daily Post*, 20th October 1888.

169 1891 census.

170 HC DEB vol. 34, 13th June 1895.

171 Ibid.

I have no direct information on this subject, and the letter of Dr Saunders has not been communicated to me. I have, however, been informed by the Holborn District Board that, on every occasion when complaints have been made to them by inspectors under the Commissioners of Sewers, of the nature referred to, they have done their best to investigate them, and have called for evidence to substantiate the charge, but that on no one occasion has evidence worthy of the name been put forward.[172]

William became ill with pneumonia late in 1900 and died on 19th January 1901 at his home at Onslow Gardens, South Kensington.[173]

The City Press wrote:

To him we owe in a great measure the improvement that has taken place in the sanitary condition of the City in the past quarter of a century.[174]

He was buried in Chapel Avenue at the City of London Cemetery, the same cemetery that is the last resting place of Catherine Eddowes. His plot is very close to the entrance, along the central pathway on the right hand side. His headstone cannot be missed, for it stands tall amongst the greenery behind it in a form of red granite. On top sits an angel draped over a cross.

Considering how close William is to the main entrance of the cemetery, once you start walking along the central path you are instantly engulfed in quietness, a sort of peacefulness that governs the whole area of the cemetery, including the plot where Catherine Eddowes lies.

One wonders if on that afternoon of 30th September 1888, when William was at the Golden Lane Mortuary and stood in front of the body of Catherine Eddowes, whether he could possibly have imagined that he would eventually rest only a few yards away from her, for all time...

---

172 HC DEB vol. 34, 13th June 1895.

173 Obituary in the *British Medical Journal*, 26th January 1901.

174 *City Press*, 19th January 1901.

Sir Henry Smith:
'Yes, the Ripper Had all the Luck'[175]

Sir Henry Smith was the Assistant Commissioner of the City of London Police at the time of the Ripper. Sir Henry Smith travelled to Mitre Square on the morning of 30th September 1888, after the news broke that there had been a murder within the boundary in which he governed. Sir Henry Smith then travelled to Goulston Street, where a piece of the victim's apron had been found next to a chalked message...

Or did he?

Some may think that writing about the life of Sir Henry Smith would be an easy task, given that he himself had written a memoir called *From Constable to Commissioner: The Story of Sixty Years, Most of them Misspent* in 1910, and although he died in 1921, the memoir does cover a fair chunk of his life.

However, we have always got to remember that someone saying something had happened and finding proof that something *did* happen can be two different things. Sir Henry Smith was writing about events 60 years after his birth and 13 years after the Ripper's crimes, so we can assume that exact dates might be out by a few years, but nevertheless the memoir should still give us a basis to work on.

Yet, let us go back to the introduction above about Sir Henry Smith for a moment. There is a question at the end of it, a question that in itself might puzzle a few of us. Of course, Sir Henry Smith was the Assistant Commissioner of the City of London Police at the time of the Ripper, of course Sir Henry Smith travelled to Mitre Square and then on to Goulston Street on the morning of 30th September 1888, we think to ourselves. For that is what we are told in every book on the subject of the crimes.

But what if we had been told something incorrectly, all these years? What would that mean?

---

175 *From Constable to Commissioner, The Story of Sixty Years, Most of them Misspent* by Lieut. Col. Sir Henry Smith K.C.B., 1910. A quote from Henry about Jack the Ripper.

When is Sir Henry Smith not actually Sir Henry Smith? The answer would be apparently from birth, because Sir Henry Smith was not born 'Henry Smith', he was born under another name.

A little shocking isn't it? We first come across this problem quite early on into research of 'Henry's' life, for there seems to be no birth or baptism record for a Henry Smith born between 1831 (the date in which he claims he was born in his memoirs) and 1836 (the year given as his birth year in later census returns), in Dumfriesshire, Scotland.

We may think, well, not every Victorian family registered the birth of a child, yet alone baptised them and you would be correct in thinking that. However, when you throw into the mix that 'Henry's' father was a well-known Minister of Scotland, as was his grandfather and great-grandfather, it would seem a little odd for the child not to be registered.

So let's look into the family background at a time before Henry was born, to get an idea of the family and his parents as this may give us an idea of what had happened at the time of Henry's birth.

His grandfather was Reverend George Smith, who was born on 2nd March 1749 to Reverend William Smith, Minister of Cranston, and Jane Baird.[176] George attended Glasgow University before marrying Marion Freer.[177] They had a number of children: Henrietta Scott Smith,[178] William Smith, Adam Smith, George Smith, David Smith and John Smith.[179]

Henrietta married Lewis Balfour, a Minster of Sorn and then of Collinton, and would in time become the grandmother of the novelist Robert Louis Stevenson.[180] This connection is made through Henrietta and Lewis's daughter Margaret Isabella, who was born in

176 The history of Galston Parish Church (Scotland's Church Trust).

177 Ibid.

178 Ibid.

179 *From Constable to Commissioner, The Story of Sixty Years, Most of them Misspent* by Lieut. Col. Sir Henry Smith K.C.B., 1910.

180 The history of Galston Parish Church (Scotland's Church Trust).

181 Birth record.

1829.[181] She married Thomas Stevenson, a lighthouse engineer, and they had a son who was baptised 'Robert Lewis Balfour Stevenson', later dropping the 'Balfour' part of his name and changing the spelling of 'Lewis' to 'Louis'.[182]

George Sr became Minister of Galston, East Ayrshire, in 1778 and served until 1823, when he passed away, and his son George Jr took over. George Sr was quite well known, being mentioned in various Robert Burns poems, such as *The Holy Fair*. He was buried in Galston Parish Church and there is a plaque addressed to him and his wife on the south wall of the church.[183]

George Jr was born on 18th February 1793. Like his father, he was educated at Glasgow University and gained his M.A. in 1812. He was made the Second Charge in Kilmarnock on 16th September 1824,[184] and married Jane Hogarth there on 2nd August 1825.[185]

The couple's first child, George Freer Smith, was born on 9th March 1827.[186] Their second son, David, came along in 1828,[187] and their third arrived on Christmas Day 1829, whom they named Hamilton Lee Smith.[188] In 1831 the Smith family had to deal with heartbreak

182 *The Life of Robert Louis Stevenson* by Graham Balfour, 1901.

183 The history of Galston Parish Church (Scotland's Church Trust).

184 *Fasti Ecclesiae Scoticanae: The Succession of Ministers in the Church of Scotland from the Reformation*. Vol 1 pg. 121.

185 Marriage record.

186 He became a Civil Engineer and died in India. *Fasti Ecclesiae Scoticanae: The Succession of Ministers in the Church of Scotland from the Reformation*. Vol 1 pg. 121.

187 1841 census.

188 *Fasti Ecclesiae Scoticanae: The Succession of Ministers in the Church of Scotland from the Reformation*. Vol 1 pg. 121. Hamilton Lee Smith was a well-known civil engineer who worked with Mr Turnbull, who was an engineer of the London end of the Great Northern Railway during its construction. Hamilton Smith became Mr Turnbull's assistant in 1852 and they travelled to India, where Hamilton was put in charge of the railway being built at the Agra district. In 1865 he worked for the Indian Government, helping to design the Lahore and Peshawar Railway, returning to England in February 1869, where he worked for the Indian Office until 1872. In 1878 he was appointed Chief Engineer of the Egyptian Railways at Cairo, filling this role until 1881 when he again returned to England, marrying a year later in Islington. In 1888 he was sent to Spain by the Honduras Company, but the tropical conditions left him seriously ill and he returned to England six months later. He took to his bed and passed away on 3rd September 1889 of heart disease. Information from an obituary published in *The Engineer*.

as their only daughter, Beatrice,[189] died on 2nd September 1831, only seven months after her birth.[190] They welcomed another son, Adam Smith, in 1832.[191]

It's unknown whether the death of their daughter prompted the Smith family to move, but George transferred to Penpont in Dumfriesshire on 16th April 1833.[192] It was here that a fifth child, another David Smith, was born in 1834.[193] Next came Walter Francis Montagu Smith, born on 13th September 1834,[194] followed by a seventh child on 15th December 1835, given the first name William.[195]

Let us for a moment leave the Smith family life and go back to the question at the beginning of this section: why can we not find a birth record for Henry Smith? George and Jane do not have any more children - George died in 1866 and Jane in 1873,[196] and a search of the census returns between 1841 and 1871 shows no more children.

This means that one of the sons must have changed his first name for some reason. The leading candidate is William Smith, born on 15th December 1835.[197] Although this is not the birth year that Sir Henry Smith gave in his memoirs, that being 1831, and also not the birth year recorded in later censuses, that being 1836, it does sit nicely in between those two dates.

What helps us further are the facts that William was listed as an apprentice to an accountant on the 1861 census, an occupation our 'Henry' admits to doing, and perhaps even more importantly William

189 Born on 21st February 1831.

190 Death record.

191 1841 census.

192 *Fasti Ecclesiae Scoticanae: The Succession of Minsters in the Church of Scotland from the Reformation.* Vol 1 pg. 121.

193 1841 census.

194 Walter Francis Montagu Smith became Captain of the Royal Artillery and died in London in 1873. *Fasti Ecclesiae Scoticanae: The Succession of Minsters in the Church of Scotland from the Reformation.* Vol 1 pg. 121.

195 Birth record.

196 Death records.

197 Birth record.

had the middle name 'Henry'. After the 1861 census, William Henry Smith disappears and Henry Smith appears. However, with no birth record found to date, can we assume this is our 'Henry' Smith?

It was while looking into the history of Henry's father George that the author discovered a book called *Fasti Ecclesiae Scoticanae: The Succession of Ministers in the Church of Scotland from the Reformation*, that not only gives a detailed description of George Smith but also a few members of his family. On page 122 it states, 'Sir (William) Henry Smith Chief Superintendent of Police for the City of London 1885-1890 and Commissioner 1890-1901,'[198] providing confirmation.

In the 1841 census, the Smith family was living at the Vicarage at Penpont, Dumfriesshire in Scotland. With George and his wife Jane are children George, David, Walter, 'William' Henry, Adam and David, along with servants Catherine McCraig, Isobella Walker, Agness Whigham and Jane Sharp.[199]

According to Henry's memoirs, soon after his birth the family moved to live in Edinburgh, 'in the place which is now the Assembly Hall.'[200] It was a loose definition of 'soon', as George Smith did not actually transfer to Tolbooth in Edinburgh until 15th August 1844 to become the Minister of that parish,[201] a full eight years and eight months after Henry's birth.

In 1846, Henry was sent to Edinburgh Academy, where he joined what was commonly known as the 'Geits', a first class society of students. Henry quite proudly admitted that he was the head boy.[202] He claimed he left this school in 1850 and had a French and German teacher for a year before attending Edinburgh University in 1851.[203]

---

198 *Fasti Ecclesiae Scoticanae: The Succession of Ministers in the Church of Scotland from the Reformation.* Vol 1 pg. 122.

199 1841 census.

200 *From Constable to Commissioner, The Story of Sixty Years, Most of them Misspent* by Lieut. Col. Sir Henry Smith K.C.B., 1910.

201 *Fasti Ecclesiae Scoticanae: The Succession of Ministers in the Church of Scotland from the Reformation.* Vol 1 pg. 121.

202 *From Constable to Commissioner, The Story of Sixty Years, Most of them Misspent* by Lieut. Col. Sir Henry Smith K.C.B., 1910.

203 Ibid.

By the 1851 census the Smith family had separated a little. George Jr had moved down to London to be with his brother, Hamilton Lee Smith, and the pair were living at Harpur Street in Holborn, a lodging house owned by Louisa Dixon.[204] They were both civil engineers by this time.[205]

George Sr and Jane, along with sons Walter and Henry, were living at 6 Randolph Cliff, St Cuthbert's in Edinburgh. George was now 53 and still Minister of Tolbooth Parish; Jane was 50, and the two remaining sons, Walter and Henry, were both scholars. The Smith family had four servants at this time, namely Elizabeth Walker the laundry maid, Margaret Milne the cook, Ann Stewart the housemaid and Catharine Mclean, the table maid. Visiting on 30th March 1851, when the census was taken, were Archibald Dickson, William Dickson, William Pott, Charles Fairlie and Henry Fairlie.[206]

Henry Smith wrote that he started his studies at Edinburgh University later in 1851, spending two years under a teacher called Kelland.[207]

By 1853, Henry had left his studies and became an apprentice to a firm of accountants called Brown and Pearson in George Street, Edinburgh. Although he claimed that he stayed there for five years, he admitted that he 'found the work too contiguous' and spent most of his time at his desk.[208]

Around the same time Henry joined St Andrew's Boat Club, later writing how in that year, "a sailor was sentenced to death and I was determined to go up to the High Street to see the execution. My mother implored me not to go to such a demoralizing spectacle; my father, on the other hand, took a different view of the question, thinking it would turn me sick, 'let him go, he'll never wish to see

204 Born 1808 in Kensington (1851 census).

205 1851 census.

206 Ibid.

207 *From Constable to Commissioner, The Story of Sixty Years, Most of them Misspent* by Lieut. Col. Sir Henry Smith K.C.B., 1910.

208 Ibid.

another."[209] Henry recalled that that the hangman was William Calcraft,[210] who gave the sailor the short drop.

In 1858, Henry had finished his apprenticeship at the accountants, passing his C.A.s, and was offered a job as a bookkeeper in Glasgow House, on Buchanan Street. He earned a salary of £100 per year, working shifts from 9:30am to 6:00pm.[211] He was living in a lodging house owned by a landlady named Bullock at this time, situated on Sauchiehall Street. The lodging house was above the local grocer and Henry stayed on the first floor. According to his memoirs, he came home one day and found the landlady dead and leaning against the front door, so he moved to Bath Street in Glasgow.[212]

In 1860, Henry returned to Edinburgh, but wrote that he was not there for long as he 'was sent to Harrogate to recruit' and claimed he was in the Suffolk Artillery Militia, his training being in Harwick, halfway between London and Flixton.[213] However, the year seems a little out as on the 1861 census, William H. Smith was still an apprentice to an accountant at the age of 25 and living in Melville Street, Edinburgh.[214] The years are not that far off, however, and Henry can be forgiven if he was writing from memory.

The title of Henry's memoirs is interesting. "From Constable to Commissioner" seems to suggest that Henry worked his way up to Commissioner but it was known that he entered the City of London Police force at a high rank. So where does the 'constable' part fit into his story? Was he adding it for embellishment, to add a more impressive-sounding promotional ladder to his career?

---

209 *From Constable to Commissioner, The Story of Sixty Years, Most of them Misspent* by Lieut. Col. Sir Henry Smith K.C.B., 1910.

210 William Calcraft was born on 11th October 1800 and died on 13th December 1879. In a 45 year career he hanged approximately 450 people. The short drop method he used meant that the people being executed died a long and painful death as they were being slowly strangled.

211 *From Constable to Commissioner, The Story of Sixty Years, Most of them Misspent* by Lieut. Col. Sir Henry Smith K.C.B., 1910.

212 Ibid.

213 Ibid.

214 Ibid.

It is easy to think this was the case; after all, there had been no real mention of him being a constable, and Henry himself certainly does not mention it within his memoirs. However, a look at the newspapers at the time of Henry's death brought surprising results. A short paragraph in the *Aberdeen Journal* of 4th March 1921 reports the passing of Sir Henry Smith, and in mentioning his career states that "He served in the Suffolk Artillery Militia and subsequently became a constable in a Scottish local police force."[215]

This is also mentioned in the *Edinburgh Evening News*,[216] however neither reports state which local police force, which year or even the area in which he served, but this snippet of information does give us a suggestion as to why Henry Smith called his memoirs *From Constable to Commissioner*... - he was a constable in a Scottish police force and Commissioner in the City of London Police force.

The new information does not stop there. The *Aberdeen Journal* stated that Henry also then served in Newcastle before travelling to London in 1879.[217] Again, this information was not mentioned in his memoirs, nor is it mentioned in what way he served - was it with the police, or the army?

All we can do is to give a rough date as to when this might have happened.

He claimed to have joined the Suffolk Artillery Militia in 1861, and in 1871 was living with his older brother, Hamilton Lee Smith, at Inverness Terrace, Paddington in London.[218] This gives us a ten-year window for Henry serving in a Scottish police force and then being in Newcastle.

On 10th June 1866, Henry's father died. He was buried in Waltham Abbey, Essex,[219] suggesting that George and Jane had moved to

---

214 *From Constable to Commissioner, The Story of Sixty Years, Most of them Misspent* by Lieut. Col. Sir Henry Smith K.C.B., 1910.

215 *The Aberdeen Journal*, 4th March 1921.

216 March 1921.

217 *The Aberdeen Journal*, 4th March 1921.

218 1871 census.

219 *Fasti Ecclesiae Scoticanae: The Succession of Ministers in the Church of Scotland from the Reformation.* Vol 1 pg. 121.

London before that date. Henry wrote in his memoirs that his mother decided to move to Alnmouth, Northumberland, in 1867 soon after the death of his father, but Henry himself felt reluctant to leave London at this time,[220] suggesting that he had been living with his parents before the death of his father.

This would fit in well with the 1871 census, which has him living with his brother in London. We can easily imagine that with his mother having left London and Henry preferring to stay in the capital, he moved in with his brother, who was living in Paddington.

Now we have Henry living in London, at the latest from 1865, so the gap in which the two events could have happened can be decreased to a possible three or four years, between 1862 and 1865.

Henry wrote that he suffered an accident after a horse bolted and struck him.[221] The exact date of this accident was not mentioned, but Henry does state that it was before his father passed away. A doctor named Warburton-Begbie considered that Henry was suffering from Bright's Disease,[222] which Henry disagreed with but took the medication the doctor gave him and recovered. Could this accident or illness be the reason he left Newcastle, from whatever position he held there, and saw him move back to live with his parents?

In 1872, Henry received word that his mother was not well and moved to Northumberland to help her.[223] Jane died on 20th June 1873,[224] and sadly the Smith family also had to cope with the death of Henry's brother Walter in London that same year.[225]

---

220 *From Constable to Commissioner, The Story of Sixty Years, Most of them Misspent* by Lieut. Col. Sir Henry Smith K.C.B., 1910.

221 Ibid.

222 The symptoms of Bright's Disease were thought to be inflammation, haemorrhages, apoplexy, convulsions, blindness and going in and out of a coma. See *A Treatise on Bright's Disease of the Kidneys; Its Pathology, Diagnosis and Treatment* by Henry B Millard (1884). It is interesting to note that Henry was given this diagnosis, given that after her post-mortem Catherine Eddowes was said to have suffered from the same disease.

223 *From Constable to Commissioner, The Story of Sixty Years, Most of them Misspent* by Lieut. Col. Sir Henry Smith K.C.B., 1910.

224 Death record.

It was in 1879, while he was still in Northumberland, Henry wrote, that he received his first call from the City of London Police, when the retiring Chief Superintendent Major Bowman was seeking his replacement. He believed that Henry would work well with Commissioner Fraser. Henry appears to have been keen to accept the position, but wrote in his memoirs that the Commissioner was not so excited, taking six years to give his agreement.[226]

Henry wrote that he did not leave his mother's home until 1885,[227] which fits in well with the 1881 census, which records him at The Tower, Alnmouth, Northumberland.[228]

It is interesting to note that this census was the first time that Henry described himself as 'Captain of Suffolk Artillery Brigade Militia (Army Officer).[229] He never mentions that he was a Captain of the Suffolk Artillery Militia in his memoirs, in fact he does not go into great detail of his time there. One would assume that if you were a captain, you would have at least mentioned it, and Henry seems proud enough in 1881 to describe himself as such on the census, and yet doesn't mention it twenty years later. Was it the case that because he was not working at the time, as he states in his memoirs,[230] he wanted the census taker to believe he was a man of importance? Or had Henry paid for that title? If so, the cost would have been the pricey sum of £1,800.[231]

Henry claims that in 1885 he was given a position in the Liverpool Police force within the Detective Department, only for his role to be ended quickly because he had no experience working against Fenian activity, which was a serious threat at the time. However, he

---

225 Died in London in 1873.

226 *From Constable to Commissioner, The Story of Sixty Years, Most of them Misspent* by Lieut. Col. Sir Henry Smith K.C.B., 1910.

227 Ibid.

228 1881 census.

229 Ibid.

230 *From Constable to Commissioner, The Story of Sixty Years, Most of them Misspent* by Lieut. Col. Sir Henry Smith K.C.B., 1910.

231 *The Purchase of Officers' Commissions in the British Army* by John Armatys and Robert George Cordery.

soon took on the role of Chief Superintendent of the City of London Police, with Inspector Tillcock showing him the area and stations of that force.[232]

Henry recalled an occasion when he and Inspector Tillcock visited Snow Hill Police Station one night, and witnessed the arrest of a woman:

> The female in question, brought in for pickpocketing in a Bayswater Bus, failing to appreciate the comfortable quarters provided for her by the 'grand old corporation' and having somewhere about her a thin, strong cord, which a culpably careless search had failed to discover, proceeded to hang herself, not ten minutes after her admission... Inspector Tillcock (who was visiting with me) ran to the cells and when we got there, it looked as if she was dead. Tillcock, a splendid policeman had his knife ready. She suffered a cut to her throat but survived to which Tillcock asked, 'Did you suffer much?', 'Not a bit' she replied, 'it was like going to sleep.'[233]

Writing of another incident, Henry provides valuable information on other City officers known to us:

> On the morning of January 24th 1886, snow lay to the depth of three or four inches in the streets of the City and Constables who had been on duty for eight weary hours were longing for relief. The police are very thick on the ground in the 'one square mile'. There was always a man in Bishopsgate Churchyard, and another less than a hundred yards from him, in Broad Street. Suddenly, a man named Hutt thought he saw the pavement rise within a short distance of where he was standing and going cautiously forward stood to attention. Presently, the pavement – a cellar flap in front of a jeweller's shop – rose again. Stepping on top of it, he whistled for assistance and was instantly joined by the constable in the Churchyard. Lifting the flap, they saw a man of 30 years of age and pulling him up, marched him off to Old Jewry with 80 watches and 219 rings on him. Sagar, the 'stick it' doctor, I instructed to see the case and endeavour to find the antecedents of the man arrested. Nothing was known in those days of 'fingerprint' identification; all we had to aid us were photographs, many of them taken by the force – for criminals used to fight and struggle in order to prevent a correct representation being got of

---

232 *From Constable to Commissioner, The Story of Sixty Years, Most of them Misspent* by Lieut. Col. Sir Henry Smith K.C.B., 1910.

233 Ibid.

their features and nearly all faded and unreliable. There were many albums filled with them at the Old Jewry, but Sagar was not long before he appeared in my room, 'that's David Grant, Sir' he said.[234]

In 1887, Henry was living in Cloak Lane Police Station, where he learnt how to pick the lock of his door using tweezers, having been told how to do so by "a young American who got five years at the Old Bailey for burglary" that year.[235]

Henry was quite open in his opinions, thoughts and even actions regarding the Jack the Ripper case in his memoirs, to the point where the reader feels they are with him on the night of 29th September, with his vivid description of events:

> The night of Saturday, September 29, found me tossing about in my bed at Cloak Lane Station, close to the river and adjoining Southwark Bridge. There was a railway goods depot in front and furriers premises behind my rooms; the lane was causewayed, heavy vans were going constantly in and out and the sickening smell from the furriers skins was always present. You could not open the windows and to sleep was an impossibility. Suddenly the bell at my head rang violently. 'What is it?' I asked putting my ear to the tube. 'Another murder Sir, this time in the City'. Jumping up, I was dressed and in the street in a couple of minutes. A hansom – to me a detestable vehicle – was at the door and into it I jumped, as time was of the utmost consequence... we got to our destination – Mitre Square – without upset, where I found a small group of my men standing round the mutilated remains of a woman.[236]

After leaving Mitre Square and going to Leman Street Police Station, where news had been received about the chalked message in Goulston Street, Henry attended the scene and viewed the message before returning to Mitre Square.[237]

Henry wrote:

---

234 *From Constable to Commissioner, The Story of Sixty Years, Most of them Misspent* by Lieut. Col. Sir Henry Smith K.C.B., 1910.

235 Ibid.

236 Ibid.

237 Coroner's Inquest (L) 1888, No. 135, Catherine Eddowes's Inquest.

I was convinced then, and convinced now, that had my orders been carried out in the spirit – they may have been to the letter – the reign of terror would have ceased that night.[238]

His orders were that every man and woman seen together were to be accounted for.

The murder of Catherine Eddowes and the City of London Police investigation was apparently not the first time the Ripper had bothered Henry, for he states:

In August 1888, when I was desperately keen to lay my hands on the murderer, I made such arrangements as I thought would ensure success. I put nearly a third of the force into plain clothes, with instructions to do everything which, under ordinary circumstances, a constable should not do. It was subversive of discipline; but I had them well supervised by senior officers.[239]

He continued:

After the second crime, I sent word to Sir Charles Warren that I had discovered a man likely to be the man wanted. He certainly had all the qualifications requisite. He had been a medical student; he had been in a lunatic asylum; he spent all his time with women of loose character, whom be bilked by giving them polished farthings instead of sovereigns, two of these farthings having been found in the pocket of the murdered woman. Sir Charles failed to find him. I thought he was likely to be in Rupert Street, Haymarket.[240]

It is a little difficult to know where Henry was living from 1891 to 1901, as he appeared as a visitor in two different houses when these censuses were taken, both owned by one Frances Dickson. On the 1891 census, he was recorded as a visitor at Queen's Gardens, Paddington, describing himself as the Commissioner of London City Police.[241] On the 1901 census, he was a visitor in West End, Pinner,

---

238 *From Constable to Commissioner, The Story of Sixty Years, Most of them Misspent* by Lieut. Col. Sir Henry Smith K.C.B., 1910.

239 Ibid.

240 Ibid.

and at the age of 65 was describing himself as Lieutenant Colonel, Commissioner of Police - another title which isn't mentioned in great detail in his memoirs. Could this have been another brought title? If he did buy this title, because of already being a Captain he would have had to pay around £1,314 to become Lieutenant Colonel.[242]

In 1896 Henry was made Knight Commander of the Order of the Bath.[243]

Sir Henry Smith retired from the City of London Police in 1901 at the age of 65. He would write of his time spent with the force:

> During my period of office, I met with nothing but kindness – in the force and out of it. I cannot speak in too high terms of the consideration and courtesy I have received from the Commissioner, my colleagues, the corporation and the public. There has been no jarring anywhere and I shall as long as I live look back with infinite pleasure to the twenty seven years, I have spent in the service of the City.[244]

We know that before 1904 Henry had moved back to Edinburgh, because in the *Edinburgh Evening News* of 13th January 1904 there appeared an article reporting that he had just bought part of the Hawick Estate, having previously been living at Chisholme Shooting in Muselee.[245]

In 1906, Henry showed that he hadn't forgotten the Jack the Ripper case, for he wrote an article for *Blackwood's Magazine* entitled 'More About the Streets of London', in which he states that he personally met John Kelly, partner of Catherine Eddowes. John had apparently told Henry about the trip to the hop farm, which he described as being in 'Ashford'. When Henry asked John "What was she doing about Aldgate and Mitre Square at that hour?", he received the rely that she was going to see her daughter in Bermondsey.

241 1891 census.

242 *The Purchase of Officers' Commissions in the British Army* by John Armatys and Robert George Cordery.

243 *From Constable to Commissioner, The Story of Sixty Years, Most of them Misspent* by Lieut. Col. Sir Henry Smith K.C.B., 1910.

244 Ibid.

245 *Edinburgh Evening News*, 13th January 1904.

Henry would write in the article that he was disinclined to believe this explanation, "seeing that he could not, or would not, tell where the daughter lived."[246]

Henry appeared in the newspapers later that year, this time because of an heroic act on his part. The *Edinburgh Evening News* reported that an invalid woman was on her way to church when she lost control of her wheelchair, and headed towards the road. In the act of trying to stop the wheelchair, Henry was run over by a cyclist.[247]

Henry Smith then did something that is not mentioned in any other book about him to date, something that seems very important when explaining the life of Sir Henry Smith: he married late in life, to Annie Maria Graham[248] in 1909 in St Andrews Church, Edinburgh.[249]

The couple lived at 18 Granville Terrace, Mercliston in Edinburgh, with servants Mary Harvey aged 27 and Agnes Scholar aged 24.[250] The house is still there today, situated at the end of the street, a modest house of Scottish stone.

In October of that year, Henry showed his love of animals by acting as a judge at the 33rd Scottish Kennel Club championship.[251]

In 1910 he found time to write his memoirs, amply quoted from in this chapter.

At some point between 1911 and 1921, Henry and Annie moved to 33 Kingsburgh Road, Edinburgh, another house that still stands today.

On 17th January 1921 Henry Smith fell ill with influenza, and died at his home on 2nd March at 4 o'clock in the morning.[252] His death certificate states that he had suffered a cerebral haemorrhage and a stroke, and that his nephew Lieutenant Colonel Albert Smith (who

---

246 *Blackwood's Magazine*, May 1906.

247 16th September 1906.

248 Born in 1867 (1911 census).

249 Marriage record, reference number 685/286.

250 1911 census.

251 *The Scotsman*, 3rd October 1911.

252 Death certificate.

lived at 3 Edensor Road, Eastbourne) was present at the death.[253]

The fact that his nephew had travelled all the way to Edinburgh from Eastbourne suggests that the family knew his illness was a serious one, with Henry now 85-years-old. His funeral took place two days later, and he was buried in Dean's Cemetery, Edinburgh.[254]

Henry will always be mentioned in connection with the Ripper case for his role as Assistant Commissioner of the City of London Police at the time. However, perhaps he will now be mentioned with the name he was born with - William Henry Smith - as well as the name he wanted to go by.

253 Death certificate.
254 *The Times*, 4th March 1921.

CHAPTER FOURTEEN

Call in the Detectives

*Detective Daniel Halse, Detective Robert Sagar,
Inspector James McWilliam, Detective Henry Cox,
Detective Robert Outram, Detective Edward Marriott
and Detective Baxter Hunt*

Detective Daniel Halse

Daniel Halse's role in the murder case of Catherine Eddowes was dealing with the aftermath of finding the body of a woman within the streets of the City of London. An element of shock must have washed over him when news broke that another murder by Jack the Ripper had happened, this time on his own streets, if only for a moment. Daniel, by this time, was an experienced detective policeman, so all thoughts of a madman running around the City of London had to be put to one side, so that this murder could be dealt with professionally and swiftly.

Just over ten minutes after the body of Catherine Eddowes was found by PC Edward Watkins, news of the discovery reached Daniel. At the time he was carrying out orders originally issued by his Commissioner but passed to Daniel by Chief Inspector McWilliam, and was keeping watch of the area bordering Whitechapel with Detective Sergeant Robert Outram and Detective Constable Edward Marriott. The trio were at St Botolph's Aldgate, not far from the murder scene at Mitre Square, and we can only imagine what was going through Daniel's mind as he ran towards the light of a policeman's Bullseye lamp.

This was not the only moment Daniel was involved in this murder investigation, however, for he was later called to another scene at which the killer might have left his only clue...

Daniel Halse was born in 1842, to papermaker Thomas Halse and his wife Maria, née Axtell.[1] In the baptism record it states that Daniel was baptised on 12th April 1842,[2] but his birth certificate, held within the City of London Police service file, clearly states that his date of birth was 19th May 1842, so there must be a mistake on the baptism record. Given that his birth was registered on 12th June 1842, there is a strong suggestion that Daniel was actually baptised on the date he was registered.

Daniel was the third child born to the family, following William (b.1830) and James (b.1836),[3] who by the 1851 census were both working as labourers.[4]

At this time, the Halse family was living in the small village of Abbots Langley in Hertfordshire, a place of paper mills and cottages. In fact, the Halse family was residing at Home Park Cottages, four dwellings built in 1826 which survive today and are Grade II listed. The cottages were designed as accommodation for workers at John Dickinson's nearby Home Park Mill,[5] where Daniel's papermaking father worked.[6]

John Dickinson was a well-known paper mill owner who opened Home Park Mill in 1829. He had a powerful influence in the village, helping to establish Abbots Langley train station and giving land to

1 Daniel Halse's birth certificate within the City of London Police file held at London Metropolitan Archives (CLA/048/AD/01).

2 Baptism record for Daniel Halse.

3 James stayed at the same village and worked as a papermill worker, like his father, for the rest of his life.

4 1851 census.

5 Home Park Mill is mentioned in Daniel's City of London Police file.

6 History of Abbots Langley records.

build the school which it is highly likely that Daniel attended.[7]

In 1851 Daniel was a six-year-old scholar.[8] The nearest educational facility to his home was Abbots Langley School, which still exists today, but by the age of ten he had left school and was working with his father in the Home Park Mill. We know this because within his City of London Police service file held at the London Metropolitan Archives, in a reference supplied by Daniel from Mr Henry Darke, it is claimed that Daniel was a labourer at the mill from 1855 to 1863, and the reason he was hired was because Daniel's father had worked for the firm for over thirty years.[9]

Although the Halse family is missing on the 1861 census, on 27th June 1863[10] Daniel applied to become a detective within the City of London Police force, and was awarded collar number 607.[11] We already know that one of the references for this change in career was from his previous place of employment, and the other was from the clerk at the vicarage at Kings Langley, a Mr H.W. Hodgeon, who confirmed that he had known Daniel from '1856 to the current time' (of 1863).[12]

Daniel was not the only member of the Halse family to have travelled to the capital to become a policeman, for in the 1861 census we find a certain William Halse, aged 31, living at the police station on Paradise Street in Rotherhithe. Daniel's elder brother was a Constable of the Metropolitan Police in M Division.[13] Ten years later, in 1871, William had moved out of the police station because he had married Martha, and they were living at Claremont Place in St Pancras.

William was at this time a Police Sergeant, but by 1873 had

7   History of Abbots Langley records.

8   1851 census.

9   Daniel's City of London Police file (CLA/048/AD/01).

10 The date on his application form within Daniel's City of London Police file (CLA/048/AD/01).

11 Old Bailey Court records show that his collar number was 607.

12 Daniel's City of London Police file (CLA/048/AD/01).

13 *Lloyd's Weekly Newspaper*, 23rd May 1875.

been promoted and was Inspector Halse. He was involved with a number of cases, including investigating the murder of William Judd in Southwark,[14] and the more mundane unlawful sale of beer and spirits in Southwark by a couple called John and Alice Cross.[15]

By 1881, William Halse had left the police force, claiming his pension, and had taken himself and wife Martha back to his birth town of Abbots Langley. Ten years later, at the age of 61, he was working as a Rate Collector.[16] He died eight years later on 17th August 1899.[17]

On brother Daniel's application to the City of London Police, he stated that he was living at 10 Blackburn Mews, Upper Brook Street, an address at which he must have been living for only a short time as he left his employment at Home Park Mill in March 1863 and by June he was living within the City boundary, as per force requirements.[18]

On 1st April 1869, Daniel was called to the Old Bailey as a witness in the case against Daniel Kelly, John Kelly and Michael Costello, who sometimes also went by the name of Michael Kelly, for theft from Mr John Greenwood at Messrs Taylor and Black's factory, 107 Cannon Street.[19]

It was on the evening of 19th March that Daniel was called to watch the Taylor and Black factory with City Policeman 655 Thomas Baldwin. Baldwin had just arrested Daniel Kelly and Michael Costello after seeing both of them carrying sacks from Cannon Street to Red Lion Court. Baldwin asked what was in the sacks, receiving the reply 'brushes' from Daniel Kelly, who then claimed to have brought them somewhere in the City, but did not know where. PC Baldwin was not happy with this reply and took the men to Bow Lane Station, which was where Daniel Halse was on duty at the time.

After travelling back with PC Baldwin to the factory on Cannon

---

14 *Illustrated Police News*, 6th May 1876.

15 *Daily News*, 19th February 1873.

16 1891 census.

17 Death record.

18 Application form held in Daniel's City of London Police file (CLA/048/AD/01).

19 Old Bailey Records (t18690301-347).

Street, Daniel saw that the door was still ajar. Both policemen watched the building and at about 9:45pm another man left the premises. Baldwin and Daniel followed him as far as Bow Lane and then asked why he had left the factory so late. The man, who was named John Kelly, gave an unsatisfactory explanation so he was also taken to the station.

Daniel was then asked to visit John Kelly's house with PC Baldwin, where his wife pointed out to the two policemen a box full of brushes without labels. Daniel then went to Daniel Kelly's abode at 10 Plough Court, Fetter Lane, where he found some more brushes which still had the price tag on them.

The outcome of the case was that Daniel Kelly was found guilty and had to serve eighteen months imprisonment. John Kelly was also found guilty and received only nine months due to having a previous good character, and Michael Costello was found not guilty.

In the 1871 census Daniel is stated as living at Bow Lane Police Station,[20] which was used more as an office by the City's Detective Department than a normal working police station.[21] By this time he would have got to know other detectives who were also living in the same place. One of these detectives, who also had links to the night the Ripper killed within the boundary of the City, was Detective Baxter Hunt.

On 3rd February 1873, Daniel was called to the Old Bailey with another case of stealing, this time by George Pross, George Manning, Charles Buckmaster and John Watson from Mr Charles Bell.[22]

Mr Bell was one of the partners of "Pimm's" oyster rooms in the Poultry, which was already being watched by Detective Sergeant William Green because of regular thefts. On the morning of 15th January 1873, Green and Daniel Halse saw Buckmaster, Pross and Watson arrive with a barrow loaded with sacks full of oysters. Manning came out and began unloading. The detectives watched

---

20 Although it was named Bow Lane, it was actually situated at 1 Great St Thomas Street. Bow Lane was the main street running alongside it, and is now called Garlick Hill.

21 1871 census.

22 Old Bailey Records (t18730203-168).

as all except one sack was unloaded from the barrow, and Manning carried this inside on his back.

Soon afterwards the men came out with what appeared to be empty sacks. These were placed on the barrow, which was then carted off by Buckmaster and Watson. They were followed at a distance by George Pross, who joined them in Lombard Street and the trio turned into Philpot Lane. Halfway down they stopped, and Buckmaster and Watson placed a basket containing a sack onto Pross's head. The latter was followed by William Green as far as Talbot Court, where the detective demanded to know what was in the basket. Pross admitted that they were oysters, supposedly being taken to a Mr Hughes near the Monument, but when asked where he had got them replied: "Little Jack, from Marlow's, gave them to me in Thames Street." At this Green took him into custody, and at the police station opened the sack to discover 260 oysters.

Detective Daniel Halse meanwhile, had followed Buckmaster and Watson, the latter pleading on being arrested for receiving stolen goods: "I hope you are not going to make me answerable for another man's actions, I don't know anything about it, I only gave him a push up."

At the Old Bailey, Manning and Watson were found not guilty. Buckmaster and Pross pleaded guilty, with the latter being sentenced to twelve months' imprisonment. Buckmaster had been convicted of a previous offence in October 1866 and was sentenced to seven years.

Two months later, on 7th April 1873, Daniel was again at the Old Bailey and this time it was a case of burglary by John Keegan, Joseph Smith, Charles Bearfield and William Mead, who broke into the premises of Mr George Tueskie, a hat maker of 42 Jewin Street,[23] and stealing seven hundred yards of silk and other items.

At 8:45am on 7th March 1873, Mr Tueskie found that his back door had been forced open, the lock broken. 700 yards of silk had been stolen, and several desks had been forced open.

---

23 A place that Daniel would come to know very well, as by 1881 he was living in Jewin Crescent, a side street from Jewin Street.

City Detective Henry Randall received certain information, from whom it is unrecorded, and as a consequence he and fellow Detective Joseph Fawke attended the home of the prisoner Keegan at 1 Banner Street on 20th March. They waited for him to return and stated that they were police officers. They then asked about the missing items. Keegan declined to say anything so was taken to Snow Hill Police Station, where a number of items were found on his person. On the journey to the Police Court, Keegan became unwell, and on the urging of his wife confessed to receiving the stolen items from Charles Bearfield at Cliff Street, New North Road, and that he was supposed to receive a commission on them.

City Detective Frederick Downs had already been sent to Bearfield's premises, and the previous day had observed a cab pull up and have a number of parcels placed inside. Shortly thereafter, Bearfield walked to 36 Peerless Street, City Road, with a parcel under his arm. This was the home of the suspect William Mead. Bearfield then left the house without the parcel, and headed towards a public house on Bath Street, outside which Bearfield met with William Mead and the other suspect, Joseph Smith.

At this point, Detective Downs left the suspects and with Daniel Halse headed back to 36 Peerless Street. By the time the detectives arrived, Mead and Smith were already home. Downs took Smith to Old Street Police Station where he tried to escape, but was caught rather quickly.

Daniel meanwhile searched 36 Peerless Street and found a crowbar. Mead said he knew nothing of it, and was also taken into custody. The following morning Daniel returned to the address and found a fur hat and cap, as well as a key, a chisel and other items.

The outcome was that through a lack of evidence, Smith, Bearfield and Mead were found not guilty, but John Keegan was found guilty of receiving stolen goods.[24]

However, Daniel was called to give evidence on the same day over these same prisoners on a separate crime, when they had burgled

24 Old Bailey Records (t18730407-302).

the house of Joseph Engster at 27 Cheapside and stole seven quilts and 41 items of bed linen. Once again Daniel had visited Charles Bearfield's premises at 28 Cliff Street, and also the home of Joseph Smith at Peerless Street and found all the missing items in those two places. The court this time decided that Keegan was not guilty, Smith was guilty and Bearfield pleaded guilty for receiving stolen goods.[25]

On 8th June 1874, Daniel was called to court again, when George Underwood, aged sixteen, William Buncher aged 21 and Edward Mackay aged 23 had attempted to steal a watch from one John Salter.[26]

At 10:30pm on 30th May, Daniel was with City Detectives Downs and Mitchell at Broad Street Railway Station when they saw the prisoners follow a lady. The detectives watched as they walked towards Moorgate Station, where the prisoners changed tack and started to follow a gentleman to Circus Place. Underwood got in front of the man, Buncher was behind him, and Mackay a short distance behind Buncher. The prisoners seemed to be planning something, but were halted when a beat constable came along and the trio headed back inside Moorgate Street Station again.

Then, almost an hour later, the detectives saw the prisoners following another gentleman with a lady in a similar fashion. Underwood ran ahead of the couple and went around the corner of Great Bell Alley, Buncher went to the other end of the alleyway, in Coleman Street, while Mackay continued to follow the couple. Buncher whistled and Underwood sprang into action and hit the man in his chest and took his watch.

Daniel tackled Underwood and shouted out for the thief to give him the watch, only for Underwood to claim he did not have it. Detective Downs, meanwhile, had arrested Mackay, Detective William Mitchell had got hold of Buncher and Daniel managed to keep hold of Underwood and took him into custody. The outcome was that Underwood and Buncher received eighteen months'

25 Old Bailey Records (t18730407-303).
26 Old Bailey records (t18740608-411).

imprisonment, and Mackay nine months.

On 17th August the same year Daniel was called to court to explain his role in discovering a coining offence by Dennis Kent and Alexander Reede.[27]

From 19th July, Daniel and fellow detectives Frederick Downs and Isaac Gilbert had been watching the Red Hart public house on Fetter Lane and also 7 John Street, Clerkenwell, where known criminals Henry Hughes and Sarah Kite lived. The pair used the Red Hart to meet other criminals, and on 29th July the detectives watched Alexander Reede and Dennis Kent enter the pub at 3:00pm, where they spoke to Kite for an hour. Some parcels were handed over, and then the suspects left. They were followed by the detectives along Fetter Lane and through Fleet Street towards St Clement's Church, where Reede crossed to the left side of the road and Kent stayed on the right. Detective Downs followed Reede, and questioned him as to the money he had on his person. Reede claimed that he had no money, but then began to throw coins into his mouth. The detective pushed him into a nearby tailor's shop and caught him by the throat, telling him to spit out the money, but it was too late - he had swallowed them.

Daniel and Detective Gilbert followed Dennis Kent, who put his hand in his pocket and took out a parcel which he placed up his sleeve. Gilbert surprised Kent by grabbing hold of his hand. He also tried to put coins into his mouth, but in the struggle this was prevented and he was arrested. Gilbert and Daniel went back to 7 John Street and found Hughes and Kite coming out with parcels in their hands. Asking what was inside the parcel, the officers were told 'I don't know', at which point they went inside the property and found two boxes containing more fake coins. At the Old Bailey, Reede was found guilty as he had been convicted previously for a similar crime, the same was said for Kent who was also found guilty. Henry Hughes and Sarah Kite were also convicted.

On 21st September 1874, Daniel was in court explaining that John

---

27 Old Bailey records (t18440817-510).

Sullivan, aged seventeen, and John Sweeney, aged twenty, had stolen a glass case containing a stuffed bird.

Daniel was with City Detective James Keniston at Tower Hill on 1st September 1874, when they saw the two prisoners at about 3:00pm near a cart. The detectives watched as Sweeney went to the bottom end and took the glass case, placing it under his coat. He then ran across the road and along Rosemary Lane, Sullivan following him. The detectives followed, noticing the stuffed bird was passed from one man to the other and then back again, before they entered The Star public house on Dock Street. Detective Keniston took Sullivan into custody and Daniel took Sweeney to the station. At the trial both were found guilty, with Sweeney also pleading guilty to a previous offence.[28]

On 3rd May 1875, Daniel was dealing with a case of pickpocketing, the thieves being Daniel Anderson, aged sixteen, and Thomas Thompson, aged twenty seven. They stole a watch and chain from a Mr Robert Leighton.[29]

At about three o'clock on the afternoon of 19th April 1875, Daniel was with City Detectives Frederick Downs and Edward Forrester at Tower Dock when they saw a crowd forming around a man with performing cats. Robert Leighton was standing in the crowd watching the entertainment, and Anderson and Thompson placed themselves either side of him. Suddenly, both were on the move and Anderson gave something to Thompson, who looked at the item as they went through Savage Gardens and on to Mark Lane. It was here that the thieves realised they were being followed by the detectives so they started running. The detectives shouted 'Stop! Thief', but luckily the fugitives ran into a vast crowd of around 200 men who were coming out of the Corn Exchange, slowing them down. Thompson ran into a court from which there was no escape, so put his hand into his pocket and threw something into a pile of packing cases. Daniel searched through them and picked up a watch, which

28 Old Bailey records (t18740921-384).
29 Old Bailey records (t18750503-349).

had broken into pieces. Anderson appeared moments later and was trapped. Both men were taken into custody, Anderson receiving two years imprisonment and Thompson seven years, having pleaded guilty to a previous offence.

In the third quarter of 1875, Daniel married Margaret Jane Evans in West Ham. This meant that he had to leave the police home and go into private accommodation with his wife, possibly to the address where they were recorded for the 1881 census, 28 Jewin Crescent, St Giles without Cripplegate, in the City.[30]

His wife Margaret had been born in Taunton, Somerset in 1838, and had come to London by 1851 where she was living with her family at Old Norland Terrace in Kensington.[31] By 1861, at the age of 23, she had left the family home and was working as a housemaid to Henry Hardinge, a doctor, at 18 Grafton Street, Hanover Square. By 1871, she had become a cook at 15 Prince of Wales Terrace, Kensington, working within the household of an important family at the time - that of George Ward Hunt M.P., who had become Member of Parliament for Northamptonshire North in 1857. In 1866 he became Secretary to the Treasury, and two years later became Chancellor of the Exchequer under Benjamin Disraeli.[32]

On 12th July 1875, Daniel was in court again to give a statement concerning a coining offence by Elizabeth Montague, aged 23, Emma Martin, 17 and Alice Jones, 18.[33]

Montague and Jones entered a grocer's at the Barbican belonging to a Mr Edward Turner on 29th May 1875 and ordered some tea and sugar, paying with a bad coin which Mr Turner refused to take. The women said they would change the coin at another establishment,

---

30 1881 census.

31 1851 census. She was living with her father, Henry Evans (b.1816), her mother, Mary (b.1817) and her two sisters, Louisa (b.1837) and Zenobee (b.1843).

32 It was because of George Ward Hunt that a tradition started which continues to this day. He had forgotten his 'Red Box' on the day he was due to give his Budget speech, and from that day to this, whoever the Chancellor of the Exchequer is they have to hold up the 'budget box' and show it to the public before they give their speeches as proof that they have not left it at home.

33 Old Bailey Records (t18750712-498).

but when they did not he sent for the police. City officer George Reed followed the two ladies along Red Cross Street towards White Cross Street, where they stopped in a doorway. The policeman caught up with them, and a boy presumably from Mr Turner's shop pointed out Elizabeth Montague as the woman who had passed the bad coin. When asked for the florin, she readily handed it over.

On 18th June they appeared at the Guildhall but were discharged due to lack of evidence. Detectives Frederick Downs and Daniel Halse watched as Montague and Jones left the court, and followed them along Lee's Place, Westminster Bridge Road, and towards New Kent Road.

The detectives had previously kept watch on the gang, and on 10th June had observed Emma Martin carrying a bag which she gave to Elizabeth Montague on the corner of Gurney Street, and then went in the Duke of Gloucester public house. She was only in there for a minute or so before coming back out to Montague and handed her something from her purse. The latter went inside and ordered a drink, paying with the coin given to her by Emma Martin.

The two detectives entered the pub and the barmaid showed them a bad shilling. The women were later arrested on London Road and found in possession of seven bad coins. At the trial, Elizabeth Montague and Emma Martin pleaded guilty and were sentenced to fifteen months' imprisonment, while Alice Jones was found guilty and sentenced to nine months.

On 18th September 1876, Daniel was at the Old Bailey again giving evidence in the case against pickpockets William Ebell and George Lovett.[34] On 21st August at 10:00pm, Daniel had been on duty around the Old Swan Pier area watching people leaving the pier, having disembarked from the excursion boat, when he saw the suspects and a third man, not subsequently arrested, push their way through the crowd suspiciously. Ebell placed himself in front of Mr John Vernon, while Lovett was to the left of him. Mr Vernon heard a 'click' and noticed that his watch was missing, and accused Ebell of

---

34 Old Bailey Records (t18760918-434).

having taken it, who shouted back that he did not have it.

Daniel managed to get hold of Ebell and took him into custody, while another officer, George Lloyd, took Lovett to the station.

However, both prisoners were found not guilty due to lack of evidence.

Daniel would appear at the Old Bailey giving evidence in several cases on a similar nature throughout the early 1880s.

By 1881, Margaret Halse's niece Virginia Tabourit had travelled from her birthplace in France to live with her aunt and uncle.[35] Sadly, late in 1886 she died at the young age of 17. She was buried two days after Christmas, on 27th December 1886, at Abney Park Cemetery in grave 079478, a cemetery and a grave number that would become important to Daniel less than ten years later.[36]

When a series of murders had been committed in Whitechapel, just over the border in the neighbouring Metropolitan Police district, the Commissioner of the City Police, James Fraser, issued an order for that force's officers to maintain 'observation on all prostitutes frequenting public houses and walking the streets.'[37] This order was passed down by Detective Chief Inspector James McWilliam, and this was how, on the night of 29th September 1888, Daniel was patrolling the Houndsditch area with Detectives Robert Outram Edward Marriott.[38]

The position of the detectives is interesting, because it provides us with a reasonable suggestion of the route taken by the killer after leaving Mitre Square. A part of Catherine's apron was found in Wentworth Model Dwellings in Goulston Street later that morning, but the quickest route from the one place to the other would have meant passing though the area that Daniel Halse, Robert Outram and Edward Marriott were on duty.

In his testimony at Catherine Eddowes' inquest, Daniel stated

---

35 1881 census.

36 Abney Cemetery records.

37 Report by City of London Inspector James McWilliam (HO 144/221/A49301C ff. 162-70).

38 Inquest testimony of City Detective Daniel Halse.

that he was near St Botolph's at 1:58am.[39] Catherine was found at roughly 1:45am and the portion of her apron was not found until an hour later, at 2:55am, with Metropolitan Police PC Alfred Long, who discovered it, claiming that it was not there at 2:20am on his previous lap of his beat.[40]

This has been debated many times, because it is odd that the killer would take a part of Catherine Eddowes's apron and decide to keep hold of it and remain for an hour in the area where he had just killed. Given that the walk from Mitre Square to Goulston Street would have taken no more than seven or eight minutes, it seems far more likely that the item was dropped closer to 2:00am, and that PC Long missed the apron first time around.

As the detectives arrived at Mitre Square and viewed the body of Catherine Eddowes, Daniel gave orders to the other detectives to search the area close by and to stop every man they came across and to question them. Daniel did not stay at the scene - there were already policemen guarding the scene and more sent for - so he instead headed in the direction of Middlesex Street, crossing over the invisible boundary and becoming a City Detective in the Metropolitan Police district.[41]

Daniel arrived at Wentworth Street, where he met two men who gave satisfactory accounts of themselves and were moved on.[42] The fact that Daniel mentioned this brief encounter in his testimony suggests that these men were the first people he came across while searching the area. If so, this also suggests that Daniel was being detailed in his testimony, as a policeman should, for there was no important outcome to this meeting between Daniel and these two men who had nothing to do with the case, but he still mentioned it. A sign perhaps of a meticulous officer? An officer that would have noticed another policeman, perhaps? We will get to this a little later.

---

39 Inquest testimony of City Detective Daniel Halse.

40 Inquest testimony of PC Alfred Long.

41 Inquest testimony of City Detective Daniel Halse.

42 Ibid.

Oddly enough, Daniel decided to walk as far as Goulston Street in his search.[43] Why he decided to go only that far and then turn back is interesting, for we know that the Ripper also went from Mitre Square to Goulston Street.

Although Daniel never mentioned that he was following someone, and we have no reason to believe that he was, it was claimed by Metropolitan Chief Constable Sir Melville Macnaghten in what is possibly the draft version of his famous memoranda written in 1894[44] that

> No one ever saw the Whitechapel Murderer, (unless possibly it was the City PC, who was on a beat near Mitre Square).

In the same report, when describing the suspect Kosminski, Macnaghten writes:

> This man in appearance strongly resembled the individual seen by the City PC near Mitre Square.

Was this a reference to City detective officer Daniel Halse, and Macnaghten had written 'City PC' when he meant 'City DC'?

Continuing with Daniel's testimony, he stated that he was in Goulston Street by 2:20am and, seeing nothing of importance, decided to head back towards the scene of the crime, where Inspector Edward Collard of Bishopsgate Police Station had arrived. Daniel was then able to communicate what had been done and what was still left to do.[45]

However, we have another problem. Daniel stated that he was in Goulston Street at 2:20am, but does not state that he saw another policeman at this time. PC 254A Alfred Long was one of the Metropolitan Police officers who had been seconded to H Division (Whitechapel) to help with the investigation into the murders. He stated that he was walking his beat along Goulston Street at 2:20am

---

43 Inquest testimony of City Detective Daniel Halse.

44 This possible draft version is known as the Aberconway version, and was held by his daughter Christabel, Lady Aberconway after Melville Macnaghten's death.

45 Inquest testimony of City Detective Daniel Halse.

and did not see a portion of an apron in the stairway of Wentworth Model Dwellings at this time. He also failed to mention that he saw Daniel Halse, who should have been there.[46]

This could have been an understandable oversight on the part of PC Long, as Daniel was in plain clothes. However, PC Long was in uniform and yet 'meticulous' Daniel did not mention him. This would suggest that someone was wrong in their timing, if only by a few minutes or even seconds, for we do not know how long Daniel stood in Goulston Street, and we do not know for sure whether PC Long was accurate in his timekeeping on his beat.

While at Mitre Square, Inspector Collard ordered Daniel and Detective Baxter Hunt to head to Leman Street Police Station. It was here that Daniel learned that a piece of the deceased woman's apron had been found in a doorway of Wentworth Model Dwellings on Goulston Street. What must he have thought, now knowing the killer had made his way in the same direction that he himself had travelled? He and Baxter Hunt went straight to Goulston Street, where they were faced with another possible clue.[47]

Above the piece of apron, on the black part of the wall, was a chalked message. Had the killer left a clue? Did the murderer really have time to throw the apron to the floor and then write a message on the wall above it? Either way, Daniel and Detective Hunt both thought that this message should be photographed, because messages such as this were nothing new to the City of London Police.

Inside the City of London Police Museum there is a photograph taken by City officers of part of another chalked message written upon a wall, which shows the words 'I am going to do one on the 27th – Jac'.[48]

The full message was 'I am going to do one on the 27th – Jack the

46 Inquest testimony of PC Alfred Long.

47 Inquest testimony of City Detective Daniel Halse.

48 This was first mentioned in 'The Victim Photographs and Some Wall Writing' by Neil Bell and Robert Clack, *Ripperologist* 127, August 2012.

49 Report of meeting and discussions 10-17 August 1891. About a collection of photographs of writing on artisan's dwellings.

Ripper'.[49]

This proves that from the City of London Police's point of view, any important message should have been photographed, which is why Detective Hunt left the scene to return to Mitre Square to inform Chief Inspector McWilliam of the apron and the writing on the wall, which needed to be photographed.[50]

Daniel, meanwhile, stayed at Goulston Street[51] as there needed to be someone from the City of London Police there because the apron belonged to a victim murdered within the City, meaning that although Goulston Street was within the Metropolitan Police district, it was related to a City of London Police investigation.

So when Detective Hunt returned to report that a photographer had been ordered, both he and Daniel Halse appear to have started taking control of the situation by interviewing the people who lived near where the apron and message were found. Daniel made a quick note of the writing, and recorded it as being 'The Juwes are not the men who will be blamed for nothing',[52] which was different from PC Long's version of 'The Juwes are the men that will not be blamed for nothing',[53] or even City Surveyor Frederick William Foster's version of 'The Juws are not the men To be blamed for nothing.'[54]

Knowing how meticulous Daniel seems to have been on this morning through his testimony, it would be tempting to think that he had written the correct version. However, we have to remember that Daniel had, at the time he wrote it, thought that the message would be photographed, so perhaps he did not take as much care as he might have done.

In the event, however, a photograph was not taken. News of the message reached the ears of both the Commissioner and Assistant Commissioner of the Metropolitan Police force, Sir Charles Warren

50 Inquest testimony of City Detective Daniel Halse.

51 Ibid.

52 Ibid.

53 Inquest testimony of PC Alfred Long.

54 Inquest testimony of City Surveyor Fredrick Foster.

and Robert Anderson, who arrived at Goulston Street. Warren's orders were to wash the message off the wall, later stating that this was because of the social uproar that the word 'Jews' - no matter how it was spelt - would bring to the Jewish population of the East End.[55]

Daniel fought for the case of having a photograph taken and then having the message removed; he even tried to compromise by suggesting that the word 'Juwes' be washed off and the rest of the message photographed.[56] This was denied by a power that technically had no control over this scene. Is it any wonder that this action has caused many a historian to question Warren's motives and some to even accuse him as being involved in the murders themselves?

Whatever Daniel had felt about what happened that morning, he continued on his work in the detective department, and on 4th March 1889 was called to court to give evidence in a case of theft, when Matthew Taylor, George Timms, James O'Brien, Albert Salter and Alfred Salter were charged with stealing a total of 300lb of wool from the London and India Docks Company.[57]

Taylor worked for the company delivering samples, while Timms and O'Brien were also employed, often loading the van. The police had been called to observe proceedings, as there was some suspicion that a certain amount of the wool was being waylaid before it was delivered to clients.

Daniel worked again with City Detective Baxter Hunt on this case, and on 6th February 1889 the two detectives watched Taylor's delivery van on Moorgate. They saw Timms, O'Brien and Taylor enter 75 Snow's Fields in Bermondsey, a shop owned by Albert and Alfred Salter, which was not one of the scheduled delivery addresses. The detectives watched as the van was opened up and emptied inside

---

55 Report of the Whitechapel Murders: Mitre Square by Sir Charles Warren (HO 144/221/A49301C).

56 Inquest testimony of City Detective Daniel Halse.

57 Old Bailey Records (t18890304-301).

the shop.

The next day brought a repeat performance, so Detective Hunt and Detective John Jones entered the shop and found Albert Salter and Matthew Taylor weighing a quantity of wool. Detective Hunt arrested them and took them to Moor Lane Police Station, while Daniel arrested Timms and took him to the same station. All were found guilty and received eighteen months' hard labour.

Daniel was in court again on 27th May 1889, with another case of theft. This time the prisoners were John Davis, William Martin, William Ford, Patrick O'Hara and Sarah Saunders, who broke into the counting house of Richard Thron, stealing 143 Hanover medals, a bag, two pieces of lead and one shilling.[58]

Daniel went to Eldon Street, Finsbury Square (where a certain PC Edward Watkins once lived) with four other officers on 17th May 1889 and saw five men walking along the road. He saw the prisoners Davis and Martin look into a gateway at some building works and speak to the others. They loitered in Eldon Street until at least 4:30, going away a short distance before coming back again. Daniel saw all those charged enter through the gateway and John Davis broke into the office door of a building. He entered but came out rather quickly, carrying a bag. Daniel arrested all five prisoners, taking the bag off Davis to discover an amount of bronze, the large number of Hanover medals and two pieces of lead. They were taken into custody, and at trial all found guilty and receiving custodial sentences.

By the time of the 1891 census, the Halse family had moved to Norfolk Road in Hackney. Daniel was by now 50-years-old and still a detective for the City of London Police force. He and wife Margaret had taken in a lodger, a 22-year-old grocer's shopman named William J Harrison.

In August of the same year Daniel wrote to the City of London Police, telling them that he wanted to retire and asked for a pension

---

58 Old Bailey Records (t18890527-514).

59 This letter is within Daniel's service file held at the London Metropolitan Archives (CLA/048/AD/01).

of £62 7s 6d that he believed he was entitled to because of the 28 years he had worked in the force.[59]

The family moved home to 36 Farleigh Road, Stoke Newington, but in 1894 Daniel Halse died.[60] He was buried on 26th February 1894 at Abney Cemetery, in the same plot that his wife's niece, Virginia Tabourlt, and a headstone was added.[61]

The headstone is an impressive one, compared to others for the beat constables visited by the author, but over the years vines and a tree have developed around it, making it difficult to see.[62] However, with the help of the staff at Abney Cemetery, Daniel's last resting place was found, after a detour to the grave of Metropolitan PC 403 William Tyler, an officer shot in the Tottenham Outrage in 1909.[63]

After researching this man for quite some time, to visit his grave to pay respects to a detective who had fought against the Commissioner of the Metropolitan Police force to not wash away possibly the only clue Jack the Ripper might have left was memorable and well worth doing.

He is with good company, for not only is he buried with his wife Margaret Jane Halse, who herself was buried on 21st September

60 Abney Cemetery records.

61 Abney Cemetery records. The author revisited the graves of certain policemen who were buried in London on 11th February 2017, as a final goodbye to these men as work on this book was coming to an end. Daniel's headstone is now all cleaned up, without tree vines, and it is easy to see and read. Finally, Daniel's last resting place is sitting proud for anyone to visit.

62 The author would like to take this moment to thank the staff at Abney Cemetery, for not only being so very helpful with the records but also taking the time to show my father and I where the grave was and even cutting as much of the vines and tree away from the headstone as possible for me to take a photograph, but not to damage the headstone.

63 Grave Number WT89827 SQ K6. What is interesting to note is not only do Metropolitan Police officers still pay their respects to him on certain dates of the year, but they still pay for the upkeep of his grave and the grave behind him, that of a ten-year-old boy who was killed in the crossfire.

64 Abney Cemetery records.

1901,[64] but the Halse family plot is within a few feet of the graves of William Booth of Salvation Army fame and his wife.

Detective Robert Sagar:
The Disguise of a Labourer was used...[65]

The man, the doctor, the detective and the real life 'Holmes'.[66]

Four descriptions of a man who was as large in life as he was in character. However, this man was also involved in possibly the greatest 'whodunit' case of all time...

'We had good reason to suspect a man who worked in Butcher's Row, Aldgate. We watched him carefully. There was no doubt that this man was insane and after a time his friends thought it advisable to have him removed to a private asylum. After he was removed, there were no more Ripper atrocities.'[67]

The above comments from Detective Robert Sagar appeared in Reynolds's Newspaper on 15th September 1946. Who was this suspect, and did Robert actually spy on the most infamous killer of the Victorian era?

Robert Sagar was born in 1853 at Simonstone, Lancashire. The family can be traced back to 1767 and probably even further, living on the same land at New House,[68] Whalley in Lancashire, although the spelling of the name changes slightly.

---

65 Part of a report on Robert Sagar's retirement in the *Morning Leader*, 9th January 1905.

66 Robert Sagar was known as 'the real life Sherlock Holmes' due to him wearing different costumes while following criminals by fellow police officers. *Brighton and Hove Herald*, 6 December 1924 and *The City Press*, 6 December 1924.

67 *Reynolds's Newspaper*, 15th September 1946.

68 In the 1851 census this was even named Sagar House. Although it returns to New House in later census returns, the home was probably known familiarly as 'Sagar House'.

69 Died in 1861 (death record).

70 1771-1861 (birth and death records).

71 Birth record.

Robert's grandfather, also called Robert,[69] spelt the surname 'Sager', and married Jane[70] in 1816. They had only one child, another Robert, who was born in 1821.[71] On the 1851 census, Robert Sager is described as owning 29 acres of land. Robert Jr was working on the land as a labourer, and the family employed a servant named Sarah Shaw.[72] The following year young Robert married that servant girl, and in 1853 Robert Sagar, who would grow up to become a City detective, was born.

In the next census, the grandfather and grandmother had passed away and Robert's father had taken over the land, which had grown to 42 acres.[73] Robert was at school at this time, attending Whalley Grammar School, and he had also became an assistant to Dr Badley.[74] His younger brother, William, had been born in 1856.[75]

By the 1871 census, the Sagar family had grown, with Robert gaining two sisters, Sarah (b.1862) and Eleanor (b.1865). The family also employed two servants, John Aspden and Mary Moorhouse.

On Friday, 28th April 1871, Robert Sagar travelled to London to embark on his chosen profession, and presented himself at the Apothecaries Hall in Black Friars Lane.[76] He received a first class certificate of proficiency in general education, and six months later was a medical student studying at St Bartholomew's Hospital within the City of London. He worked there until December 1878.[77]

A month later, Robert was called to the Old Bailey as a witness to a coining offence by Arthur Marsh and Thomas Wood. Wood had entered a hosiery shop on Blomfield Street belonging to a Mr Camming on the afternoon of 19th December. He wanted to buy a handkerchief, so handed over a very bright half crown. Mr Thompson, the sales assistant, thought it looked very different from his other half crowns in the till, but it wasn't until a detective walked

72 Born 1832 (birth record).
73 1861 census.
74 *The City Press*, 7th January 1905.
75 1861 census.
76 *The Daily Telegraph*, 1st May 1871.
77 CLA/048/AD/01/651 (London Metropolitan Archives).

in asking about the coin that he thought it was bad, and handed it over to the detective.

On the same day, at about the same time, Arthur Marsh walked into the Auxiliary Steam Company on New Broad Street to buy a Christmas card, for which he also handed over half a crown. When City Policeman Smith came in to the store afterwards, the sales assistant thought there was something wrong with the coin, so he handed it over to the policeman as it was the only half crown in the till at the time.

At 2:30pm on 19th December, City PC 161 Charles Smith was with Robert Sagar at Finsbury Pavement when they saw Wood and Marsh acting suspiciously, so they decided to follow them. Robert was not a policeman at this time, so we can only assume he was working unofficially for the City of London Police force, something a certain fictional consulting detective might have done, no doubt helping Robert to become known as the real life version of Sherlock Holmes by his colleagues later on in his career. PC Smith entered all the shops after the suspects while Robert waited outside. However, when Arthur Marsh entered a butcher's shop on Bishopsgate, PC Smith asked Robert to go inside and see what the prisoner was buying. When Robert returned, Wood and Marsh were arrested for passing on bad coins.

At the trial, Marsh was found not guilty while Wood received twelve months' imprisonment.[78]

Robert's testimony at the trial is interesting, because not only does he tell us where he was living in January 1879, at 47 Bartholomew Close, but it is suggested that he went 'undercover' as a customer into the butcher's shop, which has a surreal connection to his involvement in the Ripper case which will be discussed later. This was the first time that Robert was called as a witness to the courts, and although it was stated that he was with PC Smith, he was not classed as a policeman or doctor anywhere in this case. With that

---

78 Old Bailey records (t18790113-144).

79 *Daily News*, 9th January 1905; *City Press*, 7th January 1905; *Morning Leader*, 9th January 1905.

in mind, it can be presumed that Robert was working voluntarily. It was said in various newspapers[79] that Robert's efforts for the City Police while at the same time working at St Bart's Hospital were so appreciated that Commissioner Sir James Fraser apparently encouraged him to join the force rather than to carry on his studies at the hospital.

According to the *City Press*, Robert was not accepted in the force straight away because of a varicose vein he had in one leg.[80] However, this was later reported to be an injury received while chasing a thief, working unofficially on that occasion with Detective James Egan.

With these two examples of Robert working unofficially for the police, him coming from a medical background and his ability to adopt a disguise when necessary, it certainly sounds as if Robert was a mixture of Dr Watson and Sherlock Holmes rolled into one.

In his service file it states that although he was a police constable with the collar number 171, he was 'not to be clothed' and he went straight into the Detective Department.[81] He was later described as working for the City of London Police but never had a uniform, and because of his background he was known as 'The Doctor' by his colleagues within the force.[82]

Robert seemed to have been well liked by many and in all different ranks within the City of London Police, as even Henry Smith, the Assistant Commissioner in 1888, had nothing but praise every time he mentioned him in his memoirs: "...a better or more intelligent officer than Robert Sagar I never had under my command."[83]

In 1880, Robert married Clara Watling,[84] the couple recorded a year later in the 1881 census as living at 10 Bridgewater Square in the City, with a newborn whose name, following the family tradition,

---

80 *City Press*, 7th January 1905.

81 Robert's service file, CLA/048/AD/01/651 (London Metropolitan Archives).

82 *Morning Leader*, 9th January 1905.

83 *From Constable to Commissioner* by Sir Henry Smith, 1910.

84 Born 1858 in Hoxton.

85 Born 9th December 1880.

86 1891 census.

was Robert.

Robert's son Robert Henry Sagar[85] was a scholar in 1891.[86] It is interesting to note that the nearest school to the family at this time would have been the Central Foundation of Boys School, and through the National School Admission Registers and Log Books from 1870-1914 we can tell that he did in fact attend here after being a pupil at St Mary Axe School.[87] This school was founded by one Rev William Rogers, who became Rector of St Botolph Aldgate in 1863, the same church near which Detective Daniel Halse was when he heard news of the murder of Catherine Eddowes.

Robert Henry Sagar became a clerk to a wine merchants at the age of 20,[88] and lived with his family before signing up for the Merchant Navy in 1918. He was given Identity Certificate Number 826791, and included with his application form is a photograph of him. He certainly looked like his father, with his hair slicked back and a thick moustache, while wearing a heavy long coat and bow tie he appeared every bit the Edwardian gentleman.[89] He died in 1950, unmarried and with no children.[90]

On 10th December 1880, his father Robert Sr was in Aldersgate Street at 6:00pm when he saw Joseph Bignold and another man pickpocketing ladies' purses. Robert managed to get hold of Mr Bignold, while the other man ran away. Robert took his prisoner into custody at Bishopsgate Police Station. At the police courts, the prisoner received one month's imprisonment and five years in a reformatory.[91]

---

87 National School Admission Registers and Log Books 1871–1914 (Tower Hamlets Local History Archives and Library: I/CFS/A/2/3/3). Robert Henry Sagar is registered as admission 1280, with his father Robert Sagar also mentioned. His address was recorded as 13 Rose Alley, Bishopsgate, and the last standard level for Robert Jr was Number 1.

88 1901 census.

89 BT350 (National Archives).

90 Death record.

91 *Morning Post*, 13th December 1880.

92 1881 census.

93 She would marry Percy Bishop in 1913.

At the time of the 1881 census, the Sagar family were joined by a lodger, a 70-year-old widow called Sarah Williams.[92] Robert and Clara's second child, Sarah Jane Sagar, was born in 1883.[93]

On 26th February 1883, Robert was called to the Old Bailey as a witness at the trial of Henry Cattell for breaking the peace. On 22nd January Robert had gone to H. Cattell and Co., a printer and publishers bookseller's shop at 84 Fleet Street. Dressed in plain clothes, he went inside the store and asked for two copies of the Christmas edition of the *Freethinker*, which the shop was not allowed to sell.[94] After supplying copies of the banned magazine, Robert later returned and Henry Cattell was arrested, and at trial found guilty.[95]

On a similar case on the same day, Robert was also the witness in a case of breaking the peace against George Foote, William Ramsay and Henry Kemp. On 16th December 1882, Robert had gone to the bookseller's shop at 28 Stonecutter Street, Farringdon. Again, Robert ordered two copies of the same *Freethinker* issue, which Henry Kemp supplied.

Robert went back to the same shop on 20th January 1883 and brought two more copies from the same person, and on 31st January returned yet again and saw Mr Kemp behind the counter. After showing him all the copies which he had previously purchased and explained that he was a police officer, Robert arrested Mr Kemp and the two owners of the shop, Mr Foote and Mr Ramsay. The outcome was that Foote received twelve months' imprisonment, Ramsay received nine months and the sales assistant, Kemp, received three months' imprisonment for selling an illegal magazine.[96]

It is worth noting Robert's statement in this case, that while he had been instructed to buy copies of the banned magazine from the shop in question by Detective Inspector James McWilliam, Robert also

---

94 The *Freethinker* published cartoons which were perceived to attack religion in an aggressive way. Not only were shops not allowed to sell the magazine, but its editor, G.W. Foote, was sentenced to twelve months' imprisonment for allowing it to be printed.

95 Old Bailey record (t18830226-333).

96 Old Bailey record (t18830226-359).

made it very clear that the money he had personally spent buying the publication had not been paid, although his travel expenses had been covered.

In the February of 1884 Robert was promoted to Detective Constable.[97] Two months later, on 5th April, he was on Liverpool Street where he saw John Thomas, aged 35, acting suspiciously. Robert followed the man onto a platform at Liverpool Street railway station, where he began talking to a sailor. Soon the two men walked off to the nearby Railway Tavern, where another man, John Harris, joined them. Strangely, Thomas and Harris left the sailor rather quickly. Robert became suspicious and raced after the pair, and discovered that they had stolen a five pound note from the sailor. The prisoners were sentenced to six months' hard labour each.[98]

In May of the same year, Robert was again in court to give evidence against Charlotte Garnham and Henry William Blackborough, who had stolen nineteen pieces of velvet from one Leon Jantzen.

On 7th May 1884, Robert received information which caused him to visit the draper's shop belonging to Charlotte Garnham on the following afternoon with Sergeant Sage. When they entered the shop the prisoner stated they knew that these two men were police officers. Sergeant Sage showed Garnham a samples book which he had brought with him, and told her he had reason to believe those samples were stolen. Henry Blackborough joined them, and he and Miss Garnham claimed that the book of samples had been shown to them previously by a man who came into the shop, but they had refused to buy any fabric from him.

Robert looked over the premises but found nothing. He then visited Mrs Smith, the mother of Miss Garnham, at Eliza Terrace in Stamford Hill. Mrs Smith gave him some of the stolen velvet. This was enough evidence that the velvet had changed hands, possibly through the draper's shop. Robert arrested Miss Garnham, the

---

97 Robert's service file: CLA/048/AD/01/651 (London Metropolitan Archives).

98 *Lloyds' Weekly Newspaper*, 6th April 1884.

99 Old Bailey record (t18840519-597).

owner and her manager, Mr Blackborough. She was subsequently found guilty and sentenced to eighteen months' hard labour, while Mr Blackborough was found not guilty.[99]

Robert's third child, Cecil William Sagar, was born in 1885.[100] On 18th May that same year, the detective was at the Old Bailey about a case of forgery and deception by Eugene Loraine and John Owen, who had uttered a fake letter in order to obtain money. Owen had sent a letter bearing his own address to a stockbroker named John Shaw. In the letter, Owen claimed to be one W. Forbes Capel, and asked for the full amount of his account to be sent to him, a sum of £4,900. Mr Shaw knew something was wrong and contacted the Bank of England, who advised him not to send the money.

Robert Sagar was called in to investigate and on 27th January 1885 waited at the address given on the letter, inside the building. At last, Owen walked in and ask if he had any letters; Robert saw the receptionist hand over correspondence addressed to 'W. Forbes Capel', which Owen put into his pocket. He was arrested and taken to Old Jewry Police Station by Robert and another officer.

It was then discovered that the letter to Mr Shaw had been written by Eugene Loraine, with John Owen acting as the go-between. Both prisoners were found guilty, with Loraine receiving fourteen years' imprisonment and Owen fifteen months' hard labour.[101]

Robert was back at court on 11th January 1886, this time on a case of the theft by William Edwards and William Bye of two thousand sheets of chronographic pictures and a wooden case from Mr Max Hepner, the owner of a stationers at 55 Aldersgate Street.

The items had been delivered and left in the passageway beside the shop, but had been stolen before the owner could get to them. Mr Hepner immediately went to the police.

On 19th November 1885, Robert received information which led him to 24 Milk Street, where a Mr Schmaltz gave him further

---

100 Cecil went on to marry Bertha A Hahn in 1912 and the couple had one child, Miss Sylvia B Sagar. The fact women do not carry on the family name means Robert's side of the Sagar family line actually ends with his granddaughter, Sylvia.

101 Old Bailey record (t18850518-360).

information which in turn saw the detective visit a waste paper shed in City Road on 9th January 1886 with Detective Wise. They did not have to wait long before both William Edwards and William Bye turned up, and Robert explained why he and Wise were there and that information given to the detectives suggested that Edwards had shown samples of the stolen items, claiming they were for sale. Both prisoners admitted their guilt and were given nine months' hard labour.[102]

In December 1887, Robert's mother Sarah died in Burnley at the age of 58.[103] Her son was granted eight days leave to attend her funeral.[104]

In 1888, Robert was at the Old Bailey on 28th May giving evidence in a case of pickpocketing by John Newton. Robert had been on Bishopsgate on 11th of May at seven o'clock in the evening when he saw Newton acting suspiciously, so decided to follow him. The detective noticed him take something out of his pocket, look at it and then show it another man. Newton headed straight towards a pawnbrokers called Alton's. Robert managed to look through the window of the shop and saw the suspect handing over a watch to the sales assistant. When Newton left the shop, Robert introduced himself and arrested him for stealing the watch, with his prisoner claiming to know nothing of it - a story he repeated at Bishopsgate Police Station. However, at court the prisoner pleaded guilty and received two years' hard labour.[105]

According to several newspaper reports,[106] Robert Sagar had many meetings with the senior officers of the Metropolitan Police force at Leman Street Police Station to discuss the Jack the Ripper crimes. After the death of Catherine Eddowes, the Metropolitan Police force thought they would have to communicate a little more with the City

---

102   Old Bailey record (t18860111-228).

103   Death record.

104   Robert's service file: CLA/048/AD/01/651 (London Metropolitan Archives).

105   Old Bailey records (t18880528-539).

106   *City Press*, 7th January 1905; *The Star*, 7th January 1905 and the *News of the World*, 8th January 1905.

Police, something they had not done previously, as now both forces wanted to be seen doing everything they could to catch the killer.

In 1905, Robert was quoted as stating that "suspicion fell upon a man, who, without a doubt, was the murderer. Identification being impossible, he could not be charged. He was, however, placed in a lunatic asylum and the series of atrocities came to an end."[107] This had also been mentioned by senior officers of the Metropolitan Police force, such as Chief Inspector Donald Swanson, who mentioned a suspect who was taken with difficulty to the Seaside Home and identified by a witness.[108] The witness, however, did not want to give evidence, so the suspect had to be let go.

Swanson also suggests that the suspect was still watched by police, or more importantly to this chapter at least, that 'he was watched by police (City CID) by day and night'.

Robert stated the suspect he was watching worked as a butcher in what was known as 'Butcher's Row' in Aldgate High Street. Butcher's Row was a short row of butcher's shops on the south side of the High Street, situated within the City of London boundary. It can be suggested that because it was the 'City CID' watching the suspect, that it was because he lived, worked or had family members within the City, and with Robert proposing that the suspect was a butcher, could this suspect have come from Butcher's Row, and was that where Robert was watching him from?

Interestingly, Detective Henry Cox was quoted as stating "we had the use of a house opposite the shop of the man we suspected and disguised, of course, we frequently stopped across in the role of customers."[109] We can only wonder if Detective Cox and Robert were talking about the same suspect, being watched at the same time, although Cox does describe a charming little scene of detectives in disguise, pretending to be customers in a butcher's shop, something we know Robert had done before.

---

107 *City Press*, 7th January 1905.

108 Chief Inspector Donald Swanson in the so-called Swanson marginalia, pencil notes in his copy of Sir Robert Anderson's book, *The Lighter Side of My Official Life* (1910).

109 *Thomson's Weekly News*, 1st December 1906.

In fact, a report in the *Morning Leader* of 9th January 1905 describes a disguise Robert had used and how effective it must have been:

> The disguise of a labourer was used, too, when Mr Sagar made investigations into the notorious 'Jack the Ripper' murders. So effectual was his disguise that he was actually tracked himself by two police-officers, who thought they had reason to regard him as a suspicious character.

It is difficult to know whether the suspect Detective Henry Cox mentions is the same that Robert was referring to in his statements, as times and dates are not mentioned. However, we can suggest that Robert was in Aldgate in April 1889, because a suspect in another crime was being followed by DS Pentin, who, with help from Robert, was able to arrest the man at 5 Duke Street.[110] Perhaps Robert was watching 'Jack' in the same area at that time?

In the 1888 Business Directory it shows that numbers 44 to 62 Aldgate High Street were butcher's shops. Number 44 was a butcher's called Scales and Leuw, owned by a Mr Levy Leuw. Numbers 48 to 52 were run by Thomas Brown, William Lankester, James Tyler and Matthew Flicker. While numbers 53-54 were a butcher's shop called Attfield and Knott, on the 1891 census Mr Attfield had left the premises and the butcher's belonged to just Mr Knott. Number 55 was a butcher's owned by Nice and Hawkins, number 56 was owned by James Killby, number 57 was owned by Cooke and Banks, and 58 was owned by George Bullas. Number 59 was owned by Solomon De Leeuw, number 60 run by George Rayment, and finally number 62 was run by Morris Bosman. 62 Aldgate High Street was situated next to some warehouses selling general goods, and past these warehouses was the railway line leading to Minories Junction.[111]

Across from this section of shops, along Aldgate High Street, was the Bull Inn at number 25.[112] This public house was reopened after

---

110 *The Times*, 3rd April 1889.

111 1888 Business Directory.

112 Ibid.

113 Mr East was also the owner of the Three Nuns in the same locale.

having a refit, and was owned by Mr Samuel East Jr.[113] It is not listed on the 1890 Business Directory, suggesting it had closed down and was possibly sitting empty for a while before being knocked down.

If we assume that Robert was watching the suspect in Butcher's Row,[114] could he have been staying across the road to keep an eye on the suspect? The Bull Inn stands 'opposite', as Detective Henry Cox stated, this row of butcher's shops, and was quite possibly empty at the time.

The Bull Inn was known to the detectives through a raid in December 1890 on the Alliance Club, which was situated in Bull Inn Yard just off Aldgate High Street. This club was a gaming house and was under observation for a time before arrests could be made,[115] perhaps from the closed public house. Could this be the answer to where Robert had situated himself?

Perhaps we can permit ourselves to explore this theory... if Robert Sagar had been watching a suspect from inside a public house at 25 Aldgate High Street, he would have been just three doors down from the building outside which Catherine Eddowes had been discovered drunk by PC Louis Robinson on 29th September 1888.

If the police's suspicions were correct, and the killer did indeed work or live in one of the shops along Aldgate High Street, was this how he first selected his victim, with Catherine being in the wrong place at the wrong time?

Or, in the knowledge that Catherine headed back to this area after her release from Bishopsgate Police Station, can we ask a more haunting question? Did she in fact know her killer? Did she have a meeting arranged? Is this why she asked PC Hutt the time upon her release? Catherine had enough time to revisit Aldgate High Street before being spotted with a man by the entrance to Mitre Square by the three witnesses.

Carrying this train of thought to the identification at the Seaside

---

114 The area in question was opposite where the Hoops and Grapes public house is situated.

115 'Inspector Robert Sagar and the City of London Police Raid on the Bull Inn Yard, Aldgate' by Scott Nelson, *Ripperologist* 103, June 2009.

Home, believed to be in Hove in Sussex, it is hard to imagine that, whatever religion the witness and suspect were, the witness would not want to help the police capture Jack the Ripper. However, for the witness to have known the religion of the suspect, it does indicate that the suspect was known to the witness, and perhaps this familiarity indicates a stronger reason for the witness to have not wanted to be involved than merely religion.

One of the three witnesses at the entrance to Mitre Square was Joseph Hyam Levy, a butcher who lived at 1 Hutchinson Street, which was just over 60 yards away from 36 Middlesex Street,[116] where another family of Levys lived and worked. The head of this family was Jacob Levy, who on 15th August 1890 was taken to the City of London Lunatic Asylum.[117]

Out of the three witnesses who saw Catherine Eddowes at Church Passage with a man, it was Joseph Hyam Levy who the newspapers reported as giving the air of someone who knew more than he was letting on - perhaps he recognised the man as a fellow Jew, a fellow butcher, who lived and worked very close to himself.

On 6th December 1888, Robert was promoted to Police Sergeant,[118] and within six months, on 8th June 1889,[119] became Detective Sergeant. On 7th September that year he made a report about a letter received which claimed that a murder had been committed in Great Prescott Street, just days before a torso was found at nearby Pinchin Street.[120] Robert stated in his report that he took the letter

---

116 1871 and 1891 census returns.

117 Jacob Levy; City of London Lunatic Asylum, Stone. Male patient's case notes 1890/91 (London Metropolitan Archives). Jacob Levy died in this asylum on 29th July 1891.

118 Robert's service file: CLA/048/AD/01/651 (London Metropolitan Archives).

119 Ibid.

120 A female torso was found by PC William Pennett in railway arches in Pinchin Street on the morning of 10th September 1889.

121 CLA/048/CS/02/373, letter number 373 held at the London Metropolitan Archives.

to Detective Inspector Reid, of the Met's H Division, whose opinion was that the author was known to him and he was insane.[121]

On 20th October 1890, Robert was once again in court giving evidence in relation to a fraud case by one Arthur Rorke, who had swindled a Mr Pompellio Valenzuella. Honduras-born Mr Valenzuella, who had moved to London in order to start a business, spoke no English and had to use an interpreter, so Rorke suggested that if he paid between £800 and 1,000 he would set up an English account with the Bank of England for the foreigner, allowing them to go into business together. Once Mr Valenzuella had handed over the money, Rorke advised that carrying a large sum of cash around London in order to buy goods for the business was dangerous, and suggested that it was much safer if the money was given to him for safekeeping. At this point, with full pockets, Arthur Rorke disappeared. Robert Sagar was called in to investigate, with a warrant issued for the prisoner's arrest on 18th September. With information received, Robert was able to find the prisoner on the third floor of 31 Great St. Helens. He arrested Rorke, and at the Old Bailey the prisoner was found guilty.[122]

The next month, on 13th November 1890, Robert was promoted to Detective Inspector.[123] According to the 1891 census, conducted a few months later, the Sagar family had moved to 13 Rose Alley, situated behind Bishopsgate Police Station, and a street which was home to many policemen's families.[124] In the *Daily News* of 9th January 1905, in a report of Robert's retirement, the reporter mentioned that the Sagar would be leaving 'the comfortable quarter in Rose Alley, Bishopsgate, which he has occupied for so long.' This description hints at a contentment experienced living within the area that was initially built for married policemen in 1876, perhaps one reason that the Sagar family were still living there on the 1901

---

122 Old Bailey Records (t18901020-785).

123 Robert's service file: CLA/048/AD/01/651 (London Metropolitan Archives).

124 1891 census.

125 Robert's service file: CLA/048/AD/01/651 (London Metropolitan Archives).

census.

Robert retired from the force four years later, having completed his 25 years' service, on 5th January 1905.[125] The family moved to 4 Surrenden, Preston Park, near Brighton in Sussex.[126]

Sadly, Clara Sagar died the following year, in September.[127] Robert himself passed away on 30th November 1924 at the aged of 72. *The Brighton and Hove Herald* reported that he had died from falling in the street.[128] He was buried at Brighton and Preston Cemetery.

It interesting to note that the Seaside Home at 51 Clarendon Villas, Hove, which has often been suggested as the scene of the identification of Jack the Ripper, is just over a 30 minute walk away from Robert's last address, and just over an hour from his final resting place. Coincidence? Maybe, maybe not...

Inspector James McWilliam:
'Many persons being of the opinion that these crimes are of too revolting a character to have been committed by a sane person.'[129]

Inspector James McWilliam was told of the murder of Catherine Eddowes exactly two hours after she was found by PC Watkins. James's first action was to contact the Metropolitan Police with news of this latest murder, proving at least somewhere in the chain of command there was communication between the two police forces. He visited Mitre Square and followed the body to Golden Lane Mortuary, where he was able to connect the piece of apron found in Goulston Street to the piece of apron missing from the body of Catherine Eddowes, then he wrote a detailed report...

---

126   1911 census.

127   Death record.

128   *The Brighton and Hove Herald*, 6th December 1924. Death certificate records cause of death as arterial sclerosis and static bronchitis.

129   Report by Inspector James McWilliam (HO 144/221/A49301C ff. 162-70).

130   1841 census.

131   James McWilliam's service file: CLA/048/AD/01/466 (London Metropolitan Archives).

Born in 1837,[130] James was the son of William McWilliam, who worked at his father's Mill in Cairnie, Aberdeenshire.[131] A birth record for James cannot be found at the present time, nor a baptism record, so with no record of a marriage for William McWilliam we do not know who James's mother was.

On the 1841 census, four-year-old James was living with his grandfather, also named James (b.1781), grandmother Jean (b.1786), an aunt, Isabella (b.1827) and a servant named Elizabeth Shearer (b.1801) at the grandfather's mill in Botary, Aberdeenshire.[132] James's father is missing from this census, but as he does not appear anywhere else on the 1841 census yet does on later records, we can safely assume that he was probably away when the enumerator called.[133]

On the 1851 census, James was now aged fourteen and living with his father (who was recorded as unmarried) and grandfather James. The latter ran a farm of six acres,[134] on which William and James worked at the time of that census.[135]

In the same month that he turned 21, on 4th January 1858, James signed up to the City of London Police force. He is described as being 6ft 1¾ inches in height, with blue eyes, dark hair, dark complexion and a 'slight mole on the left cheek.'[136]

His previous employment was listed as being at the mill at Botiary in Cairnie, Aberdeenshire, working for nine months as a miller's assistant.[137] It is interesting that although James was born in January 1837, his grandfather states in a letter held in James's service recorded that he had known his grandson since May 1842.[138]

In his application form, James states was living at the mill at the

---

132 Although the 1841 census, states Hill, which is a mistake.

133 1841 census.

134 1851 census.

135 James McWilliam's service file: CLA/048/AD/01/466 (London Metropolitan Archives).

136 Ibid.

137 Ibid.

138 Ibid.

139 Ibid.

time of applying and that he was single. He was given the warrant number 2852 and a starting wage of 21s.[139] Being single, James was placed at Great Tower Street station, West Smithfield.[140]

On 9th December 1869, James was promoted to Sergeant, with a wage of 31s. In 1871 he was still living at Great Tower Street Station,[141] and on 6th July 1872, James had become Station Sergeant there, with a rise in pay to 39 shillings.[142]

James married Ann Elizabeth Bradley in 1874 in Cambridgeshire, where his wife had been born in 1848.[143]

On 15th April 1875, James was promoted Third Class Inspector with another pay rise, this time to 66s, and in 1878 became an Inspector of Detectives. James would end his career as Superintendent Inspector following a promotion in 1890. He retired in 1903.[144]

In 1881 James and Ann were living at 13 King Edward Street, Islington, with James's sister-in-law Matilda Bradley, and boarders Joseph Moul, Mary Jane Baker and Emily Grace Dowling.[145]

From 1891 to 1901 James was living at Cloak Lane Police Station, with his wife and servant Ellen Jones.[146]

It is interesting to note that James was involved in two famous cases during his career, both of which saw the City of London Police communicate with other police forces, one being its neighbour, the Metropolitan Police force, and the other being the French Police.

The first of which was, of course, the case of the Jack the Ripper Murders...

It could be said that James McWilliam's role within the Whitechapel murders investigation actually started before the murder of Catherine Eddowes. As already mentioned in the section on Detective Daniel Halse, the Commissioner of the City Police Sir James Fraser

140   1861 census.

141   1871 census.

142   James McWilliam's service file: CLA/048/AD/01/466 (London Metropolitan Archives

143   Marriage record.

144   James McWilliam's service file: CLA/048/AD/01/466 (London Metropolitan Archives

145   1881 census.

146   1901 census.

was aware of the problems the neighbouring police force was having in solving the case, so in August he had ordered officers of his own force to gather at the nearest point to Whitechapel governed by the City of London Police, this being Bishopsgate Sub Division. These officers were told to observe 'all prostitutes frequenting public houses and walking the streets,'[147] the order being passed from the Commissioner to James McWilliam who in turn relayed it to his detectives. This meant that when the killer struck in Mitre Square, on the City's own patch, detectives carrying out this order were very close by and within minutes of the body being found and the alarm raised were on the scene.

It is unusual to know the full movements of an Inspector on any given date, but with James McWilliam and the morning of 30th September 1888, the task is made easier by him writing his own report, now held at the National Archives. In it, James remarked that the order as outlined above had been given in an attempt to prevent any further murders happening, writing 'extra men in plain clothes have been employed' within the City.[148]

James then went on describe when and where the body of Catherine Eddowes had been found, stating that it was '300 yards from the City boundary'.[149] It was at 3:45am on the morning of 30th September, exactly two hours after the body had been found, James wrote, that he 'had been informed of the murder and arrived at the Detective Office' in Old Jewry.[150]

After being told of everything that had been done at that point, James took the decision to wire the Metropolitan Police to inform them of this latest murder. Considering this was James's first move upon hearing of the crime, it shows that there was an open

---

147 Report by Inspector James McWilliam (HO 144/221/A49301C ff. 162-70).

148 Ibid.

149 Ibid.

150 Ibid.

151 George Lusk (1839-1919) was a painter and restorer of musical halls. He became Chairman of the Whitechapel Vigilance Committee, who claimed the police were not doing all they could to solve the murders.

communication between the two police forces, something repeated later when George Lusk[151] received the 'From Hell' letter, supposedly from the killer of Catherine Eddowes,[152] accompanied by a portion of a kidney. James was in communication with the Met's Chief Inspector Donald Swanson and the officers believed it was a medical student's prank.[153]

James then went from Old Jewry to Bishopsgate Police Station, and then on to the scene of the crime, Mitre Square, where he met with Assistant Commissioner Major Smith, Superintendent Foster, Inspector Collard and various detectives. It was while James was at the scene that Detective Hunt returned to the square, explaining the discovery of the apron and message on the wall in Goulston Street, at which James instantly ordered for the message to be photographed.[154]

He then told Detective Hunt to make a search of the area in which the apron and message had been discovered, while James followed the body of Catherine Eddowes to Golden Lane Mortuary. On being handed the piece of apron found in Goulston Street, he 'compared with a piece the deceased was wearing and it exactly corresponded.'[155]

James then returned to the Detective Office at Old Jewry, where he telegraphed all other divisions of the City of London Police and also the Metropolitan Police with news of the latest murder, and gave a description of Catherine and what she had been wearing.[156]

On 1st October 1888 James had a meeting with the Commissioner of the City Police and the Lord Mayor of London, the outcome of

---

152 The 'From Hell' letter was sent to George Lusk's address at 1 Alderney Road, Mile End, accompanied by a portion of a human kidney. As a portion of Catherine's kidney was found to be missing after the post mortem this letter has been deemed important by some students of the case. However, others have suggested it was a practical joke by a medical student, or even Mr Lusk himself trying to make himself more famous.

153 Report by Inspector James McWilliam (HO 144/221/A49301C ff. 162-70); report by Chief Inspector Swanson (HO 144/221/A49301C, ff. 184-194).

154 Report by Inspector James McWilliam (HO 144/221/A49301C ff. 162-70).

155 Ibid.

156 Ibid.

which was a reward of £500 to be offered for any information leading to the arrest of the murderer. A poster giving details of this reward was posted in every police station and surrounding areas.[157]

James reported on 27th October 1888 that because of these posters 'a great many communications have been received and are still coming in.'[158]

James mentioned in his report the efforts made by Detective Hunt to ascertain the identity of the murdered woman, and on 3rd October 1888 it was finally learned that that her name was Catherine Eddowes, and that she had been living in a lodging house in Flower and Dean Street with a man named Kelly. Before that, Catherine had been living with Thomas Conway and had three children by him.[159]

James goes on to mention the inquest, which took place on 4th October at the Golden Lane Mortuary, with a verdict of 'willful murder against some person unknown' returned, the Inspector admitting that 'every effort has been made to trace the murderer, but up to present without success.'[160]

James reported that enquiries had been made at all London lunatic asylums, because there were 'many persons being of the opinion that these crimes are of too revolting a character to have been committed by a sane person.'[161]

He mentioned that on 16th October, Mr Lusk had received the grisly letter and package, but 'did not attach any importance to it at the time, but on mentioning the matter to other members of the Committee on the 18th October 1888, they advised him to show the piece of kidney to a medical man.'[162]

The medical man in question was Mr Reed of 56 Mile End Road, who took the kidney to Dr Openshaw at the London Hospital. Both

---

157 A facsimile hangs on the door of the Sherlock Holmes Museum in Baker Street.

158 Report by Inspector James McWilliam (HO 144/221/A49301C ff. 162-70).

159 Ibid.

160 Ibid..

161 Ibid.

162 Ibid.

thought that the kidney was certainly human. It was then handed back to Mr Lusk, who walked with it to Leman Street Police Station and from there the kidney and letter were taken to Scotland Yard. Chief Inspector Donald Swanson 'loaned' the letter to Inspector McWilliam on 20th October 1888, showing another instance of co-operation between the two forces. It was returned on 24th October after being photographed.[163]

City Surgeon Dr Frederick Gordon Brown also examined the piece of kidney, he also believing it to be human, and with this now firmly established a concerted effort was made to find the sender of both letter and kidney. It was deemed best to not make the doctor's opinions known to the public.[164]

James ended his report by stating that 'this department is co-operating with the Metropolitan Police in the matter, and Chief Inspector Swanson and I meet daily and confer on the subject.'[165]

The second famous case in which James McWilliam was involved occurred on 15th October 1895, when he became involved in the capture of the famous forger Captain Bevan, also known by several aliases including Edmund Bevan, Charles Smith, John Bright, John Benson and John Dalton.

The criminal had made himself known to the Metropolitan Police by getting hold of banker's credit notes and making forged copies of them, occasionally claiming on the notes. As he kept using different names, he was proving hard to catch.

Bevan's luck ran out when he claimed on a note to Messrs, Cook and Son, tourist agents situated in Ludgate Circus, for the sum of £100, claiming to be Charles Smith, living in Lille, northern France. The tourist agents couldn't understand why this person was asking money from them, nor did they know who he was, so they took the credit note to James, who instantly realised this was a case of forgery. He gave orders to Detective Inspector Taylor, who consulted Messrs,

---

163   Report by Inspector James McWilliam (HO 144/221/A49301C ff. 162-70).
164   Ibid.
165   Ibid.

Brown, Shipley and Company, the bank from whom the credit notes were meant to have come. This led the police to other names the forger had used, and they eventually contacted the French Police, who arrested the criminal in Lille.[166]

By 1911, James had been retired for eight years and was living at 1 Church Road, Forest Hill in London, with his wife. There are signs that James was not well at this time, because also living with them was a sick nurse by the name of Lily Amelia Otto, along with a servant called Elizabeth Kipper.[167]

James died at the same address five years later, on 8th January 1916.[168]

James McWilliam certainly was a policeman who did not mind communicating with other police forces, perhaps going against the grain in doing so - or at least what is generally believed to have been an uneasy relationship between the two forces.

He had worked under four very different Commissioners of the City of London Police, and was highly respected.

In fact, Sir Henry Smith wrote in his memoirs that "James McWilliam was born at Cairnie, Aberdeenshire - a true Aberdonian: honest, upright, and of exceptionally good education."[169]

He wrote a detailed report of his movements and actions of the morning in which Jack the Ripper struck and the days after, giving us an insight into the workings of the detective department of the City of London Police when dealing with a murder, a message, a letter and a piece of kidney.

Detective Henry Cox: Upon the Trail[170]

Henry Cox was an interesting character, if only because he was quite

---

166 James McWilliam's service file: CLA/048/AD/01/466 (London Metropolitan Archives

167 1911 census.

168 James McWilliam's service file: CLA/048/AD/01/466 (London Metropolitan Archives

169 *From Constable to Commissioner* by Sir Henry Smith, (1910).

170 A quote from Henry Cox about his involvement in the Jack the Ripper case, published in *Thomson's Weekly*, 1st December 1906.

open in his views on Jack the Ripper and his involvement in catching him. Of course, as students of crime there are areas where we wish Henry had been more detailed in his descriptions, but when reading his words it seems clear that he was not holding anything back for secret purposes, but seems to have been talking naturally, so gives us an insight into the City of London Police detectives' investigation into the Ripper's crimes.

Henry Cox was born in the third quarter of 1859 in Camberwell[171] to William (b.1824 in Holborn), a compositor and Sophia Elizabeth (b.1828 in Westminster).[172] Henry was the fifth child to be born to this growing family, joining William Jr (b.1850), George (1852), Robert Whitmore (1856) and Arthur (1858). Henry would be followed by Frederick (1860), Edward (1864), Herbert (1866), Ernest John (1868) and Julian Charles (1870).[173] The last two sons sadly died at the same time, in the latter quarter of 1872, which indicates a disease, considering their ages of two and four.

Henry was baptised on 21st August 1859 at St Mary's church in Lambeth, and would carry on the family tradition by having a large number of children himself, as we shall see.

In 1871 the Cox family were living at 31 Southampton Street in Camberwell. William Jr was already working with his father as a compositor,[174] while only Frederick and Edward are classed as scholars, suggesting that either the family could only afford to send two sons to school or that Henry was already in work, the nature of which was not relayed to the enumerator.[175]

---

171 Birth record.

172 Sophia's maiden name was Whitmore. She and William married in the latter months of 1846 in Clerkenwell.

173 1871 census.

174 In an article interview with *Thomson's Weekly* published on 3rd November 1906, Henry stated that his was 'at one time a compositor and latterly the editor of his own paper.'

175 1871 census.

By the time of the 1881 census the Cox family had move to 169 Camden Grove North, Camberwell, and Henry was listed as a 'Zinc Worker or Plumber and Gasfitter'. This career did not last long, and on 21st July 1881 he joined the City Police force as a constable,[176] at the age of 22. He was given warrant number 5465.[177]

The following year, in the last quarter of 1882, Henry married Martha Sally Vidler (b.1866) in the City of London. Two years later their first child was born, whom they named Grace.[178] It was around this time that Henry went into plain clothes for the City force.[179]

On 25th October 1886, Henry was at the Old Bailey over a case of theft by Alfred Stevens and Alfred Ryan. On 17th September Henry had been with City Policeman Frederick Holmes in Fleet Street, when they saw the suspect Alfred Ryan acting suspiciously and decided to follow him as he walked past the offices of *The Graphic* newspaper at 190 Fleet Street. At the corner of Wellington Street, Ryan met up with Alfred Stevens, the pair then walking across Waterloo Bridge into Belvedere Road in Lambeth, at which point they spilt up. Henry followed Ryan to the Rising Sun public house where Stevens rejoined him, now carrying a parcel and a jug.

When both left the public house Henry Cox followed Stevens, while Ryan was followed and later arrested by PC Holmes. Henry told Stevens that he was a detective from the City, and asked him about the parcel he had taken into the public house. When Stevens replied that he knew nothing about a parcel, Henry arrested him and obtained his address as 16 College Street. When the officers looked inside the parcel they found copies of *The Graphic* which they had stolen from the Fleet Street offices. Both were found guilty, with Ryan pleading guilty to another felony in May 1882 and receiving five years imprisonment.[180]

---

176 Henry's service record held at Bishopsgate Police Station.

177 Ibid.

178 1891 census.

179 *Police Review*, 7th December 1906, which stated that Henry was in uniform for nearly three years.

180 Old Bailey records (t18861025-1108).

In 1887, Henry's second daughter, Florence, was born, being baptised with her sister the following year- the year of the Ripper. Son Henry Jr was born around this time.[181]

Henry's comments on the Ripper case, given in an interview following his retirement, reveal that he was on surveillance towards the end of 1888, but it was not until 'after the [Mary] Kelly murder that [the police hit] upon the trail.'[182] He even congratulated his follow detectives, one can imagine with a smile, as he was quoted as saying, "When investigations made by several of our cleverest detectives indicated that a man living in the East End was not unlikely to have been connected with the crimes."

Normally, a police officer of any force talking about their involvement in the Jack the Ripper case might stop there with an open ending, to make us, as readers, possibly think they knew more than they were letting on, but Henry did not, he actually gave a description of the man he was watching:

> The man we suspected was about five feet six inches in height, with short, black, curly hair, and he had a habit of taking late walks abroad. He occupied several shops in the East End, but from time to time he became insane, and was forced to spend a portion of his time in an asylum in Surrey.[183]

Henry stated that he was watching this suspect for over three months, in an area populated by Jewish immigrants, so used a cover story of being factory inspectors who were looking into the sweating system. He told how he followed the man in question one night, the suspect heading towards Leman Street, where he visited an address known to be frequented by criminals, and later stopped to speak with a woman, Henry anticipating catching the killer red-handed.

The retired detective stated that once this man knew he was being

---

181 The two children were both baptised on 22nd April 1888, around the same time Henry's third child, Henry Jr, was born. The baptisms took place at St Bride's Church in Fleet Street, with the baptism record stating that Henry was living at 72 Fleet Street at this time.

182 *Thomson's Weekly News*, 1st December 1906.

183 Ibid.

184 Ibid.

watched, no more crimes took place and the police were left with 'not the slightest scrap of evidence.'[184]

This, you might think, would be the end of what Henry had to say about the case, but you would be wrong. Henry continued to give his opinion that "all the published portrayals of the criminal whom the police suspected" were wrong. He stated that the theory that Jack the Ripper 'jumped over London Bridge or Blackfriars Bridge,' (believed to be a reference to Ripper suspect Montague John Druitt) was incorrect, and he certainly did not believe that the murderer was 'an educated man who had had suddenly gone mad', feeling the motive may have been revenge on womankind but not for a 'lust for blood'.[185]

Henry went on to suggest that the dates of the murders made the idea of a sailor being the killer plausible, and revealed that he believed the culprit to have been a member of the lower class, like his victims.[186]

In 1890, Henry and Martha had their fourth child, Ernest, and the family moved away from the busy streets of Fleet Street, where they had been living at least since the birth of Henry Jr in 1888, to 65 Frampton Park Road in Hackney, where Ernest's birth was registered.[187]

At the end of 1890, on 24th November, Henry was called to the Old Bailey to give evidence in a case of forgery by George Johnson, aged 70, and John Phillips, aged 74. Phillips had met a businessman called Joseph Tragheim, who hailed from the Baltic Provinces, while in Rotterdam. Phillips claimed he could help Mr Tragheim obtain some Bank of England notes, with letters of credit if Mr Tragheim visited him at 115 Hampton Road in Forest Gate, which he did on 17th February 1890, but was told that Phillips was ill. Despite there appearing to be a party underway, Mr Tragheim left.

Then, in August of the same year, Mr Tragheim arrived back

185 *Thomson's Weekly News*, 1st December 1906.
186 Ibid.
187 1891 census.

in London and met Phillips on the corner of Liverpool Street and Bishopsgate. The Englishman told him that the letters of credit had to be in circulation before anything else could be done, but he would give Mr Tragheim a chance to put them in circulation first.

At the end of August Mr Tragheim felt that something was wrong so spoke to the Governor of the Bank of England, who transferred him to a solicitor named Mr Freshfield. The result was that the police were called in.

City Detective Robert Child spoke to Mr Tragheim and was handed certain items which Phillips and Johnson had given him. Armed with this information, the police realised that the prisoners planned to defraud the bank merchants of Drexel, Morgan and Company of 22 Broad Street. Henry Cox was given the task of following George Johnson to ascertain his address. Despite losing him a few times, he discovered that Johnson lived in Bacon Street, off Brick Lane in Spitalfields. There is also a connection to a fellow detective within this case, Robert Sagar, for while Henry was following Johnson, Sagar was keeping watch of Phillips' address at 115 Hampton Road in Forest Gate. It was Detective Sagar who later arrested prisoner Phillips. Both prisoners were found guilty and received seven years' imprisonment.[188]

In the 1891 census, the Cox family had gained a servant named Ellen English, but interestingly, Henry had gained another family member in his household in the form of his sister-in-law, Lucy Vidler, who was 23.

On 6th April 1891, Henry was again at the Old Bailey, over a case of deception and fraud by Alexander Brown, Jean Baptiste Flobert and Ernest Ratier. Brown had written to a Mr Francis Artesani, asking to meet in Bishopsgate, where Brown told him that he could get hold of £1,600 worth of stolen North and South Alabama bonds within 24 hours if Mr Artesani could pay 60% per cent of the money up front. Mr Artesani spoke to his 'chief' about the deal, Lord Revelstoke. Mr Artesani met up again with Brown and told him that his 'chief' would

---

188 Old Bailey records (t18901124-38).

consider giving him 50 rather than 60 per cent. There was some discussion on how much the 'chief' should pay, with agreement being reached at £200.

However, the police were already watching Brown because of information received. On 17th March, Henry and City Detective Frederick Downs saw Brown and Mr Artesani outside Martin's Bank on Lombard Street. After Brown and Mr Artesani had entered the bank and left, Henry and Detective Downs followed them to 37&38 Mark Lane, where Brown met up with Flobert and Ratier.

The detectives saw Mr Artesani hand something over to Brown, who then ran quickly away with the other two prisoners. The detectives managed to get hold of Brown, who was carrying a bag of 200 sovereigns in his breast pocket. After being questioned by Henry, Brown explained the money was payment to find some bonds, not to actually swap them for the bonds. Brown was arrested and taken into custody at Seething Lane Police Station, as were Flobert and Ratier the following day. At the trial Brown and Ratier received five years' penal servitude, and because Flobert had a previous conviction he received seven years.[189]

On 16th November 1891, Henry was at the Old Bailey as a witness to another case of forgery, this time by one Arthur Wells. He had entered a florist at 25 Avenue, Queen's Park on the Harrow Road, on 3rd October and asked for some ferns to be sent to the Naval and Military Club to Captain Thurston, paying with a fake five pound note. Once the florist noticed the fake note the police were called, and Henry was dispatched to locate and apprehend Wells. So on 26th October, when Henry saw the prisoner with another man on Commercial Road in Pimlico, he followed them to 15 Ranelagh Grove. While they were inside Henry communicated with Inspector Wright, who arrested Wells in Henry's presence, who then searched the prisoner's room. Wells pleaded guilty to a previous crime in committed in 1881, and received eighteen months' hard labour.[190]

---

189 Old Bailey records (t18910406-350).
190 Old Bailey records (t1891116-29).

On 25th April 1893, Henry was promoted to Detective Sergeant and was based at Seething Lane Police Station,[191] and in 1895 another son, Jack, was born.

In 1896 Henry was promoted again, to Detective Inspector, and was transferred to the force's Detective Office at Old Jewry.[192] The following year, another child, Allan, was born, at Madan Road South View, Westerham in Kent. The reason why Martha Cox was in Kent is unknown.[193] This was not the end of the Cox children, however, for more would soon arrive: Estella (b.1899), Phillip (1900)[194] and Sybil (1902).[195]

Between 1901 and 1903 Henry was kept busy working on several fraud cases, including his arrest of Samuel Herbert Dougal after the latter forged a cheque in the name of Camille Holland. Dougal attempted to escape when Henry took him to Old Jewry, but managed to catch him again as he ran into a cul-de-sac.[196] Dougal would later be convicted of murdering Camille Holland at Moat Farm.

Henry retired from the City of London Police force on 26th July 1906 with a pension of £117 80d.[197] Yet another child, Donald, was born in 1911, and the family moved to 177 Stanstead Road, Forest Hill in Lewisham.[198]

They would move again by the time that Henry drew up his Will in January 1916, with his last known address recorded as 17 Park Road, Forest Hill. Henry died at Charing Cross Hospital on 18th December 1918,[199] and was buried in Ladywell Cemetery in Lewisham.

Henry had worked his way up to the rank of Detective Inspector,

191 Henry Cox's service file is missing from the London Metropolitan Archives: information from records held at Bishopsgate Police Station.

192 Information from records held at Bishopsgate Police Station.

193 1901 census and birth record.

194 1901 census.

195 Born in 1902 (birth record).

196 *Police Review*, 7th December 1906 and *Evening News*, 26th July 1906.

197 Information from records held at Bishopsgate Police Station.

198 1911 census.

199 Death record and Probate, dated 6th February 1919.

200 *Thomson's Weekly News*, 1st December 1906.

retiring with a presentation clock and medals presented to him in Queen Victoria's Jubilee year, and served at the coronations of Edward VII and George V.[200] Considering that Henry had retired in 1906, he must have volunteered his services for the coronation of 1911, where former officers assisted with security or perhaps watched certain persons known to the police.

For a policeman who investigated the murders of 1888, Henry was quite open with his views on the case. But one has the suspicion that while he carried out his duties faithfully, the crimes were as much as a mystery to him on his retirement as they were fifteen years previously.[201]

Robert Outram:
'We presently drove on to Guildhall, Mr Outram in the cab with us, and Mr Williams on the box' – Annie Besant[202]

It can be said that Robert's role within the Jack the Ripper case was somewhat small compared to his counterparts mentioned elsewhere in this book, however he was at the scene at Mitre Square, so it is worth a moment of our time getting to know a little more of this man's family and career...

There is a problem with attempting to start telling the life of Robert Outram, and that is because there is no birth record for him - or at least for 'Robert Outram' anyway. Our starting point for our research is the 1881 census, where he appeared as a Detective Sergeant of the City Police aged 36-years-old, born in Westerham, Kent. The census records Robert as having a wife named 'Rosella' Outram and a son living with him.[203]

201 *Thomson's Weekly News*, 3rd November 1906.
202 *Autobiographical Sketches* by Annie Besant (1885).
203 1881 census.

We can gauge a year of marriage from the birth of his son, so searching five years either side of that date gives us something to go on at least.

With that rough information, we are able to find Robert's marriage date, and why there is no birth record for 'Robert Outram' - because he began life as Robert Outrim, and was married under that name.

Robert Outrim was born in September 1844,[204] and baptised on 3rd November that year in St Mary's Church, Westerham.[205] He was the son of Isaac Outrim and Sophia Green, who married in 1843. The whole family is missing from the 1851 census, and it is between this date and 1861 that the Outrims became Outrams, for in the 1861 census Robert Outram was employed as a servant by the Slawson family in Mitcham Road, Tooting, at the age of sixteen. The term 'servant' is not what we first think, because the Slawson family were bakers and Robert was their delivery driver.[206]

The next year, in May 1862, Robert changed jobs and became a groom for Mr W. Carey of Tooting Hall,[207] working there for three years and three months before joining the City of London Police on 15th August 1865. He is described in his application as 20 years of age, 5ft 10in tall, with grey eyes and brown hair.[208] Robert received a good reference from his previous employer.

He was certified fit for service on 19th October 1865 and issued with warrant number 3771[209] and collar number 175,[210] and given a wage of 21 shillings.[211] On 23rd August 1866, Robert was promoted to Second Class Constable with a increased wage of 24 shillings.

---

204 In his service file it is claimed that his age was 50 years and four months on retiring in January 1895.

205 Baptism record.

206 1861 census

207 Robert's service record for the City of London Police: CLA/048/AD/01 (London Metropolitan Archives).

208 Ibid.

209 Ibid.

210 Old Bailey record (t18680406-346).

211 Robert's service record: CLA/048/AD/01 (London Metropolitan Archives).

Robert was married in the last quarter of 1866 to Rosetta Keens in East London, and the following year, on 17th October 1867, he was promoted to First Class Constable.[212]

On 6th April 1868, Robert was at the Old Bailey over the murder of John Hunt by 73-year-old Mary Newell, the landlady at 1 Denmark Court, Golden Lane, where John Hunt lived with his mother Bridget. Mary Newell lived on the ground floor, while Bridget and her son, who would have been four-years-old on the day of the trial, lived on the first floor.

On 4th March, at half past eight in the morning, Bridget went to work after giving John his breakfast, and left him in the care of a Mrs Whelan, who lived in the next room. At 4:00pm Bridget was called to the hospital where she saw her boy lying in bed. After a short time she had to return to work and eventually went home at 11:00pm.

The next morning Bridget went back to the hospital and spoke to John, who told her that the landlady had put him in the pot. Bridget subsequently questioned the landlady, to which Mrs Newell shouted: "I don't care what ye say, ye can hang me if ye like, there was no witness to see me put him in the pot, if you do not like it, you can go." She then shut the door in Bridget's face and went to her room.

The house surgeon of St Bartholomew's Hospital saw the child when he was brought in, and noted that he was heavily scalded from his toes to his navel.

John Hunt died from his injuries on 7th March 1868.

After the first inquest was heard, PC Robert Outram called at Mrs Mary Newell's address and asked to see the saucepan she had used. She produced two saucepans and a pot in which she had been washing sheets. When Robert told her that he was going to take those items with him, Mrs Newell begged him not to do so. Ignoring her pleas, Robert removed the items and they were produced in court as evidence.

One wonders how Robert felt dealing with a woman who was accused of scalding a young boy, when in the same year his first son,

212 Robert's service record: CLA/048/AD/01 (London Metropolitan Archives).

Robert William Outram had been born.[213]

Margaret Norton, the Mrs Newell's ten-year-old granddaughter, claimed she had seen the boy slip on her grandmother's saucepan while she was washing, and boiling water fell on him.

The jury returned a verdict that Mrs Newell was guilty of scalding the child, but as there was no apparent malice behind it she received only five years' penal servitude.[214]

On 12th July 1869, PC Robert Outram was again in court over a case of breaking the peace and the wounding of Mary Ann Beckett by Thomas Connell. Interestingly, Robert gave evidence that he saw the victim at the corner of Golden Lane. This quite innocent statement could suggest that as Robert Outram was still a PC at this time, Golden Lane might well have been a part of his beat.

Mary Ann, who lived at 2 George Yard, Golden Lane, was a widower and had known her attacker for about five weeks, as he had been living with her. They had an argument on Friday, 30th April, but everything seemed fine afterwards until the following Monday, when Mary played a prank on Mr Connell in order to get him out of bed. When he discovered it was a prank, Connell put one hand on Mary's forehead and drew a knife across her throat with the other. She managed to run out into the street and across to the lodging house where she used to live.

Robert had seen Mrs Beckett at the corner of Golden Lane at 1:30am on 4th May. She was in her nightdress and holding her throat, and he saw blood on her neck. The officer took her straight to St Bart's Hospital, while PC 142 Henry Todd ran up the stairs of 2 George Yard, where he saw that the Connell had slit his own throat, with a knife on the floor. PC Todd called for the doctor, Dr George Eugene Yarrow, who was the police surgeon of G Division. Connell's wound was five inches in length but although the skin was cut, the windpipe, which was exposed, was unharmed, and the prisoner was also taken to St Bart's.

213 Birth record.
214 Old Bailey record (t18680406-346).

There, the house surgeon Ernest Evans saw the wound inflicted to the woman's throat, which was also five inches in length with a main artery exposed. The knife had divided the muscle on the side of her neck.

Connell claimed that Mary Ann Beckett had made him angry on the Friday before the incident when he found her with another man, and that on the day of the attack he had forgotten that he had a knife. His father and brother appeared at the trial to state that the prisoner was generally of good character, even though his mother and aunt were insane. Thomas Connell was found guilty and sentenced to five years' penal servitude.[215]

By the 1871 census the Outram family had moved to New Union Street in the City.[216] Although Robert was recorded as a Police Sergeant, there is nothing in his service file to confirm this. Instead, the official file seems to indicate that he goes from Police Constable to Detective Constable.

In the same year, Robert appeared at the Old Bailey, on 1st May, on a case of forgery by James Tier. Tier worked for Merriman and Pike Solicitors at 25 Austin Friars, his role being cashier and bookkeeper. He was also in charge of the cheque books, and had faked signatures on one cheque, which he exchanged for gold with a William Pritchard, a cashier at the London Joint Stock Bank. It was not realised that the cheque was a forgery until a fortnight afterwards.

Tier then travelled to the Weaver's Arms in Sun Street, Finsbury, where he quite openly showed the bag of gold. This worried Ann Walker, the landlord's wife, so she asked whether it might be best that she look after the gold and he picked it up the following morning to take to the bank. As Tier was getting quite drunk, he agreed.

At home later in the day, however, he changed his mind and took his wife to the public house, telling Ann Walker to hand the bag of gold over to his wife to look after, which she did. After visiting various shops and more public houses, spending the loot and

---

215 Old Bailey record (t18690712-666).
216 1871 census.

making a scene in various places, the City of London police were called to watch Tier at his home at 8 Finsbury Avenue.

One of these officers was Robert Outram, who was ordered to observe Tier on 18th January. He was unable to find his target until later that evening, when he was seen in the Prince of Wales on South Street, Finsbury. Robert introduced himself as a police officer, telling Tier that he was taking him into custody for forging a cheque. At Bow Lane Police Station the prisoner asked to speak to Robert alone. He offered 25 sovereigns if Robert would let him go, to which the officer replied: "Certainly not." Tier then asked Robert not to mention the attempted bribe.

Robert subsequently searched the house of the prisoner, where he found Tier's wife and five children, as well as two letters which had been signed by his bosses at Merriman and Pike Solicitors which the prisoner had used to make forged cheques, copying their signatures. He was found guilty of forgery and sentenced to five years' penal servitude.[217]

This case is interesting, as it shows Robert to be of honest character, turning down an offer of 25 sovereigns, which was a tidy sum for a police constable.

A year later, on 28th October 1872, Robert was at the Old Bailey again, this time over a case of theft by one John Connor. At 5:00am on 24th September, Robert was walking a beat which had him entering Hamsell Street, when he heard a suspicious noise and then saw Connor appear from where the sound had come from, carrying a carpenter's basket. Robert stopped him and asked what he had in the basket, receiving the rely: "My tools, I am a carpenter and am going to work over the water." The officer asked for a more detailed description of the tools, and when the items given by Connor failed to match what Robert could see in the basket, he asked the prisoner for his address, being told 131 Upper White Street. Robert then asked Connor to take him to his home, but he was unable to do so, resulting in Robert escorting him to the police station.

---

217 Old Bailey records (t18710501-358).

Mr Henry Snowden later came forward and stated that he had left his tools at Mr Crabb's warehouse on Hamsell Street at 5:30 the previous evening, but when he arrived for work the following morning they were missing.

Connor was found guilty of stealing, and having been convicted of a similar crime in 1870, received a sentence of seven years' penal servitude.[218]

A month later, on 30th November 1872, Robert was awarded 10s for his 'vigilance', and one wonders whether this relates to the arrest of John Connor.

At the Old Bailey on 5th April 1875, Robert appeared to give evidence in a case of theft by James Sexton and John Joyce. The officer had received information which resulted in him visiting Foster's Parcels Delivery Office on Bennett's Hill with City officer Mitchell. They saw Sexton and Joyce, and introduced themselves as police officers. Robert explained that they had information that a case of umbrellas which had been sent to Ipswich had been broken into, and asked if the pair knew anything about it, or a second case found broken into in the basement of the factory.

The two suspects told Robert that they knew nothing of it, but on searching Joyce the officer found three silk handkerchiefs. Asked how he accounted for the items, Joyce claimed that he'd received them from a man named Fowler, but that 'Sexton had them first'. Robert decided to take Joyce to Fleet Street Police Station, where a key was found upon his person and the prisoner admitted that the missing umbrellas could be found at his home at 2 Scarsdale Road, Camberwell, and he had also taken the handkerchiefs.

Robert went to Scarsdale Road, where he found a green box containing two more handkerchiefs, six scarves, ladies gloves, braces, a piece of velvet, 29 linen collars and umbrellas, all of which he took back to Fleet Street Police Station. He showed them all to Joyce, who admitted that he had stolen them all.

Robert then returned to Foster's factory and spoke to James Sexton,

218 Old Bailey records (t18721028-724).

asking whether he had any objection to his home being searched, Sexton said he did not, but after visiting the abode Robert found two handkerchiefs, a ring and an umbrella, all of which Sexton claimed had been given to him by Joyce. Nevertheless he was tried along with his accomplice, and both received five years' penal servitude.[219]

Interestingly, the Old Bailey transcripts record Robert as 'City Detective', but his City of London Police service file states that he did not become a Detective Constable until a year later, on 2nd March 1876. His salary increased to 31s 6d. Amazingly, he was then promoted again, to Detective Sergeant, just eight weeks later on 25th April.[220]

The following year Robert arrested the famous Annie Besant[221] for publishing *The Fruits of Philosophy*, a banned publication written by the American birth control campaigner, Charles Knowlton.

Annie would write:

> Detective-Sergeant R. Outram was the head officer, and he produced his warrant at Mr Bradlaugh's request; he was accompanied by two detective officers, Messrs. Simmons and Williams. He was armed also with a search warrant, a most useful document, seeing that the last copy of the edition (of 5,000 copies) had been sold on the morning of the previous day, and a high pile of orders was accumulating downstairs, orders which we were unable to fulfil.

She continued describing the day, stating:

> We started for the police-station in Bridewell Place, arriving there at 10.25. The officers, who showed us every courtesy and kindness consistent with the due execution of their duty, allowed Mr Bradlaugh and myself to walk on in front, and they followed us across the roar of Fleet Street, down past Ludgate Hill Station, to the Police Office. Here we passed into a fair-sized room, and were requested to go into a funny iron-barred place; it was a large oval railed in, with a brightly polished iron bar running round it, the door closing with a snap. Here we stood while two officers in uniform got out their books; one

---

219 Old Bailey records (t18750405-266).

220 Robert's service record: CLA/048/AD/01 (London Metropolitan Archives).

221 Annie was famous for being involved in union action in the Bloody Sunday riot of 1887 and the Match Girl strike of 1888. She was a prominent socialist, theosophist, women's rights activist, writer, orator and supporter of Irish and Indian self-rule.

of these reminded Mr Bradlaugh of his late visits there, remarking that he supposed the 'gentleman you were so kind to will do you the same good turn now'. Mr Bradlaugh dryly replied that he didn't think so, accepting service and giving it were two very different things. Our examination then began; names, ages, abodes, birth-places, number of children, colour of hair and eyes, were all duly enrolled; then we were measured, and our heights put down; next we delivered up watches, purses, letters, keys--in fact emptied our pockets; then I was walked off by the housekeeper into a neighbouring cell and searched--a surely most needless proceeding; it strikes me this is an unnecessary indignity to which to subject an uncondemned prisoner, except in cases of theft, where stolen property might be concealed about the person. It is extremely unpleasant to be handled, and on such a charge as that against myself a search was an absurdity. The woman was as civil as she could be, but, as she fairly enough said, she had no option in the matter. After this, I went back to the room and re-joined my fellow prisoner and we chatted peaceably with our guardians; they quite recognised our object in our proceedings, and one gave it as his opinion that we ought to have been summoned, and not taken by warrant. Taken, however, we clearly were, and we presently drove on to Guildhall, Mr Outram in the cab with us, and Mr Williams on the box.[222]

The first case at which Robert was called to give evidence at the Old Bailey following his promotion was on 21st October 1878. It was a case of stealing from by Thomas Enness, Samuel Cohen and Cornelius Carey.[223]

Robert had received information from Thomas Enness on 19th September which prompted him to visit Cornelius Carey, whose address was given vaguely as 'a court in the Minories'. Robert told Carey that he was a detective officer, and that Carey was to be charged with receiving two pieces of cloth on Saturday, 14th September 1878.

As Robert was taking his prisoner into custody, Carey stated: 'Me receiving cloth; I have not received cloth'. Robert decided to take him to Cohen's cloth and trimming shop and asked the proprietor whether he had seen the man before, but received a reply in the

222 *Autobiographical Sketches* by Annie Besant (1885).
223 Old Bailey records (t18781021-862).

negative.

However, a sales assistant named Mr Pritchard confirmed that the two pieces of cloth shown to him were indeed the pieces that had gone missing. At this Mr Cohen changed his story: "I will tell the truth, I did have the two pieces of cloth and sold them to him [Carey] and he gave me twelve shillings for them." An argument broke out between the two men, and both were taken to the station.

At court, all three prisoners were found guilty, with Cohen receiving eight years' imprisonment, Carey five years, and because Enness had given up the names of the other two prisoners, he received only two years.

By 1881, the Outram family had moved to 30 Palatine Road, Stoke Newington. Son Robert Jr was now thirteen and going to school.

On 14th September 1885 Robert was again at the Old Bailey, at a case of deception and fraud by a group of men: Paul Klein, Paul Klein Jr, Alexander Grant, Albert Hodder, William Gould and Robert Kitchener.

Their crime was to rent certain premises throughout London, using faked bank letters to convince the landlords that they were trustworthy, then hire furniture to fill these shops, again using fake letters to secure the items. These men would earn money for the short period of time that they were open for business, disappearing when the rent and bills were due at the end of the month.

Robert and City Detective John Mitchell went to 6 Garrick Street, near Covent Garden, armed with a warrant for all the men involved in this scam. The two policemen had been watching the address for two hours, before they saw Paul Klein Jr and his father enter the premises. DS Mitchell knocked on the door and the officers were greeted by Klein Jr, who asked them their business. After explaining they were plainclothes officers with a warrant, he said 'I know nothing of it'. DS Mitchell then asked to see the Klein Sr as they had a warrant for him too, and they were allowed into the front room of the building.

Robert and DS Mitchell were then greeted by Klein Sr and two other men, and his warrant was read out to him. He claimed he had paid all his creditors, handing DS Mitchell a pile of papers as proof. Within the documents was a book containing the names of others involved in the frauds. At this, both Kleins were taken into custody.

As Klein Sr's book recorded the addresses of other premises being used in the scam, Robert was able to visit these and was greeted by the other prisoners, whom Robert also took into custody.

At the trial, Klein Sr, Grant and Hodder were found guilty on all counts, with Klein Sr receiving five years' penal servitude, while Grant and Hodder received two years each.

Klein Jr was also found guilty on all counts, but because of his previous good character received just three months' hard labour. Kitchener and Gould were found guilty on the first, thirteenth and twenty-third counts of conspiracy, Kitchener receiving six months' hard labour and Gould eight.

Within the Old Bailey record of this case it states that 'the court commended DS Mitchell, Outram and other officers', echoed in Robert's service file, which states: '1885 September 29th – Awarded one pound for the creditable manner in which he conducted a case of fraud,' and was signed by the Commissioner of the force.[224]

On the night of 29th September 1888, Robert was with Detectives Halse and Marriott on the corner of Houndsditch by St Botolph's Church, Aldgate, when at 1:58am they received news of a murder that had occurred just a few streets away in Mitre Square.

They all rushed to the scene of the crime, no doubt in total shock that Jack the Ripper had killed just a short distance from where they were, but had escaped. After seeing the body in the light of a policeman's lamp, Detective Halse gave orders for the area to be searched and every man they come across to be examined, and this is what Robert did. He located a man and two women in a lodging house in Spitalfields and took them to the mortuary in an attempt to identify the body. One of the women identified her as 'Mrs Kelly', a

224 Old Bailey records (t18850914-851).
225 *Evening Standard*, 1st October 1888.

name that Catherine sometimes went by.[225]

On 29th September 1890, Robert received his 15% pay rise, making his wage a healthy 56s 6d, and on 13th November that year he was promoted to Detective Inspector. However, according to his service file, there was no increase in pay to accompany this promotion.[226]

In 1891 the Outram family were still living at Palatine Road, Stoke Newington, and Robert Jr, now 24, was still living with his parents and working as a Merchant Clerk.[227]

On 9th January 1893, the Detective Inspector gave evidence at the Old Bailey over a case of deception and fraud by one Alexander Lisber, who had entered the department store of Spiers and Pond on 3rd November 1892. He ordered a cape, returning the next day to order a pair of trousers, saying he was good for the money as he was an inspector of music halls. He stated he would be back on Saturday to try the clothes on, but failed to appear until the Monday, explaining he had been in Brighton.

After trying on the clothes, Lisber seemed pleased and almost walked out of the shop with them until the sales assistant stopped and asked him to make an account with the store. The customer claimed he had already paid the one pound deposit to the manager, but the sales assistant could not find it, so Lisber wrote out a cheque.

When the cheque turned out to be fake, the police were called and on 16th November Robert obtained a warrant for Lisber's arrest. Unable to find him, Robert discovered that he had actually been held at Wormwood Scrubs serving on another conviction. When the prisoner was released on 9th December, Robert read his warrant to him, with Lisber admitting to everything. At the Old Bailey he was sentenced to twelve months' hard labour.[228]

Robert Outram retired from the City of London Police force on

226 Robert's service record: CLA/048/AD/01 (London Metropolitan Archives).
227 1891 census.
228 Old Bailey Records (t18930109-189).
229 Robert's service record: CLA/048/AD/01 (London Metropolitan Archives).

31st January 1895, at the age of 50 years and 4 months. He had given thirty years of service, and received a pension of £99 8s 10d. His record of service was recorded as exemplary.[229]

With the feeling that 'you can never keep a good policeman down,' retirement was not a peaceful life of relaxation for Robert, for in the 1901 census the Outram family are recorded at 97 Alkham Road, Hackney. Robert Jr was still living with his parents at the age of 53 and working as an Accountant, while Robert himself was working as a Private Enquiry Agent.[230]

He died six years later, in the second quarter of 1907, at his home in Hackney.[231]

Edward Marriott: An Air of a Detective

Edward was the third person in plain clothes in the group completed by Detective Halse and Detective Outram that was situated at the corner of Houndsditch by St Botolph's Church in Aldgate when the news reached them of another murder, this time in Mitre Square, only a few yards away from them...

Once again with a policeman's early life story, we as researchers have to put our detective hats on.

On the 1871 census, 'Edward Marriott' cannot be found. But searching with different spellings of both 'Edward' and 'Marriott' we find an 'Edwd Marriot' born in 1862 in Middlesex, living with his mother 'Ann Marriot' (b.1831) and brother 'Samal Marriot' (b.1868) at 48 Havelock Road, Hackney.[232] As Edward's mother was listed as a widow, we will for the moment leave Edward, the future policeman, and try to find his father.

230 1901 census.
231 Death record.
232 1871 census.

Our first port of call is to follow Ann's line further along in the census returns. However, 'Ann Marriot' disappears, but we do have 'Samal Marriot', who would have been thirteen at the time of the next census, if he had not passed away within this ten year period. We can hope that being thirteen he might still be living with his mother, and assume that 'Samal' was actually 'Samuel'.

With this information, in the 1881 census we are able to find a Samuel Marriot, born in the correct year of 1868 and the right place, Hackney. He is stated as son to a widow who was born in 1832 in Middlesex, whose name was recorded not as Ann, but as Annie Marriot.

So on the 1881 census, we have Annie Marriot, a widow living with her four children, Averil (born 1858 in Stratford, Essex) working as Brush Finisher; *Edwin* (born '1864' in Hackney) working as a Plumber's Labourer; Thomas (born 1864 in Hackney) working as a Railway Porter, and finally Samuel (born 1868 in Hackney) working as a Shoemaker's Assistant. The family were living at 108 Morning Lane, Hackney, East London.[233]

However, 'there are difficulties, but then there are always difficulties...'[234] first of all, where is Edward? Well, we have an *Edwin* Marriot, could this be him? A look at the original document of the 1881 census return, does show that the transcription of 'Edwin' might not actually be correct, as there does seem to be an incomplete letter 'd' at the end. Also on the original document, we can see that the transcribed 'Averil' is actually 'Annie'. The enumerator appears to have made Thomas and Edwin twins, almost certainly another mistake, for there is no birth record of an Edwin Marriot born in 1864.

By 1891 we know that Edward had moved away, as mentioned shortly, but where was the rest of his family? Thomas had married and moved away from London due to his work as a railway porter.

---

233 1881 census.

234 A quote from Sherlock Holmes in *The Sign of Four* by Sir Arthur Conan Doyle (1890).

235 1891 census.

He was living in 1891 in Red Cross Street, Brighton, with his wife Isabella (born in 1861 in Brighton) and his children Thomas (b.1888) and Edmund (b.1890), both children having been born in Brighton.[235]

Brother Samuel had also moved away from his mother, having married Louisa (born in 1869 in Twickenham). They were living at Ludwick Road, Greenwich, with Samuel working as a Dining Room Manager.[236]

The daughter, 'Annie', had married George Ventham (born in 1860 in Islington), who was a House Decorator, interestingly so because Annie was at one time a Brush Finisher. In 1891 they were living at Church Road, Hackney, and had one child, a daughter also called Annie (born in 1884 in Hackney).[237]

However, also living with the Ventham family in 1891 was George's mother-in-law, an 'Anna Marriott', a widow, born in 1831 in Hackney.[238] So, in the space of 30 years, Edward's mother goes from being 'Ann' to 'Annie' and finally 'Anna'.

Returning to our original mission of finding Edward's father, we are now therefore looking for a man whose surname was Marriott or Marriot who married a woman with a variation of those first names.

What could be a difficult task is made easier by using the birth year of Edward's sister Annie, 1858, and the fact that his mother was born in 1831. We have a window of between 1848 to 1858 in which it would be reasonable to assume that the marriage of Edward's parents took place. Victorians are known to have followed the tradition of naming their first son after the father, so is it possible that an Edward Marriott or Marriot married an Ann, Annie or Anna between 1848 and 1858?

A search brings only one couple to light, an Edward Marriott who married Anna Lane in the second quarter of 1854 and adding to

236 1891 census.
237 Ibid.
238 Ibid.
239 Marriage record.

the likelihood that that this could be Edward's parents is the fact that this couple were married in Hackney, East London, where the mother and all the children with the exception of Annie were born.[239]

With this information, can we take it a step further back and locate in the 1861 census an Edward Marriot or Marriott, married to an Ann, Annie or Anna who was born in 1831/32 in Hackney, with a daughter called Annie born in 1858 in Stratford?

The answer is yes. Living at 11 Greenwood Row, South Hackney, East London is Edward Marriot, born in 1831 in Hackney, working as a labourer, with his wife Annie Marriot, born in 1832, also in Hackney. There is a daughter called Elizabeth Marriot, born in 1859 in Bow, but more importantly to us there is another daughter, Annie, born in 1858 in Thetford, Essex. A close look at the original document reveals that the transcription of 'Thetford' is wrong, and the entry is actually Stratford.[240]

This presents two issues which need resolving: what happened to Elizabeth Marriot, for she does not appear on the 1871 census? Sadly, she died in the last quarter in 1861, after that year's census was taken.[241] Secondly, did this Edward Marriott Sr die between the birth of the youngest child Samuel and the 1871 census, when Anna was recorded as a widow? Sadly, again the answer is yes, for Edward Marriott's father passed away in the third quarter of 1868, in Whitechapel.[242]

We now have the complete story of Edward, the future policeman's beginnings. His parents married in 1854, and four years later this couple have their first child, who they named Annie after the mother. Sadly, Elizabeth, the second child, died at just two-years-old, and then Edward Jr was born in 1861. Thomas, Edward's younger brother, is missing from the 1871 census, but he returns ten years later and by 1891 has married and moved away. Samuel was born in 1868, the same year Edward's father died.

240 1861 census.
241 Death record.
242 Death record.

Edward Marriott Jr became a plumber's labourer, only to have a change of career by 1885.

Between April and June of that year Edward worked for a Mr Joseph Wilman, a builder of Wilman Road, with Edward employed as an engine driver.[243] It was also around this time that he married Emily Jones in Hackney.[244]

Edward joined the City of London Police on 13th July 1885, at the age of 21, and of course because he was already married he did not go into a police residence.[245]

He was certified fit of service for the force on 11th September 1885 on a wage of 25s, and was awarded warrant number 5830 and collar number 860.[246] At the time of his application, Edward and his wife were living 55 Balls Pond Road, London.[247]

Edward's former employer, Mr Wilman, was one of his references and he gave a satisfactory record. The other references were Mr Jones, a chimney sweep of Prout Road, Upper Clapton, who stated that Edward was a 'highly respectable young man', Rev. Shelford, Vicar of St Matthew's Church, Upper Clapton, and also Mr Sentland, a builder of 67 Church Road, who stated 'known him since childhood to the present time and believes him to be a sober, honest and respectable man'.[248]

On 16th September 1886, Edward was promoted to Second Class Constable with a rise in wages to 28s.[249]

On 22nd November 1886, Edward was at the Old Bailey giving evidence in a case of coining offences by Henry Devenish aged only seventeen. Henry had entered a cook's shop at 19 and 20 Aldgate on

---

243 Edward's service file for the City of London Police: CLA/048/AD/01/478 (held at the London Metropolitan Archives).

244 Marriage record.

245 Edward's service file: CLA/048/AD/01/478.

246 Edward's collar number changed throughout the years as recorded in his service file; in addition to 860 he had 628 and 386, ending on 1137.

247 Edward's service file: CLA/048/AD/01/478.

248 Ibid.

249 Ibid.

19th October and had some tea, which he paid for. He then asked the waiter, John Beck, if he had change for half a crown and passed over a shilling. The waiter gave him the change and Henry walked out of the shop. It was only afterwards that the waiter noticed the shilling Henry had given him was bad. The waiter then separated the bad coin from the rest of the change.

Devenish later used the same shop to buy some sausage and bread from Mr Peter Matzoni, paying with another bad shilling. Mr Matzoni noticed the bad coin and went to his boss, a Mr Joseph Nana, who called in the police, while preventing the crook from leaving the shop. PC Edward Marriott answered that call, and was told by Mr Nana: "I will have this man locked up for passing this two shilling bit, last Saturday, he also passed a bad shilling to one of my chaps." Edward then asked the prisoner what he had to say about this, receiving the reply, "I carried a gentleman's parcel this morning and he gave me that, I was not near the place Saturday." Edward escorted him to the nearest police station, and at the trial Henry Devenish was found guilty but strongly recommended to mercy by the jury on account of his youth, at which judgment was respited.[250]

In 1887, Edward's first child was born in Aldgate, named Emily after her mother.[251]

On 2nd June 1888 Edward was awarded a one pound reward for 'apprehending a notorious receiver of stolen goods.'[252]

Edward's role in the Jack the Ripper investigation is an interesting one, not so much for what he did, but because of his rank at the time. He is often described as Detective Constable Edward Marriott, which may seem normal to students of the case as he was indeed a Detective Constable by the time he ended his career, but his service file held at the London Metropolitan Archives states that he didn't officially become a Detective Constable until 21st January 1904. In fact, Edward was not even a First Class Constable until 14th

---

250 Old Bailey records (t18861122-34).
251 Birth record.
252 Edward's service file: CLA/048/AD/01/478.

May 1896, which means that he was not a 'detective' by certified standards in 1888. Yet, we students of the case generally think of him as such.

How can this be? Well, it doesn't help that Detective Daniel Halse was quoted as saying at the inquest that he was 'in company with Detectives Outram and Marriott',[253] which was picked up by several newspapers.

Edward raced to Mitre Square with Daniel Halse and Robert Outram, and saw the dreadful sight of Catherine Eddowes' body. That would be the extent of his involvement as he was not asked to appear at the inquest.

On 4th February 1889, Edward was at court over a case of theft by Mary Ann O'Connor, who stole a watch chain and medal from Mr Atkins Smith, the landlord of the Britannia public house on Bishopsgate.

On 24th January at 11:00pm, O'Connor went into the Britannia and demanded to be served. However, Mr Smith thought she had drunk enough already and refused her. He tried to take her outside, but she struggled and then laid down on the floor. After picking her up and placing her by the door, Mr Smith noticed his watch chain was gone, so he told someone to hold her while he went for the police.

Edward was walking his beat along Bishopsgate when he saw O'Connor burst out of the public house, running down the street with people shouting 'Stop thief!' The officer stopped her and brought her back to the Britannia, and while searching her heard the chain fall to the floor.

Amazingly, Mary Ann O'Connor was found not guilty, probably due to the fact that she was very drunk and the item had been returned to Mr Smith within moments of it being taken.[254]

On 12th May 1889, Edward was in trouble himself through drink, when he was found drunk on duty in plain clothes while taking

---

253 *The Daily Telegraph*, 12th October 1888.

254 Old Bailey Records (t18890204-208).

255 Edward's service file: CLA/048/AD/01/478.

an improper charge to a Metropolitan Police station in R Division. Edward was severely reprimanded and given a caution, and ordered to pay a fine of 1s 6d.[255]

On 29th September 1890, Edward received his 15% pay rise, bringing his wage to 32s 2d. On the 1891 census, seven months later, the Marriott family were recorded as living in Spital Square, Spitalfields,[256] and had a new addition, a boy named Samuel not yet a year old.[257] The child was registered in Bishopsgate, most likely because it was easier for Edward, it being on his way to work.[258] Sadly, Samuel died the following year in Bethnal Green.[259]

On 18th September 1892, Edward was cautioned for allowing the escape of a young man who had broken into a shop. This caution did not affect his future work, for just a month later, on 29th October, Edward received another reward of one pound, this time for intelligence in dealing with a marine store dealer. It is interesting to note that this reward was given to Edward by the Commissioner of the Metropolitan Police force - another example of the two forces working together going against the grain of the myth that they never worked well together.[260]

On 18th May 1893, Edward returned to his Second Class Constable rank. After his 15% pay rise and the new level on constables were introduced, his wage was now 34s.[261]

Edward was reduced in rank to Third Class Constable on 14th May 1894, also losing two shillings from his pay, because he had received money from a woman in his custody. He was seen drinking with the same woman in several public houses after her discharge by the magistrate. As a further punishment, he was also put back into

---

256   1891 census.
257   Presumably after Edward's brother.
258   Birth record.
259   Death record.
260   Edward's service file: CLA/048/AD/01/478.
261   Ibid.
262   Ibid.
263   Birth record.

uniform.[262] One wonders what his wife thought of this, especially as she had given birth to another child at this time, a son named Charles.[263]

However, a year and two days later, on 16th May 1895, Edward was returned to the rank of Second Class Constable, and on 14th May 1896 was promoted to First Class Constable with a salary of 36s 3d.[264] The extra money had certainly come at the right time, for his wife gave birth to another child in this year, a daughter named Evelina.[265]

On 20th January 1898, Edward was pardoned for being 45 minutes late at a 5:45am muster. One wonders what the case was, and why Edward was late, but sadly his service file does not go into any detail.[266]

It is interesting to note that the first mention of Edward officially being 'appointed to Plain Clothes Patrol' within his service file was on 1st July 1898, but Edward certainly had had moments in his career where he was in plain clothes, as previously mentioned. His rate of pay at this time was 41s 3d.[267]

On 31st October 1899, Edward was commended for his 'energy and prudence' in the arrest of a woman for larceny from children,[268] and on 24th December 1901 he was commended by the Acting Commissioner of the City force, for his 'intelligence, detecting and arresting' three men for larceny from a warehouse.[269]

Again, any extra money was timed well as in 1899 Edward's wife had given birth to their fifth child, who they officially named George,[270] but who may not have been referred to as such at home, as discussed later. He was the first of their children to be registered

264 Edward's service file: CLA/048/AD/01/478.
265 Birth record. She was recorded as 'Eva' in the 1901 census.
266 Edward's service file: CLA/048/AD/01/478.
267 Ibid.
268 Ibid.
269 Ibid.
270 Birth record.

in Hackney, and as the Marriott family were living in Hackney by the time of the 1901 census, one wonders if they had actually moved to the area by 1899.

On the 1901 census, the family were living at 30 Terrace Road, Hackney, with yet another addition, Edward Jr.[271]

As stated in his service file, due to 're-organization' Edward was finally promoted to the rank of *Detective* Constable on 21st January 1904, with a salary of 45s.[272]

He was again at the Old Bailey on 13th September 1904, over a case of theft and simple larceny by Thomas Allen. On 19th August a porter named Frank Dickenson, working for Waterson and Sons on St. Bride Street, left his truck briefly while he went inside a warehouse on White Street and upon his return found a man called Middleton lifting a parcel out of the back of the truck. The thief turned and walked across the road, disappearing down a court. Mr Dickenson followed, and arriving in the court saw another man, Thomas Allen. The cab driver managed to grab hold of Middleton and thought that Allen would help him, but instead the other man turned on Mr Dickenson. After a struggle Allen fled, but Mr Dickenson still managed to hang on to Middleton and take him to a police station.

Detective Edward Marriott saw Thomas Allen in custody at Bethnal Green Police Station on 1st September, the latter having been arrested by the Metropolitan Police on another matter. Edward took the prisoner to Moor Lane Police Station in the City for his part in assisting Middleton with the theft of the parcel, and he was subjected to an identity parade. He was immediately picked out of the line up by Frank Dickenson, but at the trial several witnesses swore that Thomas Allen was at the King's Arms on Pritchard's Road at the time of the robbery, so he was found not guilty and released.[273]

On 18th September 1907, Edward was again commended, this

---

271 1901 census.
272 Edward's service file: CLA/048/AD/01/478.
273 Old Bailey records (t19040913-643).
274 Edward's service file: CLA/048/AD/01/478.

time by the Commissioner of the City Police, for 'praiseworthy conduct in arresting three men for a warehouse breaking.'[274]

Less happily, a year later, on 6th November 1908, Edward was on duty when he received an injury which caused him to suffer epileptic fits. He was sent to the police surgeon, whose report to the Commissioner dated 21st April 1909 declared Edward unfit for service, and to retire him.[275]

The incident causing the injury was recorded in Edward's service file. On 6th November 1908 he was with Detective Sergeant Digby, walking along Basinghall Street, when he was knocked down by a horse and cart driven by Henry William Martin[276] which hit him in the chest, and as he fell down he had hit his head on the road. An ambulance was called and Edward was taken straight to Bishopsgate Police Hospital, suffering from 'concussion of the brain' and a grazed elbow. He was discharged from hospital on 19th November 1908.[277]

On 2nd March 1909, Edward was back at work and at the Old Bailey giving evidence in a case of theft and embezzlement by Annie Cleverley, a 33-year-old waitress at Mr Henry Crane's restaurant at 35 Barbican. Mr Arthur Watson, the manager of the restaurant, gave Annie a cheque for eight pounds, asking her to cash it at a nearby bank. This she did, but failed to return with the money.

She was arrested and brought to Lambeth Police Court on a different matter for stealing clothes, but Edward was able to re-arrest her as she was coming out of that court on 11th February. When told the reason why, Annie claimed: 'When I came out of the bank someone knocked up against me and it [the money] fell into the road.' The excuse did her no good: she was found guilty and sentenced to six months' imprisonment.[278]

275 Edward's service file: CLA/048/AD/01/478.

276 Sometimes recorded as just William Martin, several witnesses stated he was driving recklessly.

277 Edward's service file: CLA/048/AD/01/478.

278 Old Bailey record (t19090302-15).

279 Edward's service file: CLA/048/AD/01/478.

On 21st March 1909, Edward had a fit at home, and eight days later had two attacks in the street.[279] He was found lying unconscious on the pavement in Redcross Street on 29th March at 12:15pm by PC 374 Henry, who with PC 382 Night carried Edward to the local police station,[280] from where he was taken by ambulance to St Bart's Hospital. Edward was there seen by the House Surgeon, who stated that he had just recovered from an epileptic fit, and allowed him to leave the hospital.[281]

PC 32 Redwood took Edward from Bart's to Bishopsgate Police Hospital, where he was seen by City Police Surgeon Dr Frederick Gordon Brown. The reason they had not taken him straight to Dr Brown was because they didn't think the Divisional Surgeon would have been at the police hospital before 1:00pm.[282]

Edward was retired 'unfit' on 6th May 1909, with a pension of £78 5s 4d and a certificate stating that his conduct had been 'very good'. He was 47-years-old, his height recorded as 5ft 10in and he had grey eyes with brown hair.[283]

However, retirement seemed to not be for Edward, because on 30th October 1909 the City of London Police received a letter from the Keeper of the Guildhall explaining that that the former detective had applied for a temporary role, possibly as a Time Keeper, the profession he was recorded as having on the 1911 census, and a reference was requested as to his trustworthiness.[284]

On the 1911 census, the Marriott family were living at 34 Albert Road, Ilford, son Charles working as a Draper's Porter and daughter Evelina as a Confectioner's Shop Assistant.

This census entry is interesting for three reasons, firstly because a 'Matilda Marriott' appeared on this census as Edward's daughter,

---

280 Which particular station is not mentioned in the report, although it was probably Bishopsgate Police Station because of its proximity to Red Cross Street and Bishopsgate Police Hospital.

281 Edward's service file: CLA/048/AD/01/478.

282 Ibid.

283 Ibid.

284 Ibid.

born in 1897 in Hackney. However, there is no birth record of this Matilda, nor does she appear in the previous census or the special census taken in 1939. However, that is not to say she didn't exist, because being a female her surname could have changed through marriage. A search of grave records between 1911 and 1980 shows one Matilda Marriott, who was buried in Nottingham in 1919. Whether this is Edward Marriott's daughter is uncertain.

Also strangely on the 1911 census return, 'Stanley Marriott' and 'Reggie Marriott' appear in Edward's household. Their ages and place of birth are the same as George and Edward Marriott given on the previous census, and there are no birth records for either 'Stanley' or 'Reggie'. How 'Stanley' can become a nickname for 'George', or 'Reggie' can replace 'Edward' is a mystery, although as the 1911 census was the first to be completed by the head of the household rather than the enumerator, could Edward have written the nicknames of his two youngest children? He was not a well man - did he get confused?

Edward Marriott died in Romford in the third quarter of 1916 at the age of 55.[285] In his service file is a letter to the City of London Police dated 19th August 1923 from his daughter, Miss Evelyn (Evelina) Marriott, who asked whether her mother, Emily, was entitled to the widows' fund after Edward's passing in July 1917. The reply to this letter, dated 28th August 1923, explains that Emily was not entitled as 'only widows of members serving in the force on or after the 1st September 1918 are entitled.'[286]

Detective Baxter Hunt:
I Discovered the Pensioner Conway Belonging to the 18th Royal Irish.[287]

Baxter Hunt's involvement with the investigation into the death of Catherine Eddowes was that he was called to the murder scene, and

---

285 Death record.

286 Edward's service file: CLA/048/AD/01/478.

287 Baxter's statement at Catherine Eddowes inquest, reported in the *Daily News* of 12 October 1888.

therefore one of the few men who saw the body of this poor woman as she was left by the killer. He was one of the very few men who actually saw the now famous message on the wall in Goulston Street before it was washed off. He was also the detective who sought out the former partner of Catherine...

Born in North Witchford, Cambridge, in the last quarter of 1845,[288] Baxter was the third child to be born to Baxter Sr, a blacksmith,[289] and Alice Hunt.[290] He appears not to have been baptised. His siblings were Mary Ann (b.1842) and Nathan (b.1844). One imagines the Baxter Jr did not get to know his father, who died in the last quarter of 1847, being buried on 3rd February 1848.[291]

On the 1851 census the Hunt family were living at Church End, March in Cambridgeshire. This is the first census on which Baxter Hunt appears, at the age of five. It seems at first that Baxter disappears by the 1861 census, as he does not emerge on any record. We know he did not pass away, and being a male his surname would not have changed had he married, so how can this be? What can we do to solve this problem?

Searching the 1861 census for Baxter's mother, we find Alice Hunt recorded as a widow, now aged 48. She had moved to Whittle End, March, and was working as a Charwoman. Living with her were son Nathan aged seventeen, who was working on the local farms as an Agricultural Labourer, and another young male listed as her son, also working as an Agricultural Labourer. This 15-year-old was recorded as 'Buster', obviously a mistake on the part of the census enumerator, who probably misheard the name given to him verbally.[292]

288 Birth Record.

289 1841 census. Baxter Hunt Sr was born in 1811 in Cambridgeshire.

290 Alice was born in 1813, also in Cambridgeshire. Before Baxter Jr was born, the family were living at Doddington Mill, North Witchford, Cambridgeshire.

291 Birth and death records.

292 1861 census.

293 Baxter's City of London Police service file: CLA/048/AD/01/360 (held at the London Metropolitan Archives).

By March 1866 Baxter had moved to London and joined the Metropolitan Police force, in which he stayed for one year and five months. He left on 4th July 1867,[293] and just eighteen days later, on 23rd July, joined the City of London Police. He is described on his application as being 21-years-old, 5ft 9in tall, with grey eyes and brown hair. He was single and living at 4 Commercial Road, Lambeth, at the time of his application.[294] This address was within the Metropolitan Police district, no doubt because of his previous employment, and one can imagine that this soon changed once Baxter was accepted into the City Police.

On 3rd October 1867 Baxter was classed as 'fit for service' and given warrant number 4088, with a wage of 21s. Just over a year later, on 4th November 1868, he was advanced to Second Class Constable, with his salary increased to 24s. He was promoted to First Class Constable on 2nd June 1870 with a rate of pay of 28s.[295]

An appearance at the Old Bailey on 2nd May 1870 gives us Baxter's collar number - 559 - for on this day he gave evidence in a case of pickpocketing by Mary Jones, Charles Johnson and Edward Beech.

At 1:30 in the morning of 31st March, City PC 461 William Simmons was in Fleet Street when he saw Mary Jones stop and speak with a number of men, always with Johnson and Beech standing nearby.

Eventually she spoke with a Mr Thomas Saunders, who was about to hail a cab but was taken by the arm by Mary Jones and led away into New Bridge Street, followed at a distance by her accomplices and PC Simmons, unnoticed in plain clothes. Jones led Mr Saunders as far as Blackfriars Bridge, then onto William Street, where, after a couple of minutes of conversation, she coughed twice loudly, an obvious signal for Beech and Johnson. PC Simmons, who had been sitting on a nearby window sill watching, intervened at this and took Jones by both wrists, saying that he believed she had just robbed Mr Saunders.

The prisoner struggled, so PC Simmons called for assistance. City

294 Baxter's service file: CLA/048/AD/01/360.
295 Ibid.

Police Sergeant John Gellatlt had seen Charles Johnson and Edward Beech on the corner of William Street, and at PC Simmons' alarm apprehended both.

Simmons searched Mary Jones and found a watch and chain in her pocket, which Mr Saunders confirmed were his. He later admitted to being quite drunk and had not noticed the items being stolen.

Baxter Hunt was called to testify that he had previously watched the thieves - on 8th March 1870 - for two hours on Cannon Street, confirming a connection between the prisoners.

Mary Jones received fifteen months' imprisonment and Johnson nine months, while Beech received seven years' penal servitude because of four previous convictions.[296]

By the time of the 1871 census, Baxter was living in the police station at 172 Great St Thomas, in the City of London.[297] This police house accommodated many police officers who worked at Cloak Lane Police Station, including Daniel Halse. In fact, on the census record Daniel's name sits just one entry above Baxter's.

On 4th September 1873, Baxter was rewarded one pound for his 'energy and tact in watching suspected persons' by Commissioner Sir James Fraser.[298]

On 2nd March 1874, he was in the Old Bailey over a theft by David Peck from his master, Charles William Meiter.

Mr Meiter was an India rubber manufacturer with a warehouse at 87 Gracechurch Street. David Peck, an employee at the warehouse, had been discovered committing a number of embezzlements from the firm's accounts over a period of time.

City Detective Robert Outram was called to the warehouse by Mr Meiter and took Peck into custody. He was charged at the Royal Exchange with stealing some pouches.

Baxter, appearing on behalf of the police, answered a question

---

296 Old Bailey records (t18700502-415).

297 1871 census.

298 Baxter's service file: CLA/048/AD/01/360.

299 Old Bailey records (t18740302-203).

from the prisoner by saying: 'Mr Meiter said you were a thief and had been robbing him.' Peck denied any involvement of stealing money, and was found not guilty.[299]

On 23rd November 1874, Baxter was again in court over a case of breaking and entering and burglary by one Richard Clark.

On the morning of 31st October 1874, City PC 170 Thomas Hickmore was in Gresham Street when he saw a light burning at a window of nearby 114 Wood Street, a counting house. He caught the attention of a beat constable and rang the bell of the next door building, waking the housekeeper.

PC Hickmore sent for Sergeant Honister, who arrived with Baxter, who searched number 114, having entered the building from the roof of the next door property, and then climbed through a window. He had found Clark on the second floor staircase, covered by a canvas. When Baxter told the prisoner to get up there was no response, and, being grabbed in order to get him to his feet, the prisoner exclaimed 'Wait a moment, I am asleep and very queer'.

On searching the prisoner, Baxter found 40 skeleton keys, three screwdrivers, a hand chisel, a centre punch, a hammer, a hand vice, a file, a piece of candle and many matches.

The safe had been opened, and marks on the door matched the tools found upon the prisoner. He was taken into custody, and at the trial received six months' imprisonment.[300]

On 4th April 1875, Baxter married Mary Jane Sayer (b.1836) in Bromley, Kent.[301]

On 1st March 1879, Baxter became a Detective Constable, with his rate of pay being 31s 6d. He would remain at this rank until three months after the murder of Catherine Eddowes.[302]

On 5th August 1879, Baxter was giving evidence at the Old Bailey, in the trial of Frederick Anderson and James Miles, who had stolen

---

300 Old Bailey records (t18741123-29).
301 Marriage record.
302 Baxter's service file: CLA/048/AD/01/360.

16 dozen bottles of Eno's fruit salt on 4th June 1879 from Edward Mountsteven Wright, their employer at Barclay and Son, a wholesale chemists and druggists.

Arthur Matthews, a bricklayer's labourer working on the rebuilding of Anderton's Hotel, had on several occasions passed the rear delivery door of the company on Fleet Lane while going for his meal breaks, and had observed suspicious activity with a number of parcels being removed by Frederick Anderson and James Miles.

As a result the police were informed, and Baxter Hunt visited Arthur on 5th June, the labourer taking the detective to the delivery door at 8:25am. Baxter watched the prisoner Miles, dressed like a porter, acting suspiciously, and returned five days later with Detective Parsons.

Baxter followed Miles to the end of Fleet Lane, where he left Detective Parsons watching the suspect and then walked to the other end of the lane in Ludgate Hill, which took him around three minutes. He met Miles walking towards him, carrying a parcel.

The detective explained that he was a police officer and asked Miles where he was going, receiving the reply 'to my master at 18a Giltspur Street.' Baxter's next question, who gave Miles the parcel he was carrying, was met with the unsatisfactory response 'a man'.

At this, Miles was taken into custody and two dozen bottles of Eno's fruit salt was found on his person. Baxter visited the prisoner's home at 11 Haig Street, Bethnal Green Road, where he discovered more bottles of the same. On being asked about these, Miles admitted that he had stolen them, with the assistance of Anderson. At the trial, both were imprisoned for twelve months.[303]

In the 1881 census Baxter was classed as a Detective and his wife a housekeeper, the couple living at 21 Cannon Street. A few months later, on 23rd July, Baxter was awarded another pound for 'detecting and apprehending two men for stealing goods from doorways', and on 1st March the following year received another reward of a pound

303   Old Bailey records (t18790805-707).
304   Baxter's service file: CLA/048/AD/01/360.

for 'detecting and apprehending a man robbing children in the streets'.[304]

On 28th July 1884, Baxter was once again at the Old Bailey for a case of theft by Horace Forancisco. At the Farringdon Hotel, on 10th July, the prisoner had asked for a glass of gin and then handed over half a sovereign, which he later asked to be returned if the barmaid would accept some silver instead. This was a scam known as 'ringing the changes', because the silver offered was either too light in weight or a fake.

When the manager overheard what was happening he called in the police, and Baxter arrived quickly enough to be able to follow Forancisco as he left the hotel and arrested him. The criminal received two years' hard labour.[305]

On 20th April 1885, Baxter was a witness at a case of theft by Solomon Garcia aged 67, who had stolen some 310 boxes of cigars from the warehouse of Herbert Grattan on Jewry Street.

The cigars were noticed as missing on 11th March. Nine days later, one of the firm's travelling salesman, a man named Edward Oram, was in the Horse and Leaping Bar public house in Whitechapel collecting on the account his company had with the landlord, a Mr March, when he saw a box of the same brand of cigars behind the bar. While asking the landlord about this, he saw Garcia enter with a parcel under his arm. Ironically, Garcia then took Mr Oram to one side and open the parcel in front of him, offering two boxes of cigars for 50s. Mr Oram purchased the two boxes and left them with Mr March and went to inform the police.

Baxter Hunt had already been assigned to the case, and on the morning that the theft had been discovered had visited the warehouse. On the first floor entrance he found some jemmy marks, suggesting that a break-in had taken place.

On receiving the two boxes of cigars from Mr Oram on the 20th, he compared them to those at the warehouse and, quite happy that they were from the some batch, waited at Mr March's public house

305   Old Bailey records (t18840728-793).

for Solomon Garcia, who walked in at 7:00pm.

He was questioned by Baxter and admitted that he had sold the boxes to Mr March and Mr Oram, and was taken into custody. He claimed that he had not stolen the cigars from the warehouse, but had bought them from another man at the Ship public house on Anthony Street, Commercial Road, and at the trial the landlord of that establishment confirmed the story. The jury decided that although Mr Garcia had bought and sold the cigars, there was no evidence that he had known the cigars to be stolen, and was found not guilty.[306]

On 11th June 1885, Baxter received another award of one pound, for his 'vigilance in re-apprehending J. Oxley who had escaped from prison', the award being made by the Commissioner.[307] This was not the last of his bonus pay that year, for exactly one month later, on 11th July 1885, Baxter received a further three pounds for 'assisting to trace and arrest Mr W. Vale and others for a warehouse breaking.' The size of the reward was suggested by the Council of Aldermen.[308]

On 31st January 1887, Baxter was in the courts again over another case of theft, this time by one Henry Fowler. He had stolen a coat and other goods from Evan Humphreys, a medical student who lived at 14 Ella Road, Crouch Hill.

He had visited the Birkbeck Literary and Scientific Institution on Chancery Lane on 11th January, spending two hours there, and had placed his coat on the third hook, close to the door.

Mr Humphreys had seen Fowler enter the building at 3:30pm, and noticed that he was wearing a black coat but no overcoat. Mr Humphreys took no more notice of the man and carried on reading, but at 4:00pm left the room for five minutes to get another book and on his return noticed that Fowler had gone, and so had his coat.

Baxter was called in and, after obtaining information, staked out

306 Old Bailey records (t18850420-486).
307 Baxter's service file: CLA/048/AD/01/360.
308 Ibid.
309 Old Bailey record (t18870131-239).

the Birkbeck Institute and waited for the thief to reappear. After spotting him, Baxter arrested him and took him into custody. At the trial Henry Fowler was sentenced to six months' hard labour.[309]

Detective Baxter Hunt's involvement in the investigation into the murder of Catherine Eddowes was very similar to Detective Daniel Halse's, his former fellow lodger at St Thomas the Apostle. He went with Detective Halse and Constable Marriott to Mitre Square, and conducted searches of the nearby area. He eventually went with Detective Halse to Leman Street Police Station,[310] where they heard of developments in Goulston Street.

Baxter left Detective Halse at Goulston Street while he returned to Mitre Square, in order to tell his superior Chief Inspector James McWilliam about the apron piece and to ask whether the message on the wall should be photographed. McWilliam confirmed that it should, and while a photographer was sent for Baxter returned to Goulston Street to tell Detective Halse and the Metropolitan Police officers at the scene. As we have seen, before the photographer could arrive the Met's Commissioner, Sir Charles Warren, ordered the removal of the chalk writing, despite the protests of the City detectives.[311]

Baxter's involvement in the case did not end there, for it was he who was tasked with locating Thomas Conway, Catherine Eddowes' former partner, with whom she had had three children. Catherine's sisters told the detective that Conway was a member of the 18th Royal Irish Regiment, and although a man of that name belonging to the regiment was found, the sisters were unable to confirm it was the same man that had been Catherine's companion. Baxter continued to try to find him,[312] but following newspaper reports of the inquest stating the detective's difficulty in locating the man, Thomas Conway came forward himself.

---

310 A Metropolitan Police station, but although the apron piece was found at Goulston Street in the Met's H Division, it related to City investigation and the City Detectives were therefore informed of the discovery.

311 Inquest testimony of City Detective Daniel Halse.

312 *Freeman's Journal and Daily Commercial Advertiser*, 12th October 1888.

Around this time, Baxter was actually grieving in his private life, as the death records show that his wife Mary Jane died in the last quarter of 1888.[313] It is a reminder that all those mentioned in this book were not just policemen, machines trying to catch a serial killer, but were real people with real lives.

Despite this personal tragedy, Baxter's career had to continue and around the same time of his wife's death he found himself promoted to Detective Sergeant on 6th December 1888, with a rate of pay of fifty shillings.[314]

On 30th May 1890, Baxter married again, this time to Abigail Asplin[315] in Westmorland, Kendal, at St Mary's Church, in front of Abigail's brother John Asplin and Jane Robinson.[316] The couple lived at Alfred Buildings, Cartwright Street, St Botolph-without-Aldgate.[317]

On 29th September 1890, Baxter received his 15% pay rise, so that he was now earning 57s 6d. Six weeks later, on 13th November, he was promoted to Detective Inspector at the age of 44.

On 12th December 1892, Baxter was at the Old Bailey again, explaining his involvement in a case of theft by William Collins, who had stolen a coat and handkerchief from Mr Joseph Birnie Low.

At 3:00pm on 3rd November, Mr Low had entered his place of work at the Clydesdale Bank at 30 Lombard Street. He headed downstairs to the basement, where he hung up his coat, with a handkerchief in one of its pockets. At 4:45pm Mr Low returned to the basement and noticed that his coat was missing.

A messenger at the bank, a Mr William John Copper, saw William Collins in the basement at 3:30pm, leaning against the front door. Mr Copper did not see Collins take anything.

Two weeks later, on 19th November, Detective Inspector Baxter Hunt was called to another bank on Lombard Street, that of Messrs.

---

313 Death record.
314 Baxter's service file: CLA/048/AD/01/360.
315 Born in 1856 in Bluntisham, Hampshire.
316 Marriage certificate within Baxter's service file: CLA/048/AD/01/360.
317 1891 census.

Glyn, Mills and Co. When he arrived he found that William Collins had been detained by the manager, a Mr Harvey, who stated:

> This man has been in our house three times this morning, twice on the second floor and once on the ground floor, at the top of the steps leading to the basement.

Collins claimed he was hanging around the bank because he had been sent to get some money for a Mr Williamson, but he had been unable to find the person he was meant to speak to. He was searched, and the handkerchief belonging to Mr Low was found on his person. At the trial, Collins admitted committing a similar offence in April 1887, in the name of Ryland, and was sentenced to five years' penal servitude. For the present case, he had nine previous convictions taken into account and received a further three years' penal servitude.[318]

On 28th May 1894, Baxter gave evidence in a case of forgery at the Old Bailey, committed by John Russell aged 61 and Benjamin Benjie aged 75. Both had attempted to secure large amounts of money by selling their supposed interest in forged land registry documents, and were eventually arrested by Baxter on 13th March. Both were found guilty, and because of previous convictions, Russell received five years' penal servitude and Benjie four.[319]

Detective Inspector Baxter Hunt retired from the City force on 12th September 1895, after twenty eight years' service. He was awarded a pension of £98 18s 10d, and his certificate of service was recorded as 'Exemplary'.[320]

By 1896, Baxter had three sons by Abigail, James B Hunt,[321] Sydney W Hunt[322] and John R Hunt.[323] By this time, the family had moved to

---

318 Old Bailey records (t18921212-106).

319 Old Bailey records (t18940528-508).

320 Baxter's service file: CLA/048/AD/01/360.

321 Born in 1892 in London.

322 Born in 1893 in London.

323 Born in 1896 in Ambleside, Westmorland.

324 1901 census.

Compston Road, Ambleside, Kendal.[324]

However, even though Baxter had retired from the City of London Police force, he was still of good health and he played cricket for the force against Reading Borough Police in June 1899, turning out alongside another retired officer, George Izzard. Baxter chipped in with thirty runs for the City of London Police.[325]

On the 1911 census, Baxter was described as a Police Pensioner and Old Clerk aged 65, with Abigail now 55. They were still living at the same address as given in the previous census, and all three sons were still living at home. James was now aged nineteen and working as a joiner's apprentice; Sydney, 18, and John, 15, were both employed as draper's apprentices.

Baxter Hunt died on 17th October 1924, at the age of 79.[326] He passed away at his home in Compston Road, Ambleside. According to Dr Houghton Mitchell, the cause of death was bronchitis and heart failure.[327] Son James Baxter Hunt was present at the death.[328]

Baxter had paid into the Widow's Fund, so his wife, now aged 69, was entitled to a pension of 14s a week.[329]

Detective Constable Baxter Hunt was one of the few policemen who saw how Catherine Eddowes had been left in Mitre Square. He was one of even fewer policemen who saw the message on the wall at Goulston Street, and how it had been written. He would have seen the handwriting, which words had actually been used and their spelling, something that we students of the case will never know for certain.

325 *The Reading Mercury*, 17th June 1899.

326 Death record.

327 Baxter's death certificate within his service file: CLA/048/AD/01/360.

328 James was living at 60 Furguson Road, West Derby in Liverpool at the time.

329 Baxter's service file: CLA/048/AD/01/360.

CHAPTER FIFTEEN

The Foster Family

Superintendent Alfred Foster,
Henry Edgar Foster and Frederick William Foster

Superintendent Alfred Foster:
'They were dealing with a man who was far too clever to go about boasting of what he was going to do.'[1]

Alfred Foster was called to the murder scene at Mitre Square, 'shortly before three o'clock on Sunday morning... from bed by a report that a terrible murder had been committed just inside the City boundary on the eastern side.' He arrived there with Inspector James McWilliam and Inspector Edward Collard. When he got to the spot at which Catherine Eddowes had died, he must have seen the square as a hive of activity with doctors already looking over the body, and detectives and uniformed men trying 'to detect, if possible, the murderer...'[2]

Once again we have to do a little detective thinking into the background of Alfred Foster's early life, and even his work career,

---

1 A quote from Alfred Lawrence Foster regarding the message on the wall in Goulston Street, reported in *The Star* of 2nd October 1888.

2 Alfred's interview for the *Evening News*, 1st October 1888.

because not only is there no mention of him on any birth record or the 1841 census, but his service file is missing from the London Metropolitan Archives. However, this should not prevent us from telling his story - we just have to use other means to fill in most of the missing gaps, such as the newspapers.

Born in Birmingham in 1826,[3] Alfred was educated in Warwick and at the age of thirteen worked for a local solicitor as an apprentice. After completing his apprenticeship, five years later, he found a job working for a law firm called Gregory, Faulkner, Gregory and Skirrow.[4]

Two years later, in the last quarter of 1846, Alfred married Matilda Peacock in Islington, north London,[5] and a year later the couple welcomed their first child, Sophia Mary Foster, who was born in the second quarter of 1847 in Islington.[6]

We know that by 1851 that Alfred and his family had moved to Clerkenwell, with him ending that year as Deputy Governor of Clerkenwell House of Detention.[7] When did Alfred start working at this prison? We cannot know for sure, but we can fairly confidently state that it was between 1847 to 1850 because when Sophia was born in 1847 the family were still living in Islington, but by 1850, when Henry Edgar Foster was born, the Fosters had moved to Clerkenwell.[8] We will leave Henry Foster here, but will return to him later in this chapter.

Clerkenwell Prison was designed to detain prisoners awaiting their trials,[9] and was situated on Bowling Green Lane. Formerly known as the New Prison, when Alfred took up his position it would felt like a new building because it had been rebuilt twice, once in 1818 after

---

3   1851 census.

4   *The Times*, 15th December 1897 and the *Police Review*, 7th January 1898.

5   Marriage record.

6   Birth record.

7   The *Pall Mall Gazette* of 19th May 1892 reports that he was a Prison Officer but "sometime afterwards he was elected Deputy Governor of the House of Detention - a post which he held till the 29th September 1864."

8   Birth record.

9   *The Penny Illustrated Paper and Illustrated Times*, 31st March 1877.

being destroyed in the 1793 Gordon Riots, and then again in 1847, when it was renamed Clerkenwell House of Detention.[10]

On the 1851 census, the Foster family were living at Rawstorne Street, Clerkenwell. Alfred was now 25 and described as a Prison Officer (Warden), so he seems to not have been Deputy at the time of this census. His wife Matilda, aged 23, was an Officer's Wife and the two children were not yet old enough to go to school, Sophia being three and Henry being just one. There were two other family members living with them, Matilda's widowed mother[11] and her sister,[12] both called Susannah Peacock.[13]

In 1852, Alfred and Matilda had another child, whom they named Matilda,[14] and in 1857 a boy, Charles, was born. The following year, in 1858, another son was born - Frederick William Foster, who would later be involved in the Catherine Eddowes case. We will also return to him in more detail later in this chapter.[15]

In 1861 John Foster was born to the family. At this time the family were still living in Clerkenwell, with Alfred still working at the prison.[16]

On 26th September 1863 there was an inquest into the death of a former inmate of Clerkenwell Prison, a Mr Henry Richardson, aged 29. Just before the time of his death, Mr Richardson had been transferred to Colney Hatch Asylum, where he died. Alfred stated at the inquest that the deceased had been held at Clerkenwell Prison between April and September of that year, and that 'he was often violent and excited... he was treated as a rational prisoner... it was not thought he was insane.'[17]

---

10 *The Penny Illustrated Paper and Illustrated Times*, 31st March 1877.

11 Aged 63.

12 Aged 20.

13 1851 census.

14 1871 census.

15 Ibid.

16 Ibid.

17 *The North London News*, 3rd October 1863.

Alfred left the position of Deputy Governor of Clerkenwell Prison in September 1864[18] and was presented with a silver snuff box.[19] Shortly afterwards, on 29th September, he became Superintendent of the City of London Police.[20]

The next year, 1865, Alfred and Matilda had another child, their third daughter, named Harriet.[21]

The Superintendent was mentioned that year in the *Kentish Chronicle* of 22nd July, when he raided a room of the Drapers Arms, on Talbot Court. The owner, a Mr Clawcorden, was taken to court and warned that if he were to be caught again he would be fined £100 for allowing people to illegally gamble on horse racing on his premises. For the present offence he was fined ten pounds.

Alfred's name also appeared the following month in the *Holborn Journal*, on 5th August, when he raided 60 Snow Hill in the City, which was suspected of being an illegal gambling house. The owner of this house, a Mr Benjamin Jones, was taken to the Old Bailey, found guilty and fined twenty pounds.

In 1866 another daughter was born to the Foster family, who they named Edith. Another son, Frank, was born in 1868.[22]

On 28th February 1870, Alfred raided a coffee house that was also being used as gambling house at 16 Duke's Street. The newspapers reported that he had arrived 'with a posse of policemen with a warrant.' The owner, Mr Morris Emanuel, was released on bail of fifty pounds.[23]

In 1871, the Foster family were living at 26 Old Jewry, the

---

18 Three years after Alfred had left Clerkenwell there was a gunpowder explosion at the prison when the Fenian Society attempted to free Ricard O'Sullivan Burke, killing twelve people and wounding over 120. One of those put on trial, Michael Barrett, was the last person to be hanged publicly. See *Victorian Lives behind Victorian Crimes It's a Hanging Job Now* by Amanda Harvey Purse.

19 *London City Press*, 8th October 1864.

20 Ibid.

21 1871 census.

22 Ibid.

23 *Manchester Evening News*, 1st March 1870.

headquarters of the City of London Police. Not only were all the children old enough to receive an education, but there was also a new edition to the family in the form of Thomas Foster, who had been born earlier that year. The family employed a servant named Elizabeth Walker, aged seventeen.[24]

Sadly, this was to be the last census that Sophia Foster, Alfred's oldest child, appeared on, because in the last quarter of that year she died, at the age of 24.[25]

By 1881, the family was still living at the Headquarters of the City of London Police. Son Frederick Foster had moved out by this time and was beginning a life on his own, and all the other surviving children were still at school. At this point, Alfred was 55 and his wife 53.[26]

On 30th September 1888, at 'shortly before three o'clock', Alfred was called from his bed at Old Jewry with the news that 'a terrible murder had been committed just inside the City boundary on the eastern side.' When he arrived at Mitre Square, he could see that 'measures had already been taken to detect... the murderer.'[27]

Alfred must have spoken to the officers in the square and taken a moment to study the area in which the body of Catherine Eddowes lay, because he was later able to describe it in an interview with the *Evening News*, published on 1st October.[28]

After discussing various aspects of the case, including who had discovered the body, it seems that the newspaper reporter had asked Alfred whether PC Watkins was correct about the time he claimed to have found the body, as the interview ends with Alfred stating: 'Constable Watkins is a most reliable man and is no doubt correct about the time.'[29]

---

24 1871 census.

25 Death record.

26 1881 census.

27 Alfred's interview for the *Evening News*, 1st October 1888.

28 Dated 1st October 1888.

29 *Evening News*, 1st October 1888.

It seems as if Alfred was quite happy to talk to the press whenever it was needed. This perhaps held him in good stead with reporters, as the City Police were often looked at in a more favourable light than their Met counterparts by the newspapers because of the City's apparent openness compared to the seemingly guarded views of the Metropolitan Police.

An interview with Alfred appeared in the *Star* of 2nd October 1888. Asked about the message on the wall in Goulston Street, he stated that he believed 'they were dealing with a man who was far too clever to go about boasting of what he was going to do.'[30]

Alfred also made an appearance in an article in the *Evening News* of 9th October 1888, which discussed the three witnesses at the entrance to Church Passage, and how one - Joseph Lawende - was being looked after by the police who, after 'imposing a pledge on him of secrecy', were 'paying all his expenses, and one if not two detectives are taking him about. One of the two detectives is Foster.'[31]

At the beginning of February 1889, a Synagogue Parade was organised to highlight the problems of the Jewish sweaters and the Jewish unemployed. It was to take place on Saturday, 16th March, starting at 12:30pm from 40 Berner Street, the home of the International Working Men's Educational Club. The body of Elizabeth Stride, the other victim of the 'Double Event', had been found in Dutfield's Yard next door. The march was to end at the Synagogue near Mitre Square. This caused uproar, but the police, 'under the direction of Superintendent Foster and Chief Inspector Egan',[32] were prepared, with the police outnumbering the rioters, and they were not allowed to enter Mitre Square.

In 1891, the Foster family was still living at 26 Old Jewry. Henry had left to start his own career but Frederick had returned, living under his parent's roof at the age of 32. The family employed a new servant, 19-year-old Emily Green. Alfred was recorded as Chief

---

30 *The Star*, 2nd October 1888.

31 *Evening News*, 9th October 1888.

32 *The Jewish Chronicle*, 22nd March 1889.

Superintendent for the City Police.[33]

He would not remain in his post for long, for on 18th May 1892 he retired as 'unfit for service', with a pension of £333 6s 8d.[34] The *Pall Mall Gazette* marked the occasion with an interview.[35]

An interesting note about this interview is that Alfred seemed happy to talk openly about the Ripper murders, whereas other senior officers had been more reticent:

> ...that Mitre-square murder fairly puzzled me. I have been interviewed by eminent spiritualists and others on the subject, and have had great hopes at different times of lighting upon some clue, but have completely failed. In fact that crime is as great a mystery to-day as ever it was.[36]

As well as remembering the day the Queen opened Blackfriars Bridge in 1869, Alfred spoken of various Lord Mayor's Days.[37]

As a retirement gift he was given £500.[38] The Foster family finally moved out of Old Jewry to Warwick Lodge, Alexandra Road in Kingston-upon-Thames.

Alfred died on 13th December 1897,[39] and was buried in the City of London Cemetery, where Catherine Eddowes was interred. Although they lie in different parts of the cemetery, today there are matching blue and gold plaques on their final resting places.

Alfred quite openly expressed a belief in ghosts, as stated in his retirement interview with the *Pall Mall Gazette*. If the spirit world exists, it is a nice thought that perhaps Alfred Lawrence Foster is looking after Catherine Eddowes, long after both their deaths.

In 1900, the family placed a memorial piece in the *Morning Post* of 14th December 1900. Alfred's wife, Matilda, continued to reside

---

33 1891 census.

34 Information from a file held at Bishopsgate Police Station.

35 Dated 19th May 1892.

36 *Pall Mall Gazette*, 19th May 1892.

37 Ibid.

38 *The Times*, 30th July 1892.

39 *Morning Post*, 14th December 1900.

in the Kingston home in which Alfred had died in, and in the 1901 census was listed as living there with five of her children: Matilda now aged 49, John (40),[40] Harriett (36), Frank (33) and Thomas (30).[41]

Ten years later, in the 1911 census, the Foster family are recorded as having separated. Matilda, by now 83, and daughter Matilda Jr, 59, were living together in a smaller house at 29 Berrylands Road, Surbiton, with a housemaid named Nellie Ward.[42]

Sadly, Alfred's wife Matilda Foster died the following year.[43]

Henry Edgar Foster:
Following in his Father's Footsteps

We already know that Henry Foster was born in the third quarter of 1849.[44] He had left the family home by 1871 to begin a career as a policeman in the City of London Police force, and was a lodger at 41 Selforde Street, Clerkenwell.[45]

By the 1881 census, now aged 31, Henry had become Station Sergeant at Snow Hill Police Station, where he was then residing.[46]

In the third quarter of 1889, Henry married German-born Maria Barbara Overlack, twenty years his junior, in Kingston.[47] The couple welcomed their first child, Alfred Edgar Foster, in 1891. The boy was presumably named after his grandfather, and took his father's middle name.[48]

It is difficult finding Henry in the 1891 census, but with a little change in the way his surname is spelt we find a Henry 'Faster', born in the same year and place, who happened to be an Inspector of the

---

40 Following in his brother Frederick's footsteps by working as a surveyor.
41 1901 census.
42 1911 census.
43 Death record.
44 Birth record.
45 1871 census.
46 1881 census.
47 Marriage record.
48 1901 census.

City Police. He was recorded as living in Bridewell Place in the City with his wife Maria and their son Alfred.[49]

A year later Henry and Maria had another child, a daughter named Katherine Matilda Foster, with the middle name perhaps chosen after Henry's mother.[50]

In 1901, Henry was a Chief Inspector of the City Police and living with his wife and two children at Cloak Lane Police Station. They have one servant, 15-year-old Annie Hetteridge.[51]

By the time of the 1911 census, Henry had retired from the City of London Police. His children had moved away, and perhaps to help with the finances, the family had taken in a boarder, a schoolmistress named Jessie Brown. Also living with the family as a boarder was Henry's brother Thomas, a London County Council Clerk, now aged 40.[52]

Frederick William Foster:
The Map Man of Mitre Square

Frederick was the son of Superintendent Alfred Foster, but did not become a policeman. So why are we mentioning him in detail within this chapter? Well, although Frederick did not join the City police, he certainly had a role within the investigation into Catherine Eddowes' death, and whether he knew it at the time or not, his role was as unique as it was important to the case...

Frederick was born in the fourth quarter of 1858, in Islington, north London.[53] He lived with his parents until 1878, when he married Juliana Mary Atkens in Holborn.[54]

By the 1881 census he was already describing himself as an architect, and possibly working away from his home, because on the

---

49 1891 census.
50 Birth record.
51 1901 census.
52 1911 census.
53 Birth record.
54 Marriage record.

return he was listed as a lodger to the Sharp family at Model Cott, Halton, Aylesbury in Buckinghamshire. Although his wife Juliana was not with him, his status is given as being married.[55]

However, the couple were certainly living in London by the first quarter of 1888, for at this time Juliana sadly died, aged just 29. Her death was registered in Islington.[56]

Three years later, in the 1891 census, Frederick was recorded as living back with his parents, at the age of 32.[57]

We have briefly touched on the fact that Frederick was an architect, and in fact by 1888 he was the City's Surveyor. His job would collide with that of his father, Superintendent Alfred Foster, on the morning of 30th September 1888.

Once Catherine Eddowes' body had been discovered and the alarm raised, the City of London Police did not rush to return Mitre Square to normality. Instead, they wanted everything at the scene recorded, and this was why the City Police brought in Frederick.

Not only was Mitre Square cordoned off from the viewing public until that afternoon to allow Frederick enough time to draw a somewhat detailed map of Mitre Square and its exits, but he was also able to make some very detailed sketches of the way Catherine's body lay and even the injuries inflicted to her body and face.[58]

Two of Frederick's maps - one a plan and the other a three-dimensional sketch of Mitre Square which includes sketches of Catherine's injuries, are held at the London Hospital Museum. The plan of the square is on public display, whereas the detailed sketch is not.[59]

Frederick Foster was called to appear at Catherine Eddowes' inquest, and gave a description of the work he had done, stating:

---

55 1881 census.

56 Death record.

57 1891 census.

58 *The Evening News*, 1st October 1888.

59 The author would like to thank both Mehzebin Adam and Richard Meunier of the London Hospital Museum for permission to view both maps and to reproduce them in this book.

I have made the plans produced - I have them in three sections, one 8 feet to an inch, another 200 feet to an inch from an Ordnance map of the City - I have marked on an Ordnance Map of the same scale from Berner Street to Mitre Square - that would be 1144 yards about ¾ of a mile - it would take about 12 minutes to walk it from one to another.[60]

However, he not only gave a description of the killer's route to Mitre Square, but also discussed the possible routes he may have taken in order to get to Goulston Street, where the apron piece had been left:

It is the nearest route that anyone unaccustomed to it would take - There are 2 routes to Goulstone Street [sic] one from Church Passage through Duke Street crossing Houndsditch through Gravel Lane, Stoney Lane crossing Petticoat Lane and through to Goulstone Street [sic]. A person going from Mitre Square to Flower and Dean Street would go as the most direct route across Goulstone Street [sic] - it would take within ¼ of an hour to get there.[61]

In the April 1966 edition of *The London Hospital Gazette*, Professor Francis E. Camps wrote an article about Frederick Foster's maps and sketches called 'More about Jack the Ripper'. He described the last known movements of Catherine Eddowes and how his assistant, Sam Hardy, had found Foster's maps in the basement of the London Hospital. Professor Camps also wrote that the kidney which was possibly taken from Catherine Eddowes was sent to Dr Thomas Openshaw, the Pathological Curator of the London Hospital in 1888, stating that Dr Openshaw

reported that it was a portion of human kidney and that it had been placed in spirits within a few hours of its removal. It was a 'Ginny kidney', i.e. alcoholic and it belonged to a woman of about forty five and had been removed within three weeks. Two inches of the renal artery were in the body and one inch attached to the kidney. It is of interest that both the kidney left in the body and the 'postal' kidney showed severe Bright's disease.[62]

60 Coroner's inquest (L) 1888, No.135, Catherine Eddowes Inquest, 1888.

61 Ibid.

62 A portion of Catherine's kidney was taken away by the killer and purportedly sent [PTO]

In 1891, Frederick was living with his parents and siblings at the headquarters of the City of London Police force at Old Jewry. He was now 32-years-old, and although the census records him as single, we now know that he was in fact a widower.[63]

One can imagine that Frederick stayed with his parents, even when his father retired from the force a year later, and moved from Old Jewry to live in Kingston. One wonders whether Frederick was at his parent's home when his father passed away in 1897 and was buried in the same cemetery as the woman that Frederick had spent one morning back in 1888 capturing her horrific injuries.

In March 1901 Frederick was living with the Clarkson family at 175 Park Road, Kingston. He was 41 years of age, still working as an architect and recorded as single,[64] but by that June he married Mabel Roper Blinkhorn in Gloucester.[65] She was twenty years his junior.

In the 1911 census the couple were recorded at 52 Seymour Street, Marylebone. Frederick was 52-years-old and still working as an architect.[66]

Frederick died in Uckfield in the first quarter of 1939, at the age of 80.[67] In the special census of September 1939,[68] his wife Mabel had moved down to Bournemouth, where she lived out the rest of her life before passing away in 1964 in Huckfield, Sussex.[69]

It is often noted in books relating to Jack the Ripper that Frederick Foster drew a map of Mitre Square after the death of Catherine Eddowes. In this book the author has attempted to make the people

---

to George Lusk, the Chairman of the Whitechapel Vigilance Committee along with a letter addressed 'From Hell'. Although the kidney was confirmed to be human, it is debatable whether it was Catherine's. 'More about Jack the Ripper' by Francis Camps, published in *The London Hospital Gazette*, April 1966.

63 1891 census.

64 1901 census.

65 Marriage record.

66 1911 census.

67 Death record.

68 Carried out to obtain a record of the population people at the outbreak of WWII.

69 Death record.

who were involved in the investigation of Catherine Eddowes's death seem more real and human to us. It is therefore sad to note that while Frederick was doing his job as 'the Map Man of Mitre Square' and recording the way in which a woman was killed, he was dealing with his own grief of losing his first wife.

CHAPTER SIXTEEN

Lost Policemen

*Sergeant William Miles, Inspector George Izzard,
Sergeant Alfred Izzard, Sergeant Amos Dudman
and PC Richard Pearce*

Sergeant William John Miles:
Going to the Mortuary

*Sergeant Miles is indeed a lost policeman. He is only ever mentioned
briefly, and for two concise reasons, in the aftermath of Catherine
Eddowes' murder. He is only ever mentioned as Sergeant Miles,
without a warrant number or collar number, or even a first name!*

*Should we give up on finding him? The short answer is no: whoever
this Sergeant Miles was, he did have an involvement in the City force's
Jack the Ripper murder case. He may not have met the victim while
she was alive, he may not have been called to the murder scene or
made any house-to-house searches in the vicinity of Mitre Square, but
what he did do was to meet John Kelly, the man that by all accounts
loved Catherine in the last years of her life.*

*However, John Kelly was also the man who had walked into
Bishopsgate Police Station, where his partner had been shortly before
she died, believing that the woman who had been murdered a few
streets away, in Mitre Square, at that stage still unidentified, was 'His
Kate'.[1]*

It was Sergeant Miles's role to take John Kelly to Golden Lane Mortuary, and to soothe the distraught partner of the victim as he looked down at the disfigured face of his loved one...

With this in mind, Sergeant Miles's role was quite an important one, so the little problem of not knowing his first name shouldn't stop us from finding out who this man was and his family background.

So where do we go from here? Somehow we need to get hold of a file which lists details of everyone who joined the City of London Police force from its early beginnings up to 1888. Did such a file exist, and if so does it survive today? The answer to both questions is yes. Within the vaults of Bishopsgate Police Station sits this very file, and the author was lucky enough to have been allowed to access it while researching for this book.[2]

This is a step forward, but we are a long way from reaching our goal as there could be hundreds of officers named Miles. In fact, if you pardon the pun, there could be miles of Miles within the file. We do not even have Sergeant Miles's age to go on, so we don't even know what year to start looking from. Consequently, we should start at the very beginning and work our way through...

Astonishingly, as it turns out, between the start of the file and 1888, there are only three policemen with the surname Miles, all unrelated to each other.[3]

We have William Robert Miles, who joined the City of London Police on 19th August 1876 and left on 22nd August 1907. The dates are promising, but this William Robert Miles, sometimes stated as just Robert Miles, became a Sergeant after 1888.

A Nathan Miles did make Sergeant before 1888, but he joined on

---

1   A reference John Kelly had made, published in an article in the *Echo* of 3rd October 1888.

2   The file is not available for public scrutiny. The author would like to thank Sabine Thornton and Richard Thomas for allowing me to access it on 5th February 2016.

3   Confirmed through later research.

20th May 1875 and resigned on 29th May 1879 due to the city smog disagreeing with his health.

So we are left with William John Miles.

William John Miles was born in 1855 to Edward (b.1829)[4] and Mary Louisa Miles (b.1831). William was the first child born to this family, with siblings Louisa Jane (b.1858), Edward Israel (b.1860), Henry Jesse (b.1862), Charles Alfred (b.1865), Eliza Matilda (b.1867) and James Arthur (b.1870) coming later.[5]

In the 1871 census, the Miles family were living Cape Place, Dorking in Surrey, with William's grandfather, another William Miles.[6]

This is the address that William gave when he signed up to the City of London Police force on 27th March 1873. On his application form he stated that his previous job was as a foreman for Mr Charles Chambers' company at Lethem Grange, Sydenham, where he worked from 20th January 1872 to 24th March 1873, leaving three days before he joined the City force. Mr Charles Chambers was also William's reference, stating that he 'knows nothing whatever against the candidate in question', so he must have left on good terms. William's rate of pay at the start of his new career was 25s. He was given warrant number 4694.[7]

On 1st November 1873, William was caught drunk on duty. There is no further information in his service record held at the London Metropolitan Archives to go further into this incident, with not even a punishment recorded. That is not to say that a punishment wasn't given, but perhaps it was not recorded or William was given just a stern talking to, as this was his first and only offence.[8]

On 27th June 1875, William married Sarah Ann Mills at St George's church in Hanover Square. However, because he was just 20-years-old and Sarah nineteen, they were both classed as minors and had

---

4   A greengrocer, according to William's second marriage certificate held in his City of London Police service file: CLA/048/AD/01.

5   1871 census.

6   Born in 1787. 1871 census.

7   William's service record: CLA/048/AD/01.

8   William's misconduct record within his service record: CLA/048/AD/01.

needed permission from their parents to marry.[9]

Three years later, in 1878, their first child, Emily Louisa Miles, was born. She would later write, at the age of 60, to the City of London Police force, revealing that she was born at Sparrow Corner, Minories.[10]

William and Sarah welcomed their second child, William E Miles, in 1880. According to Emily's letter, the family were living at King William Street at the time of her brother's birth.[11] They moved shortly afterwards to 6 Northumberland Alley. This is an interesting location for the City of London police officer, for he was just a three minute walk from Mitre Square. William was also a nine minute walk away from Bishopsgate Police Station, where he met John Kelly before taking him to Golden Lane Mortuary.[12]

William's wife Sarah died some time between 1880, when her last child was born, and 1886, when William remarried.[13]

There are three women named Sarah Miles who passed away within that time period, however the Sarah Miles who was buried on 11th March 1882 at Nuthead Cemetery in Southwark seems to be the closest to her last known address.[14]

On 1st January 1885, William was promoted to Second Class Sergeant with a rise of pay to 36s.

Then a year and two months later, on 18th March 1886, he married Sarah Judd, who at the time was living at 13a Jewry Street, immediately behind William's own residence and therefore only a minute's walk away from each other,[15] and the following year William's second daughter, Eliza or Elizabeth Louisa Miles, was

---

9 Marriage record.

10 Letter written by E.L. Miles within William's service record: CLA/048/AD/01.

11 Ibid.

12 The address given on his second marriage certificate held within William's service file: CLA/048/AD/01.

13 He claimed to be a widower on his second marriage certificate, dated 18th March 1886. Held within William's service file: CLA/048/AD/01.

14 Death record.

15 Marriage Certificate dated 18th March 1886. Held within William's service file: CLA/048/AD/01.

born.[16]

Following the murder in Mitre Square, the identity of the victim was not immediately known. John Kelly walked into Bishopsgate Police Station on 2nd October 1888 and related how he believed the woman, who had been described as having a pawn ticket bearing the name 'Mary Kelly' among her belongings, was his partner.

William was then ordered to take John Kelly to Golden Lane Mortuary to see whether this was the case. Once inside, William took John over to a wooden casket, inside which the body lay.

It's possible that William felt sorry for Kelly: although he had not lost a partner in such a horrific way, William had indeed lost a wife, so perhaps with a heavy heart the officer made sure John was prepared for the awful sight.

It must have been a shock. He broke down and cried, and William had to ask him if he was certain this was Catherine. John was sure, saying the tattooed 'T.C.' on her forearm confirmed it.[17] He told William that although Kate and he were never married, they had lived together for several years.[18]

If William thought his part in the investigation in Catherine's murder ended there at the mortuary he was mistaken, for that evening a man named William Bull, who lived at 6 Stannard Road, Dalston, walked into Bishopsgate Police Station. He was quite drunk.

Bull made his way to Inspector Izzard and told him that it was he who had killed the woman found in Mitre Square. After making a statement, Mr Bull was asked where the clothes he had worn the previous night were, answering 'in the Lea.' He claimed to have thrown the knife away.

Sgt William Miles was tasked with finding out whether Mr Bull was known at any of the local hospitals, but he was not. His parents were well known and 'respectable' people. Bull later retracted his

---

16 Birth record. By the time of the 1911 census Eliza was working as a domestic parlour maid, although still living with her family.

17 We know this happened because the following day, 3rd October 1888, John spoke to a reporter from the *Echo*.

18 *Evening News*, 3rd October 1888.

statement, claiming he was 'mad drunk and could not have done the murder'.[19]

In 1889 William and Sarah had another child, Edward Henry Miles.[20] In later years Edward would become a tourist clerk, possibly working for his elder step-brother William Jr, as he and his wife were both working within that industry while still living at the family home.[21]

In December 1889 William was called to the Old Bailey as a witness at the trial for coining of Thomas Wood and Elizabeth Clark.

City Detective Walter Outram was in Finsbury on 26th November with another officer named Alfred Scrivener, when they saw Elizabeth Clark acting suspiciously and decided to follow her. She met Thomas Wood on the corner of Fore Street and the pair exchanged something. The detectives continued to follow them along London Wall, and watched Clark enter Mrs Bourne's stationer's shop. On leaving she walked towards Bell Alley, with Wood following a few yards behind. They stopped to talk for a moment, and then Clark entered a confectioner's in Bell Alley, then exited and walked to Angel Court, where the couple stopped and spoke again.

The detectives watched as Elizabeth Clark walked up Bartholomew Lane, then Threadneedle Street and into Bishopsgate, with Thomas Wood following twenty years behind.

Eventually she went into the Golden Grain Bread Company's shop, and Detective Scrivener followed her inside. Wood looked in through the window, and as Clark and Scrivener were about to leave the shop, William Miles seized Wood, stating, "I am a police officer; you will be charged with being concerned with this woman in uttering counterfeit coin."

His prisoner claimed not to know the woman and in a struggle fell through the window of the shop.

Both Wood and Clark were taken to the station, where they were

19 *City Press*, 6th October 1888.
20 Birth record.
21 1911 census.

searched and more than 20 coins discovered in his pockets. While the majority of these were good, Wood must have felt nervous because when some shillings were placed on the counter he grabbed them and put them in his mouth. William rushed at him, threw him to the floor and put his fingers inside the prisoner's mouth to stop the coins being swallowed, but to no avail.

Thomas Wood complained of his rough treatment by William, to which the detective pointed out that he should not have swallowed the bad coins in the first place.

Both prisoners were found guilty and sentenced to eighteen months' hard labour.[22]

1890 saw William receive two promotions. On 24th January he was made First Class Sergeant, with a pay rise to 39s. On 6th March he became Station Sergeant, with pay of 50s, and on 29th September his 15% pay rise saw his salary rise to 59s.[23]

The following year, William and his family moved to Beauford Road, Tottenham, with his eldest two children now at school.[24]

On 31st May 1894, William was promoted to District Inspector, with a pay rise to 69s. His final child, Kate Ethel Miles, was born the following year.[25]

William Miles resigned from the City of London Police on 31st March 1898, after serving his 25 years in the force. He was awarded a pension of £108, and received a certificate rating his conduct as 'very good' from Commissioner Henry Smith.[26]

By the time of the 1901 census the family had moved back to William's birth town of Dorking, and were living at 34 Rothes Road.[27]

In 1911 they were at 68, Cobden Road, South Norwood near Croydon, William now being 56-years-old.[28]

22 Old Bailey record (t18891216-72).

23 William's service record: CLA/048/AD/01.

24 1891 census.

25 Birth record. She would become a bookkeeper at the age of sixteen (1911 census).

26 William's service record: CLA/048/AD/01.

27 1901 census.

28 1911 census.

Within William's service record held at the London Metropolitan Archives is his death certificate, sent by his son Edward Henry Miles as evidence of his father's death, as Edward hoped that Sarah, his mother, might be able to claim on the Police Widows' Fund. Sadly, because William 'withdrew' from this fund at some point, the police could not pay anything his widow.[29]

William's death certificate shows that he died on 21st April 1931 in Croydon General Hospital. The cause of death was an enlarged prostate and uremia, and his daughter 'E. Miles' was present at the death. His last address was given as 12 Woodside Green, South Norwood.[30]

We will never know how William felt dealing with the distraught John Kelly as he had to show him the body of his loved one, Catherine Eddowes. The author hopes that now we know who 'Sergeant Miles' was, and his family background, William John Miles will now not be a lost policeman ever again within the Ripper case.

Inspector George Izzard and Sergeant James Izzard: The Problem with the Izzards

Many believe it was Inspector George Izzard who was called to the scene of Catherine Eddowes's murder, and who gave orders to Sergeant Dudman and Sergeant Phelps to guard Mitre Square.

It has also been believed for some time that this same George Izzard was the 'Inspector Izzard' mentioned in The Times of 4th October 1888, in a report about a William Bull who had entered Bishopsgate Police Station, claiming to the man who had murdered the woman found in Mitre Square, as described above.

This was a natural assumption, as we already knew of an Inspector Izzard with the first name George who had been involved in the case. However, over time it has been suggested that this was not the case, as there is another Inspector Izzard who worked for the City of

---

29 A letter from Edward Henry Miles held in William's service record William's service record: CLA/048/AD/01.

30 Death certificate within William's service record: CLA/048/AD/01.

London Police who, because members of the Bull family attended his retirement party,[31] may have been the 'Inspector Izzard' who took William Bull's confession. This second possibility is Inspector James Alfred Izzard.

Whichever of the two Izzards was the Inspector who attended Mitre Square - and the author will investigate this shortly - were they in some way related?

George Izzard was born on 15th January 1842[32] to John Izzard (b.1809)[33] and Sarah Pratt (b.1806),[34] who married in Redbourn on 17th February 1828.[35] George was the fourth child born to the Izzard family, following Mary Ann (b.1835), Elizabeth[36] (b.1837)[37] and Louisa (b.1839).[38] George would be later joined by two siblings, William (b.1846)[39] and John (b.1849)[40]

George Izzard first appeared in a census in 1851, where he was

---

31 *The Times*, 9th January 1901.

32 Baptism record.

33 Birth record.

34 Birth record.

35 Marriage record.

36 Baptism record. Mary Ann Izzard was born on 3rd February 1835 and baptized in Welwyn on 8th March. By 1851 she was working as a servant at the Dunsdale Arms public house on Fore Street, All Saints, Hertfordshire. Ten years later she had changed careers and was working as a cook for the Harrison family in Dunstable Street, Ampthill in Bedfordshire. After this she disappears from all records.

37 Elizabeth Izzard was born on 3rd February 1837. She was not baptized until 1842, presumably at the same time as brother George and sister Louisa, 13th February.

38 Louisa Izzard was born on 31st May 1839 and baptized on 13th February 1842 in Welwyn. She appears on the 1841 census at two-years-old but sadly died the following year.

39 William Izzard was born on 20th October 1846 and baptized on 17th December that year. He died aged five, and was buried on 2nd May 1852.

40 John Izzard was baptized on 30th September 1849 in Welwyn. By the age of 21 he had moved to London and was living as a lodger at 20 Edmund Place, St Botolph, in the City. One of the other lodgers at this address, was one Alfred Aldridge, possibly known to the family due to his relationship with the man who would later marry John's older sister, Elizabeth. John died at the age of 25 in Lambeth.

nine-year-old scholar. The family was living at 85 Fore Street, Welwyn in Hertfordshire. Around this time there were three private schools on Fore Street; at number 16 there was a private boys school run by a Reverend Thomas Ray. This was not a big school, as by 1851 it had only eighteen pupils, although George was not one of them.[41] Further along the same street was another private school at number 20, but again this was a small school consisting of children mainly from one family, which was not George's, and the other private school was exclusively for girls.[42]

However, near to where the Izzard family was living, in Great North Road, was the National School, oddly named The London Road. This school was built in 1850 when the railway came to Hatfield, bringing more families with it, and in 1854 the school was extended to take in boys from the closed school at Puttocks Oak.[43] As this was the biggest public school in the area and was very close to where the Izzard family was living, it can be reasonably assumed that George attended this school.

We know that at the age of fifteen George was working as a miller for Mr John Carman, as this is stated in his application to join the City of London Police, and indeed Mr Carman would provide his reference.[44]

George joined the City force on 11th May 1859, being described as aged twenty, 5ft 9¼in tall, with blue eyes and light brown hair.[45] He was awarded warrant number 2951.

The following year he married Elizabeth Pilgrim in Clerkenwell.[46] On the 1861 census taken a year later, the couple were listed as living at 11 Bartholomew Close, West Smithfield, with George recorded as

41 1851 census.

42 History records of Hatfield.

43 History records of the London Road School.

44 George's application form for the City of London Police force: CLA/048/AD/01/61 (held at London Metropolitan Archives).

45 George's application form for the City of London Police force: CLA/048/AD/01/61. His recorded age seems to be a mistake, as he was actually 17-years-old.

46 Marriage record. Elizabeth was baptized on 16th June 1839 in Shoreditch.

a 'police constable'.[47]

That year their first child was born, a daughter called Louisa, who was possibly named after George's sister who had died at a young age.[48] A second child, George Jr, was born in 1863 and registered in the City of London.[49]

George's third child, Charles, was born in 1865 at St Botolph's Aldgate. He would follow in his father's footsteps and become a City of London Police officer on 1st July 1885.[50]

His references were from a Mr Joseph Jopling of Messr Perry Company, whom Charles had worked for from June 1883 to June 1885 as a carpenter, and his own father, George Izzard, who by this time was an 'Inspector of City Police' living at 1 Ball Court, Giltspur Street. Charles was described as 5ft 10¾in tall, with grey eyes and light brown hair, and living at 6a St Andrew's Street, Wandsworth Road, Clapham. He would enjoy a successful career, retiring in 1913 as a District Inspector.[51]

George Izzard's fourth child, Samuel, was born in 1867 in the City of London.[52] A fifth child, Lizzie, was born in 1870. She sadly died at

47 1861 census.

48 Louisa would later marry Henry Andrews in Wandsworth in 1886, the couple going on to have four children: Henry Jr (b.1888), Albert (b.1889), Florence (b.1891) and Elizabeth (b.1898).

49 Birth record. George Jr worked as a seed merchant before passing away in 1933 in Battersea.

50 Charles's application form for the City of London Police force: CLA/048/AD/01/20.

51 Charles's service record: CLA/048/AD/01/20. He was promoted Second Class Constable 9th September 1886 and First Class on 16th April 1891. He was made Second Class Sergeant on 20th June 1892, and Station Inspector on 30th December 1897. His final promotion was to District Inspector on 31st December 1907. He retired on 6th March 1913 with a pension of £135 6s. Charles Izzard married Mary Ellen Cull in Wandsworth in 1892, the couple having two children, Charles Jr (b.1893) and Ellen (b.1898). According to a letter from Mary held in his service file, both children were born at the 'City Police Buildings in Bishopsgate', which suggests that the family were living in Rose Alley or perhaps Bishopsgate Police Station itself. Charles Izzard died on 3rd May 1913, with his last address being 31 Green Lane, Penge, The letter from Charles' widow to the Commissioner, dated 26th April 1934, paints a picture of him being quite ill in the final years that he spent in the force, and that just before he retired he was actually working within the headquarters of the City Police at Old Jewry.

52 Birth record. He would later become a postman, before passing away in 1931 in Wandsworth.

the age of two.[53]

In the 1871 census the Izzard family were living at 20 Edmund Place, St Botolph in the City.[54] George was recorded as a 'police officer', and all of his children that were old enough were at school.[55]

In 1872, George's sixth child, Alfred, was born.[56] Like his brother Charles, Alfred also followed in his father's footsteps and joined the City of London Police force, on 3rd March 1892, after previously working as a bookkeeper. Alfred was issued with warrant number 6307, and would be promoted to Acting Sergeant on 2nd May 1901 and then Sub Station Inspector on 7th April 1909. He retired on 28th August 1919.[57]

Alfred Izzard married Charlotte Mary Pettett on 19th September 1898 at All Saints Church in Hatcham Park, London. According to a copy of the marriage certificate held in Alfred's service file, he and Charlotte were both living at 39 Besson Street, and his father George acted as a witness to the marriage, describing himself as a police pensioner.[58]

The couple had five children, George (b.1899), Alfred Jr (b.1905), Ernest (b.1908), Doris (b.1910) and Alice (b.1912).[59]

Alfred Izzard died at Middlesex Hospital on 2nd September 1938 of cardiac failure, coronary thrombosis, hypertension and diabetes. His last address was at Nector Road, New Marford in Hertfordshire.[60]

Interestingly, Alfred's oldest child George Edwin Izzard also joined the City of London Police, making it three generations to have served in that force, a span of 80 years from grandfather George joining in

---

53 Death record.

54 A popular address with the Izzards, with several members of the family living here at different times. Not only did George and his family live here, but his brother William had resided here, as had a nephew, mentioned later.

55 1871 census.

56 Birth record.

57 Alfred's service file for the City of London Police force: CLA/048/AD/01.

58 Ibid.

59 Birth records.

60 Death certificate.

1859 to George Jr's retirement in 1939.[61]

George Izzard Sr welcomed his seventh child, William, in 1874,[62] and his eighth, Alice, in 1876.

An 'Inspector Izzard' is mentioned in a newspaper report of an attempted burglary on 15th November 1878, when at quarter to two in the morning the officer was walking along Carrol Road, Highgate, with a Sergeant and Constable when they heard a noise coming from the back garden. Investigating the noise, the policemen saw one James Clark and another man jump over the railings and run off. When Inspector Izzard caught up with him, Clark claimed he hadn't been in any garden, but had just returned from Holloway. He was escorted to Marylebone Police Station, where after a search he was found to have a chisel, a skeleton key and a rope on his person.[63]

Although there is speculation whether this could be George Izzard, we cannot know for sure as much of his service file is missing from the London Metropolitan Archives. On the 1881 census three years later, he is described as a Police Sergeant, not an Inspector.

A ninth and final child, Florence, was born in this year, with the family recorded as living at 482 Wandsworth Road, Clapham.

On 24th January 1884, Inspector George Izzard was involved in case of mistreatment of a horse. Like the Metropolitan Police, the

---

61 George Edwin Izzard's application form for the City of London Police force (CLA/048/AD/01/014). He was a cadet with the Royal Flying Corps from 22nd August 1917 to 31st March 1918, the following day transferring to the Royal Air Force, which he served as a Second Lieutenant. He spent seven months overseas before leaving on 16th June 1919. George joined the City of London Police on 20th January 1920 and was given warrant number 8072 and collar number 242C. He advanced his rate of pay regularly over the next four years, until 17th January 1924 when he was on the ninth rate of pay of 78s. He passed his educational examination for promotion on 19th February 1924, but failed his examination of police duties. He retired on 24th August 1939 due to bad health, and was awarded a pension of £91 14s 1d. George married Minnie on 23rd December 1925 at the City of London Registry Office, and on 7th January 1930 the couple welcomed daughter Leila. Like his father and Uncle Charles, George Jr seems to have suffered with poor health, his file recording a long list of medical complaints from catarrh lunfleeyia to a stomach ulcer. He died on 11th February 1941 at St Bart's Hospital of cerebral haemorrhage hypertension.

62 Birth record. William would later marry Alice Pettett in 1904, having three children: William Jr (b.1905), Alice (b.1906) Ernest (b.1908).

63 *The Echo*, 15th January 1878.

City force had rules about cruelty to animals. The *Police Code* stated that:

> A constable witnessing the perpetration of any gross act of cruelty upon any animal whatsoever (including birds) may, without warrant, apprehend the offender and take him before a Magistrate.[64]

James Hatch was seen by George driving his omnibus along Newgate Street with a chin iron attached to the horse which seemed to be too tight. The officer had already warned the driver of this previously, so took Mr Hatch before Alderman Gray. The horse was checked over by the Veterinary Surgeon, Mr William Sangster of Long-Lane, Smithfield, and no injury was found, so James Hatch was released.[65]

George was possibly involved in a case of shooting, when on 4th June 1885 Mr Walter Foss-Smith, a solicitor of Bedford Row, Bloomsbury, shot himself in a cab. Mr Foss-Smith had entered the cab at Holborn and asked to be driven to Liverpool Street station. Not long into the journey he shot himself dead. 'Inspector Izzard' was given the weapon used, and discovered that four of the chambers were loaded with ball cartridge, and a fifth had evidently been discharged. A verdict of Suicide while Temporarily Insane was passed at the inquiry held at St Bartholomew's Hospital.[66]

Now, we come to the murder of Catherine Eddowes. George was called to Mitre Square and gave orders for the scene to be protected from members of the public, this being achieved by officers Sergeant Dudman and Sergeant Phelps.

It is interesting to note that George appeared in an article published in the *Star*, where the reporter compared the attitude of the Metropolitan Police to that of the City force with regard to newspaper men attempting to learn details of the murders. The reporter complained that the Met did not give out any information,

---

64 *Sir Howard Vincent's Police Code, 1889* by Neil R A Bell and Adam Wood (2015).
65 *Lloyd's Weekly Newspaper*, 27th January 1884.
66 *The Centaur*, 6th June 1885.

while 'Inspector Izzard' was pleasant and more than happy to pass on any information he had.[67]

George handed his uniform back to the store rooms on 23rd January 1890. He was now 51-years-old. His conduct was recorded as 'very good',[68] and he was awarded a pension of £112 6d.[69]

In the 1891 census George was listed as a Licensed Victualler at the George and Dragon Inn in his hometown of Hitchin, Hertfordshire. Daughter Louisa and her children were visiting on the day the census was taken. Son William was employed as a barman at the public house, while Alice, Florence and Minnie were all at school. Also living with George was his father-in-law Samuel Pilgrim and his sister-in-law, Mary Pilgrim.[70]

Both the City and Met forces were heavily into their sports and actively promoted participation across the ranks. Although retired, George Izzard played for the City of London Police in a charity cricket match against Reading Borough Police at Elm Park, Berkshire, in June 1899.[71] One of his teammates was Detective Baxter Hunt, who was also involved in the Ripper investigation of 1888.

Sadly, in the first quarter of 1900, George's wife Elizabeth died at the age of 62.[72] Accordingly, on the census taken the following year George was recorded as a widower, now working as a postmaster. Still living with him at this time were George Jr, Alice, Florence, Minnie and his grandchildren Henry and Elizabeth.[73]

Now we have the question of how Inspector George Izzard was related to Inspector James Alfred Izzard...

---

67 *The Star*, 1st October 1888.

68 George's service file: CLA/048/AD/01/61.

69 Bishopsgate Police Station file.

70 1891 census.

71 *The Reading Mercury*, 17th June 1899.

72 Death record.

73 1901 census.

Now we have looked at the life of George Izzard, it's time to investigate the other possibility for the 'Inspector Izzard' of Bishopsgate Police Station, James Alfred Izzard. Were the two men related?

Our first major clue comes from George Izzard's police service file, held at the London Metropolitan Archives. There is a letter dated 8th February 2000 from his great granddaughter, asking for information about her family, in which she states that James Alfred Izzard was George's nephew. This seems to confirm that the two were indeed related, but we must investigate further.

For James to be George's nephew, our first thought would naturally be that James's father was one of George's brothers. George had two brothers, William and John. However, James' second marriage certificate recorded his father as also being named 'James'.[74]

How can this be? Let's go back to George's sister Elizabeth, mentioned briefly earlier. Born on 3rd February 1837, she was the second child born to John and Sarah Izzard. She was listed on the 1851 census working as a servant at the Wellington Inn in Welwyn, Hatfield, at the age of fourteen,[75] but then seems to disappear. There is no death record, but after some investigation it becomes clear that she had started using a diminutive version of her name, and was now calling herself 'Betsy'.

On 11th April 1857, a 'Betsy' Izzard married an Edward Aldridge in Welwyn;[76] Aldridge is a surname we already know, it being the name of a man who lodged with her brother William.

James Alfred Izzard was baptised on 1st February 1856, almost a whole year before Betsy married Edward Aldridge. On the baptism record, it records the mother as Betsy Izzard, with father unknown.[77]

Further evidence is found in the 1861 census, where Betsy Aldridge was recorded as living with her husband Edward, a blacksmith, at

74 James Izzard's service file for the City of London Police force: CLA/048/AD/01.
75 1851 census.
76 Marriage record.
77 Baptism record.

Brickwall, Welwyn, with their two daughters Sarah (b.1859) and Mary Ann (b.1861). Also listed as living with the family was Edward Aldridge's 'stepson', James A. Izzard, who is a seven-year-old scholar, perfectly matching the age of James Alfred Izzard.

This means that the letter held in George Izzard's service file from his Great Granddaughter is absolutely correct: James Izzard was George's nephew, but from his sister Elizabeth, or 'Betsy'.

From February 1863 to February 1873 James was working as a warehouseman for Mr John Freshwater, a shoe manufacturer at 50 Walting Street, London, who would provide James's reference for the City of London Police force - twice.[78]

James first joined the City force on 17th February 1873, being given collar number 507 and warrant number 4829, He was living at this time at 20 Edmund Place, Aldersgate Street.[79] Just five months later, however, on 17th July 1873, he left the force. He is described in his record of leaving as being 21-years-old, 5ft 9in tall, with hazel eyes and dark hair.[80]

He returned to work for Mr Freshwater at the shoe manufacturing warehouse, where he was employed from July 1873 to August 1874. He then re-joined the City of London Police on 24th August 1874, and was recorded as still living at 20 Edmund Place.[81]

In the first quarter of 1875 James married Eliza Ellen Gates,[82] who was born in January 1852 and baptised on 1st February 1852 in Shephall, Hertfordshire.[83] It is interesting to note that on his marriage certificate, James states that his father was 'Thomas' Izzard.[84]

78 James's service file for the City of London Police force: CLA/048/AD/01.

79 The same address that William Izzard and Alfred Aldridge, James's uncle and step-uncle lived. We now know that George Izzard was living at this address at this time, with James's uncle looking after him.

80 James's service file: CLA/048/AD/01.

81 Ibid.

82 Marriage record.

83 Baptism record. Some records list her as Ellen Eliza.

84 A name changed on his second marriage certificate, perhaps another piece of evidence that James did not know his father?

85 James's service file: CLA/048/AD/01.

The next few years were eventful for James and Eliza. On 21st October 1875 he was advanced to Second Class Constable.[85] The couple's first child, Ellen Eliza, was born in 1877, and registered in the City of London.[86]

James was promoted to First Class Constable on 5th September 1878, with a pay rise to 31s 6d.[87] The following year a second child, Lily, was born, and was registered in Welwyn, James's hometown.[88] Perhaps he and Eliza were visiting when Lily was born. In 1880, a third daughter, Ethel, was born, and registered in Hackney, east London.[89]

By the time of the 1881 census the Izzard family were living at 165 Gladstone Buildings, with Ellen going to school at the age of four.[90] On 26th May that year James was promoted to Second Class Sergeant, and again promoted on 3rd April 1884, to First Class Sergeant.[91]

On 9th August 1889, James became a Third Class Inspector with an increase in salary to 60s. On 13th November 1890 he became Station Inspector First Class of B Division (Great Tower Street Station).[92] The family were recorded as living at this station on the 1891 census.[93]

On 7th October 1892, James was promoted to Chief Inspector of the same division, with a pay of 80s 6d, and his service file records an award of £230 on 7th October 1897, although the reason for this bonus is unknown.[94]

Like his Uncle George, James represented the City of London Police at sport, although for James it was the Tug of War. Ironically,

---

86 Birth record.

87 James's service file: CLA/048/AD/01.

88 Birth record.

89 Birth record.

90 1881 census.

91 James's service file: CLA/048/AD/01.

92 Ibid.

93 1891 census.

94 James's service file: CLA/048/AD/01.

in the same year that his uncle played a cricket match for the force, James was in the City of London Police's tug of war team. There is a photograph held at the City of London Police Museum of him sitting with the 1899 tug of war team. James is sitting next to the huge shield which the City of London Police still owns, and which sits proudly within the Museum.

James retired from the City of London Police on 19th July 1900, receiving a pension of £146 3s 3d. On leaving the force James also received another bonus of £230,[95] although *The Times* of 9th January 1901 reported that he received a cheque for two hundred guineas at his retirement presentation. This function was attended by Aldermen Sir J.C. Dimsdale MP, Mr Deputy Myers, Mr H. Baker, Mr W.R.C. Moore, Mr B. Aaron, Mr A. Wagstaff, Mr W. Bull and Mr C. Goldfinch. It was also reported that 'the Chief Commissioner and the Assistant Commissioner felt they had lost in Mr Izzard one of the most able, conscientious and respected members of their body.'[96]

One of these men attending, Mr W. Bull, is the reason why James Izzard has been mentioned as the possible Inspector who was at Bishopsgate Police Station when William Bull, a 27-year-old supposed medical student, walked in drunk and claimed to have murdered the woman found in Mitre Square. It was 'Inspector Izzard' who took Bull's statement that on the night in question he had met a woman in Aldgate, went along a dark street with her and gave her half a crown (which another man took from her). He then killed her, apparently because he 'could not put up with the suspense any longer'.

The *Morning Advertiser* reported that inquires had been made [by Sergeant Miles] and it was found that William Bull was connected to 'important people', but he was not a medical student. On 7th October 1888 'Inspector Izzard' made his own inquiries into the matter, but found no leads. William Bull was released, with a warning that he should be ashamed of himself.[97]

---

95 James's service file: CLA/048/AD/01.

96 *The Times*, 9th January 1901.

97 *The Morning Advertiser*, 8th October 1888.

The 1901 census shows that James was living with his wife and daughters Ethel, Edith May and Gertrude (b.1892) at 129 City Cottage, Rabley Heath near Hitchin in Hertfordshire. At the age of 47, James was recorded as a 'Police Pensioner'.[98]

James's wife Eliza died at the age of 58 in 1910.[99] A year later, on the 1911 census, he was still at the same address and now a widower, living with his daughters Edith and Gertrude, also gaining a granddaughter, Eva Blanch Izzard (b.1905 in Leybourne, Essex).[100]

James must have stayed close to his deceased wife's relations, the Gates family, because in 1912 he married Elizabeth Gates, his deceased wife's younger sister, in Islington.[101]

James died in Hitchin, Hertfordshire, in the first quarter of 1926, at the age of 72. His second wife, Elizabeth, passed away 14 years later.

We have already solved one mystery with James Izzard, now knowing he was related to Inspector George Izzard of the same City of London Police force through his mother, Elizabeth', George's sister.

But what was his involvement in the investigation into Catherine Eddowes' death? Was he indeed the 'Inspector Izzard' who took the statement from William Bull?

The *Daily News* of 4th October 1888 reports that it was an 'Inspector George Izzard' who took the statement from William Bull, but could the newspaper be wrong?

The answer to this lies in the fact that the officer 'Izzard' who was called to the scene at Mitre Square and who later met William Bull was an Inspector. Both James and his uncle George were 'Inspectors' at one point in their careers, but timing is everything.

James Izzard's service file reveals that he became a Third Class Inspector, with a pay rise to 60s, on 9th August 1889.

98 1901 census.

99 Death record.

100 1911 census.

101 It was recorded on James's second marriage certificate that his father's name was James Izzard, a change from his first marriage certificate, which states that his father was Thomas Izzard.

Before this date, James was a Sergeant. It could therefore not have been anyone other than Inspector George Izzard who took the statement from and charged William Bull.

However, James Izzard was related to the policeman who was involved in the investigation into the murder of Catherine Eddowes, and was a highly respected policeman in his own right, so time spent reading about this man's life is hardly wasted.

Sergeant Amos Dudman: On Guard...

Amos Dudman's role in the investigation into Catherine Eddowes's death may seem small, but as he was one of the City officers who went to Mitre Square and saw her body lying on the cold, hard ground, he has to be mentioned more than just briefly.

Sergeant Amos Dudman was given orders to guard the entrances in and out of Mitre Square from the growing crowd of interested members of the public. He was there until Mitre Square was opened to the public that Sunday afternoon, at which point he must have thought that his connection to the crime had ended. However, by the following afternoon he found that he was wrong.

Amos was born in the first quarter of 1851 to Richard Dudman,[102] a shoesmith, and his wife Amelia.[103] At the time of Amos's birth, the family consisted of sister Eliza (b.1839) and brothers Cyrenius (b.1844), William (b.1846) and John (b.1848). The family lived at 2 Garden Row, Camberwell.[104]

Strangely, Amos's mother seems to disappear from the 1861 census. She doesn't die until 1891, so where has she gone? Further research finds her at the same address in the 1881 census, listed as a widow. Her occupation in this census might give a clue; she was

102 Born in 1800.
103 Born 1817.
104 1851 census.

a nurse at the local hospital.[105] Could it be possible that when the census man called on 7th April 1861 and 2nd April 1871 she was away from the family home, working?

On the 1861 census Amos's father Richard was still working as a blacksmith at the age of 61. The age given for Amos's brother William in this census is strange, as he should have been 15-years-old, but for some reason was recorded as being seven. Brother John is correctly listed as being thirteen and is a scholar, as is Amos.

Nine years later, in 1870, Amos joined the City of London Police and was given warrant number 4347.[106] He moved from the family home in Camberwell into Bishopsgate Police Station at the age of 22.[107]

The 1871 census shows that John stayed with his father, but William, Amos's older brother, had moved away from the family home.

Amos Dudman was called to court on 10th July 1871 as a witness in a case of theft by Charles Clayton, Francis Duval, Jane Fielder, Mary Holmes and Sarah Allen. They had stolen 982 yards of silk from Mr Robert Nuthall, silk agents in Mitre Court, and had attempted to sell the material to Mr Parker's pawn shop in Houndsditch.

Amos was handed the case, and at 6:00pm on 5th June arrived at the pawnbroker's, where Mary Holmes was still trying to sell samples of the stolen silk. He asked her where she had got the material and was told that her sister had given it to her. Holmes was unable to say where her sister lived, however, so he took her into custody. At the station she was searched, with 13s and more samples of the silk found on her person. She refused to give her address.

The other prisoners were picked up by other policemen at different pawnshops in the area, all trying to sell silk of the same pattern.

Sarah Allen was found not guilty, while all the others were found guilty and received custodial sentences. Due to the fact that Francis

105   1881 census.
106   Bishopsgate Police Station records.
107   1871 census.

Duval had already been charged for a similar crime, he received the longest punishment at seven years.[108]

The following Amos year married Caroline King[109] so left the police station for a private residence.

In 1873, Amos's brother John married Angelina Trenberth in her hometown of Truro, Cornwall.[110] The couple went to York, where their first son John Jr was born in 1874.[111] John and Angelina soon found themselves back in the capital, and in 1876 a daughter, Emily, was born.

In the same year, Amos and Caroline welcomed their first child, a daughter named Amy.[112]

Sadly, Amos and John's father Richard passed away in 1878,[113] but more happily Caroline gave birth to her first son, Amos Jr, a year later.[114]

In the 1881 census, the two brothers are both recorded as living in Southwark, Amos at 7 Tennis Place and John at 9 Hamilton Square. Perhaps John saw the stable career that Amos enjoyed, because his occupation was recorded as a Police Constable of the Metropolitan Police.[115]

Amos himself had been promoted to Sergeant by this time, for he appeared as a witness at the Old Bailey on 26th April 1880, where he was recorded as 'City Police Sergeant 60'.

On 3rd April he had been alerted by beat constable 652 Charles Smith, who had noticed an open window at 7 Wood Street, a warehouse belonging to Mr Sidney Druiff. Amos arrived at around 8:00pm and obtained a ladder in order to reach the open window. He noticed the dust had been disturbed around the ledge, and climbing

108   Old Bailey records (t18710710-546).
109   Marriage record.
110   Marriage record. Angelina was born in 1851.
111   Birth record.
112   Birth record.
113   Death record.
114   Birth record.
115   1881 census.

inside immediately saw 21-year-old Thomas Saunders, standing by a bench with a portmanteau.

Amos asked Saunders what he was doing there, and was told 'Nothing'. The officer looked around and saw that the door behind the intruder had been forced, and desks had been broken into. He escorted Saunders to the station and at trial Thomas Saunders received eighteen months' imprisonment for breaking and entering and for stealing the portmanteau.[116]

By 1881, Caroline had just given birth to Ethel, and the Dudman family had taken in a lodger named James Powell, a 71-year-old Hearth Rug Dresser.[117]

Tragically, in 1884 John Dudman lost his wife Angelina. His two children went to live with their mother's family in Cornwall, John Jr becoming a railway labourer[118] and Emily a servant in the household of James and Edith Edwards at Killigrew Street, Falmouth.[119] Although we don't know what John did in the years following this event, he would appear to have moved nearer to his children by the 1901 census, when he was recorded as a patient in Plymouth Hospital.[120]

On the morning of 30th September 1888, when news broke of a murder in Mitre Square, Sergeant Amos Dudman was at Bishopsgate Police Station. He was ordered to go to the scene of the crime to see if there were any orders for him. On arrival he was ordered by Inspector Izzard to help Sergeant Phelps and other policeman secure the area, allowing not one member of the public to enter Mitre Square.

News had filtered through that another murder had been committed earlier that same night, that of Elizabeth Stride in Berner Street, so a crowd comprised of members of the press and

116 Old Bailey records (t18800426-374).
117 1881 census.
118 1901 census.
119 1891 census.
120 1901 census.

public alike were expected. However, the City of London Police were determined to keep the square clear long enough for the scene to be investigated fully, to allow the City Surgeon to examine the body, and for City Surveyor Mr Foster to accurately draw a sketch of the locality and the position of the body.

The City of London Police certainly did not want to take this crime lightly, nor make mistakes by rushing to wash the scene of any clues, as the press had accused the Metropolitan Police of having done with previous Ripper murders.

Interestingly, an early report in the *North Eastern Daily Gazette* stated that:

> The woman, up to the point of writing, has not been identified and the police admit that they have no information which can possible be termed a clue.[121]

This sounds as if the reporter was at Mitre Square that morning. As he was unable to enter the murder scene itself, did he ask those officers guarding the square for information? If so, could this reporter have obtained a quote from Amos?

By that afternoon, Drs Saunders, Sequeira and Brown had visited the scene and examined the body of Catherine Eddowes where she lay, the inspection of the area had been completed by the City Police, and City Surveyor Frederick Foster had made his sketches. The body had been removed to the Golden Lane mortuary and the blood had been washed away. To any local using Mitre Square as a quick cut-through on their way to or from work, it would have looked as if Jack the Ripper had never graced the City of London at all.

Amos's involvement in the case had not yet ended. According to the *Daily News* of 2nd October 1888, at the entrance to 36 Mitre Street he found what appeared to be bloodstains. The newspaper stated that the stains looked

> as if a person had wiped his fingers on the window ledge and drawn a blood-stained knife down part of the doorway.

---

121 *North Eastern Daily Gazette*, 1st October 1888.

Mr Hartig, the tenant of number 36, had noticed the stains 'quite by accident' and alerted Amos. When the officer inspected them he also noticed marks on the window of the premises belonging to Mr William Smith, situated on the corner of Mitre Square. When asked, Mr Smith thought that these marks would have nothing to do with the case because at the time of the murder the shutters had been closed. It was later claimed that these bloodstains were in fact candlewax stains.[122]

Amos was dismissed from the City of London Police force in 1889. This was unusual, as the force believed in handing out punishment which could be learned from. However, whatever Amos did (it does not give details within his file), it was considered serious enough to warrant immediate dismissal. Not only that, but Amos was dismissed with 'forfeiture of all pay,' so something quite bad must have happened.

At some point between 1883, when fourth child Mortimer Dudman was born, and the 1901 census, Amos and his wife Caroline separated. The census of that year lists Amos as living at 3 Selkirk Road, Tooting, with a 'wife' named Elizabeth Dudman.[123] However, there is no recorded marriage for Amos and Elizabeth, nor is there a divorce recorded for Amos and Caroline. Caroline is alive in 1901, living with three of their children, Amy, Ethel and Mortimer at Vintry Wharf, St James Garlickhite.[124]

Whatever the nature of Amos' relationship with Elizabeth, it had ended by 1908 for in that year he married Mary Ann Saunders in Edmonton, London.[125] Former wife Caroline did not die until 1922, and there is no record of a divorce between she and Amos found to date. There is therefore a possibility that Amos had committed bigamy.

Amos lived with Mary as man and wife, and in the 1911 census are

122 *Ripperana* 14, p27.

123 1901 census. Amos is quoted in this census as being a 'Currier Clerk'.

124 Ibid. Amy and Ethel are working in the stationery trade, and Mortimer as a junior clerk.

125 Marriage record. Mary Ann Saunders was born in 1864 in Louth, Ireland.

listed at 3 Marlborough Road, Wood Green.

He died in 1935 and was buried at Camberwell New Cemetery on 11th December that year, in a private grave, number 3805 square 110.[126]

Sergeant Amos Dudman's role within the case does seem to be a relatively small one, but his actions show not only the protection needed in order to protect a crime scene, but this in turn illustrates the morbid sense of entertainment that these killings brought to the local population. This duty also highlights the slight differences between the actions of the Metropolitan Police force and the City of London Police force.

PC Richard Pearce:
I reside at Number 3 Mitre Square[127]

PC Richard Pearce was not called to the scene of the murder of Catherine Eddowes. He had not met Catherine Eddowes on the night before she died, he did not investigate the crime. However, his role in this killing is perhaps the most haunting...

As mentioned elsewhere in this book, there were many 'what ifs' surrounding the murder of Catherine Eddowes, different ways in which at best she could have survived, or at worse, if she couldn't be saved, how the killer could have been caught.

Those last few words - 'the killer could have been caught' - is where PC Richard Pearce comes in. He did not need to be walking his beat or running through the streets in order to catch the killer, hauntingly, for all he had to do was not go to bed for another hour and look out of the window of his own home...

Born on 20th September 1850 in Whitechapel,[128] Richard William

---

126   Camberwell Cemetery records.

127   Statement by PC Richard Pearce made at the inquest of Catherine Eddowes, reported in the *Daily Telegraph*, 12th October 1888.

128   Birth record.

Pearce was the first child to be born to goldbroker Richard Pearce[129] and his wife Maria.[130] Richard Jr was to gain three sisters: Maria Clara in 1853, Elizabeth (b.1856) and Edith (b.1859).[131]

From 1859, the Pearce family lived at 162 Cannon Street Road, St George-in-the-East. Their elder children Richard Jr, Maria and Elizabeth had all been born in Whitechapel, whereas Edith, born in 1859, was registered in St George-in-the-East.[132]

One can imagine that the Pearce children could not get away from being taught in school, even if they wanted to. One reason for this was because there was another person living within the same building at the time of the 1861 census, one Ravamond Young, who was a Governess for the local school.[133] A second reason was that this local school was very close indeed.

On Cannon Street Road was a charity school, founded in 1784 by the Middlesex Society but later taken over by the National Society in 1862. The main aim of the school was to educate poor children of a Protestant background and to clothe them, at a cost of one guinea per child per year, or parents could pay the full ten guineas per child for their entire time spent at school.[134]

In 1866/67 Richard Jr joined the 94th Regiment of Foot, previously known as the 'Scots Brigade'.[135] At the time of his enlistment, the regiment was engaged in fighting in the Crimean War, at places such as Peshawar, India, Aden and Yemen, although it is not known whether Richard travelled with these units. He was in the regiment for four years and five months, but did not leave the army completely at this point as he was still counted as a reserve for a further year

---

129 Born in 1825 in Middlesex.

130 Born in 1824 in Oxfordshire. Information from 1861 census.

131 1861 census.

132 Ibid.

133 1861 census, in which all the Pearce children are listed as scholars.

134 History records of St George in the East Schools, and *The British Magazine*, October 1832.

135 Richard Pearce's City of London Police service file: CLA/048/AD/01/567 (held at the London Metropolitan Archives).

and seven months.[136]

In his service file for the City of London Police, it states that Richard was a labourer for one Thomas Halford at 9 North East Passage, Wellclose Square, before joining the force.[137] The 1871 census tells us that Thomas Halford was an engineer, with his nephew working with him as an engineer's apprentice.[138] Richard worked for Mr Halford from August 1871 until March 1873, and his former employer would provide Richard's reference, stating he was 'sober, honest and well conducted.'[139]

Richard himself does not appear on the 1871 census with his family, who were still living at 162 Cannon Street Road, with a new addition in the form of Thomas Pearce (b.1861). This is because Richard was still with the 94th Regiment of Foot, commencing work for Thomas Halford four months after the census was taken.

Richard joined the City of London Police force in March 1873.[140] His papers record him as being 5ft 10in tall, with light coloured hair, grey eyes and 'ink markings' on his arms.[141]

On 14th August the same year he was 'fit for service'. This may seem a long time between joining and being passed as fit, but a record within Richard's service file gives a possible reason. On 28th April 1873 he was 'absent from his beat' for a period of 55 minutes, and the Commissioner sought punishment. Normal practice was to impose a reduction in pay, but in this case that could not happen, so Richard's trial period was extended for another two months.[142]

This does not seem to have had the desired effect, for a month later, on 23rd May, Richard had spent another 45 minutes away from his duties in the 'water closet', so his trial period was extended

136   Richard Pearce's City of London Police service file: CLA/048/AD/01/567.
137   Richard Pearce's City of London Police service file: CLA/048/AD/01/567.
138   1871 census.
139   Richard Pearce's City of London Police service file: CLA/048/AD/01/567.
140   March 1873.
141   Richard Pearce's City of London Police service file: CLA/048/AD/01/567.
142   Ibid..

for another month in the hope that this would sort the matter.[143]

Richard was given warrant number 4690 and collar number 922, and being a Third Class Constable his rate of pay was 25s. Being single, Richard must have been living within a police home at this time. It is stated in his service file that on 8th October 1873 he had passed water in his bed and soiled the bedding, and he was charged by the force to repay the cost of new bedding.[144] The incident goes some way to explain why Richard had been missing twice during his trial period, once being found in the water closet.[145]

In the first quarter of 1874, Richard married Jane Myrtle at St George church, Hanover Square.[146]

A few months later, in July 1874, he was caught drunk on duty and fined 5s. This doesn't seem to have harmed his career advancement, because one month later he was promoted to Second Class Constable, with his rate of pay going up to 28s.

He was promoted to First Class Constable on 14th February 1878, with a rate of pay of 31s.[147]

He was recorded in the 1881 census as living at 18 Steward Street, Whitechapel, with wife Jane and their two children, William Richard (b.1880) and May Olive (b.1881).[148]

He was found drunk on duty again on 9th December 1883, this time being demoted to Second Class Constable. A year later, having committed no further misdemeanors, he was promoted back to First Class Constable, a rank he retained for the rest of his career.[149]

Another child, Alice, was born in 1883 and registered in Whitechapel,[150] indicating that the Pearce family was probably still living at 18 Steward Street.

---

143 Richard Pearce's City of London Police service file: CLA/048/AD/01/567.

144 He was charged 3s 6d.

145 Richard Pearce's City of London Police service file: CLA/048/AD/01/567.

146 Marriage record. Jane was born in 1848 in Hampshire.

147 Richard Pearce's City of London Police service file: CLA/048/AD/01/567.

148 1881 census.

149 Richard Pearce's City of London Police service file: CLA/048/AD/01/567.

150 Birth record.

At some point Richard and his family moved from Whitechapel to 3 Mitre Square, in the City of London.

In the 1881 census this address was occupied by John Smith, a 36-year-old cabinet maker and his family, wife Susannah (35) and their children Kate (8), Herbert (5) and Arthur (4). Also living with them were Susannah's mother Betsy Beaumont, and two lodgers, Mortitz Myer and Leopold Gicht.[151]

We know from a case mentioned in more detail later in this book that PC Robert Wilson of the City of London Police lived at 5 Mitre Square in 1885. He had become suspicious about one of his fellow lodgers at this address and was told to watch the man, while Detective Roper watched Mitre Square itself.[152] There was no mention in either of their statements of another policemen living in the area, let alone two doors away, which seems to indicate that PC Richard Pearce and his family moved into 3 Mitre Square around 1886.

At the inquest of Catherine Eddowes, Richard states that he 'resides at Number 3 Mitre Square. There are only two private houses in the square,'[153] before going on to relate his movements on the morning of 30th September 1888.

Before going into the timings of his statement, it is important to point out where Catherine Eddowes' body lay in relation to Richard's family home.

If you were to walk into Mitre Square from Mitre Street, just as PC Watkins did, Catherine was found in a dark corner to the right hand side. She was lying on the pavement across the entrance of Heydemann and Company's warehouse.

There were only two gas lamps within the square, one at the entrance to Church Passage down which PC Harvey would have walked, and the other attached to the Kearley and Tonge warehouse on the opposite side of the square, on the same side as Richard's

---

151 1881 census.

152 Old Bailey records (t18850420-532).

153 Inquest testimony reported in the *Daily Telegraph*, 12th October 1888.

home.

As previously mentioned, these gas lamps was not fully working at the time of the murder. But at the inquest, Richard made an interesting and potentially alarming comment. He stated:

> There are only my wife and family of small children in the house, and I keep a light burning all night in case they wake up.[154]

Richard had a light burning in his home, which overlooked the murder scene. In fact, on being asked by Mr Crawford, 'From your bedroom window could you see the spot where the murder was committed?' Richard replied 'Yes, quite plainly.'[155]

Hauntingly, these comments lead the author to consider something which perhaps Richard and his family thought in 1888: what if the light from Richard's candle, left burning all night as a comfort for his small children, gave the killer just the right amount of brightness to see what he wanted to do to Catherine?

Another thought which comes to mind, and probably Richard's as well, relates to his statement regarding his movements on the night of the murder.

At the inquest he stated: 'I retired to rest at twenty minutes past twelve on the morning of last Sunday week.'[156]

So to get the timings right, let's go over them again. Catherine was found dead at approximately 1:45am. The killer was certainly not in the square at 1:30am, even if we dismiss PC Harvey's statement.[157]

Richard Pearce, who lived opposite the murder spot, went to bed at 12:20am. Around one hour and twenty minutes later, Catherine Eddowes was opposite Richard's home with the Ripper... What if he hadn't been able to sleep, or had woken up for some reason, and happened to look outside his window - what or who would he have

---

154 *Daily News*, 12th October 1888

155 *Daily Telegraph*, 12th October 1888.

156 Ibid.

157 As discussed in the chapter on PC Harvey, there is a suggestion that his statement about his timing might have been untrue because he may have skipped a part of his beat or was running late.

seen, possibly in the light of his own candle?

It is sickening to think that in the last seconds of Catherine's life, when she perhaps knew she was about to die, that she might have wished for a policeman to come along, perhaps knowing that a policeman's beat meant there was indeed one close by, but not aware that a policeman actually lived just yards away, and who just happened to be at home at the time...

At the inquest, PC Richard Pearce stated that he was woken at 2:20am by a police constable who told him of the murder that had happened almost on his own doorstep.[158] He confirmed that neither he nor his family had heard anything until that point.

However, some newspapers,[159] reported that after PC Watkins had run to raise the alarm with nightwatchman George Morris, he had also woken Richard and they both used their lanterns to see the body more clearly. This could have been a misunderstanding of the facts, as George Morris had brought his lantern to look at the body more clearly before running off to find PC Harvey.

By the 1891 census, the Pearce family had moved out of 3 Mitre Square. Had they continued to live just yards from where the Ripper, the most wanted man in the country if now the world, had killed, for more than two years?

The answer, unsurprisingly, is almost certainly 'no'.

Sadly, in the first quarter of 1889, Richard's daughter May died at only eight-years-old. The fact that her death was registered in Hackney[160] would seem to indicate that the family had moved from Mitre Square within five months of Catherine's death.

On the 1891 census, the family were living at 10 White Lion Street, Whitechapel.[161]

Four years later, on 28th January 1895, Richard was caught 'loitering on his beat for the purpose of obtaining drink'. He had two

158 *Daily News*, 12th October 1888.
159 Such as *Evening News*, 1st October 1888; *Weekly Herald*, 5th October 1888.
160 Death record.
161 1891 census.

days deducted from his leave. Six months later, on 10th July 1895, he was found in a urinal 'for the purpose of drinking' when he should have been on his beat, and was fined 10s.[162]

PC Richard Pearce resigned from the City of London Police force on 18th February 1898. He was now 47, and described as having hazel eyes, auburn hair and being 5ft 11in tall. He was awarded a pension of £56 14s 1d, and his conduct was classed as 'good'.[163]

In 1901, the Pearce family were living at 39 Fulbourne Road in West Ham. Richard was working as a Licensed Porter at the age of 51. Daughter Alice, now eighteen, was working as a Fancy Shop Assistant, and son William is classed, for the first time, as an 'imbecile since birth'.[164] This explains why he was still living with his family at the age of 21, without a job. William sadly died in the third quarter of 1902.[165]

Richard passed away in 1907 at the age of 59 in West Ham.[166] By this time his daughter Alice had married James Little, a printer's nightwatchman born in 1875 in Walthamstow.

In the 1911 census Jane Pearce, Richard's widow, was living with her daughter and son-in-law at 5 Boundary Road, along with their children James (b.1908) and Alice (b.1910).[167]

PC Richard Pearce was a Lost Policeman because he is hardly mentioned within the investigation, obviously because he was not directly involved in it. However, his role is important because he perhaps came the closest of all the City policeman to having caught the most famous killer of his time, and all he had to do was to look out of his window...

---

162 Richard Pearce's City of London Police service file: CLA/048/AD/01/567.
163 Ibid.
164 1901 census.
165 Death record.
166 Death record.
167 1911 census.

CHAPTER SEVENTEEN
To Shawl or Not To Shawl

Metropolitan Police Officer Amos Simpson

In recent years, the name of Metropolitan Police officer Amos Simpson has become prominent in books on the Jack the Ripper case. He is alleged to have picked up a shawl in Mitre Square on the night Catherine Eddowes was killed. Claiming he was allowed to keep it, it was kept for many years in a cupboard, unwashed, because his wife did not like it. The shawl was eventually passed on through his family, until being sold at auction to certain interested parties who conducted DNA testing on it in an attempt to prove that bloodstains on the shawl matched Catherine Eddowes's DNA taken from a living descendant, and that semen found on it belonged to Ripper suspect Aaron Kosminski.

The story of the shawl has floated around the fringe of the Ripper case for some time. Initial DNA tests were very basic, with results inconclusive, but more complex and expensive testing was performed and the results have since divided Ripperologists.

Without being drawn into the scientific debate, questions exist regarding the shawl's background. Firstly, what was a Metropolitan Police officer doing at a City of London Police murder scene? Why is there no mention of a shawl in any of the records? Why was he allowed to keep the shawl? And after all these years, can we believe the shawl sat there, unwashed, when it had bloodstains on it?

Whether you believe in the shawl or not, it is an interesting story and the life of Amos Simpson deserves to be looked at…

Born in the farming village of Acton, near Sudbury in Suffolk, in 1846, the same town and year that poisoner Catherine Foster[1] murdered her husband, Amos Simpson was the son of farmer John Simpson and his wife Mary, the fourth child of eleven. Amos attended school from the young age of four, along with his siblings Susan (b.1845), Charles (b.1844) and George (b.1843).[2]

Ten years later, in 1861, Amos had ended his education and was working on the farm with his father. Perhaps times were hard for the family at this point, as none of the children were at school according to the 1861 census.

After seven years working with his father, Amos left Suffolk for the busy streets of London and a career in the Metropolitan Police, joining on 24th February 1868. His application papers record him as standing 5ft 8¾in tall. He was stationed at Platt Street Police Station, and as an unmarried constable also resided there. This was part of the newly-formed Y Division, covering St Pancras, Holloway and Highgate. Amos was given warrant number 49611.[3]

Three years later, on 5th March 1871, PC Simpson was involved in a fight while on duty. He was walking his beat on the early afternoon shift when he came across a drunken man named George Butcher in Ossulston Street, just around the corner from the police station. The drunk came running up to Amos, his hair a mess and clothes stained

---

1   In November 1846, the newly married Mrs Catherine Foster gave her husband John a meal of dumplings and potatoes, and he died painfully a few hours later. A doctor was called and stated that death was from cholera, and the body was subsequently buried. When the chickens belonging to the Fosters' neighbours also died after eating the leftover dumpling, an investigation started. Catherine's eight-year-old brother Thomas recalled seeing her sprinkle something white over the dumplings served to her husband. John Foster's body was exhumed and arsenic was found in his body as well as in the chicken feed. Catherine Foster was arrested and tried at Bury St Edmunds. She was hanged by executioner William Calcraft.

2   1851 census.

3   MEP021/22.

by some bodily function or other. Amos must have sensed danger, and he would later recall bracing himself before Butcher grabbed the policeman by the neck and punched him in the chest, without saying a word.

Once Amos was able to regain his breath, he was able to arrest Butcher and escort him around the corner to Platt Street station, learning that his assailant worked as a plasterer. George Butcher was sent to prison for fourteen days with hard labour, despite asking whether he could pay a fine instead.

The attack was recorded in the *London Police News* a week later, but this was not the first time that PC Amos Simpson had appeared in that newspaper.

Five months earlier, he was mentioned in a report of his arrest of a group of gamblers in the streets around St Pancras on 3rd October 1870. With the help of a plainclothes officer, Amos was able to stop a game of 'tossing', where participants would throw coins against a wall and generally cause a disturbance by getting in people's way. Five men were arrested and later fined five shillings each in court.

In early March 1874 Amos married Jane Wilkins in nearby St Pancras Old Church,[4] with one Elizabeth Bundy acting as witness. Amos might have met his future bride while on duty, as she was housemaid to John Bundy and his daughter Elizabeth at 46 Crowndale Road, which was close enough to Platt Street Police Station to be a part of Amos's beat.

Son Henry was born in 1878, and the couple celebrated the birth of their second child in 1881, a girl named Ellen. At this time the family were living at 21 Stanley Buildings, right by the entrance of St Pancras train station. Built in 1864 to house workers on King's Cross station, by the time Amos lived there the building was home

---

4 St Pancras Old Church was first built in the early 17th century and rebuilt in the 19th century. The famous architect Sir John Soane is buried here with his wife in the tomb he designed, which is thought to be the inspiration for the design of the famous red telephone box. Also buried here is Mary Wollstonecraft, whose daughter Mary Shelley wrote *Frankenstein*. It is said that St Pancras Old Church is where Mary and her future husband Percy Bysshe Shelley planned their elopement in 1814. Charles Dickens mentioned this church in his 1859 novel *A Tale of Two Cities*, as the scene of bodysnatching for medical schools.

to more than a hundred families.

In early 1886, Amos was promoted to Assisting Sergeant at Islington Police Station, in N Division.[5] While the increase in wages was no doubt welcome, it meant Amos leaving Y Division and the only police station he had ever known, Platt Street.

Two years later, Jack the Ripper struck in the East End.

When questioning why Amos Simpson may have been at Mitre Square despite there being no record in official files, it has been suggested by his family that he had been sent there on observation duty in connection with Fenian activity.

It will be remembered from an earlier chapter that following the Fenian bombings at the Tower of London in 1885, City PC 863 Robert Wilson entertained suspicions about a man who lodged at the same address as himself, and that after informing his superiors it was decided that PC Wilson would watch the man from inside the house, while Detective Roper would watch the vicinity from outside. The address was 5 Mitre Square, and the man was Harry Burton.[6]

According to Caroline Wilson, wife of PC Robert Wilson, they lived in two rooms on the second floor. Before his arrest, Burton had rented a small back room on the ground floor from 26th December 1884 for around fourteen days. Burton was eventually arrested at 90 Turner Road.[7]

Is it possible that the police were still keeping an address once associated with Fenians under surveillance? Even if the answer is yes, and Mitre Square was being watched, there is no evidence that an Assisting Sergeant performed the task, either in the early hours of 30th September 1888 or at any other time.

If we do accept that Amos Simpson was there, we also have to accept that he picked up a shawl associated with a murder victim. Why would a police officer of any force be allowed to keep an item

---

5   MEP021/22.

6   Unlike in 1885 when Harry Burton lived there, there is no record of 5 Mitre Square being used in 1888 as a residential address, as the only two homes were number 3, where City police officer Richard Pearce lived, and number 4, which was empty.

7   The trial for treason of Harry Burton, April 1885.

belonging to a murder scene, a potential clue?

If, as had been suggested, Amos was the first to find the body of Catherine Eddowes, why would he take the shawl and walk away, without reporting the discovery, which there is no record of him doing?

There is, and most likely never will be, any evidence of his involvement in the Jack the Ripper events of 1888.

In the 1891 census Amos was recorded as being 40 years of age. His son Henry was working as an errand boy for the local bakers, and daughter Ellen was still at school. The family had left Stanley Buildings and moved to 103 Gews Corner, Chesthunt, in Waltham Cross. The place still stands today, and is a lovely little two-up two-down cottage.

On 27th March 1893, Amos Simpson resigned from the Metropolitan Police force after completing his 25 years service. He was awarded a pension of £54 16s 2d, and his certificate records his conduct as 'Very Good'.[8]

Eventually the Simpson family moved out of London to the most natural of places for Amos, back to the little village of Acton in Suffolk. In 1901, all the family apart from son Henry, who was working at the Cheshire Cheese public house in the City of London, lived on a small farm called Barrow Hill.

His 1893 retirement was not the end of policing for Amos Simpson, however, for he received a letter from the Metropolitan Police asking him to return for extra security for the coronation of Edward VII.[9] Amos travelled to London on 12th June 1902, but when the crowning was delayed due to urgent surgery required by the new king, he served a total of 28 days as an officer in Z Division,

---

8   MEP021/22.

9   Edward VII's coronation was delayed as the new king was in urgent need of surgery on his appendix. He did not want to go to hospital and he argued strongly on the matter, but Dr Frederick Treves stuck to his guns stating that it would also be a funeral if the King did not have the operation. The coronation was therefore delayed until the abscess on his appendix was drained, and Dr Treves earned himself a knighthood for his efforts. Ironically, the surgeon himself later died from a burst appendix in December 1923, after finishing his book called *The Elephant Man and Other Reminiscences*.

being given warrant number 01285.[10]

By the time Amos's wife Jane died in 1912, daughter Ellen had already moved in to help around the family home. She had married Morris Stearns and had five children: James (b.1902), Beatrice (b.1904), Joseph (b.1905), Alma (b.1906) and Violet (b.1909).[11] They all lived with Amos until Morris joined the army during the Great War, dying in battle in 1916.[12]

Amos Simpson died a year later in 1917. A report of his passing in the local newspaper stated:

> His wife died five years ago and since then he has been attended to by his devoted daughter, who lost her husband (killed in action) on September the 13th 1916, leaving five young children. Mr Simpson was very cheerful on the Monday morning and sang 'The Last Rose of the Summer' to the monophone. He was taken suddenly ill in the evening and died on Tuesday morning at 8 o'clock.[13]

It is still debateable what Amos's actual role was in the Jack the Ripper case, if any, but he is entwined with it until evidence can be found to either support or disprove claims of his involvement, so he should be mentioned here.

---

10 MEP021/22.

11 1911 census.

12 *Suffolk and Essex Free Press*, 18th April 1917.

13 Ibid.

CHAPTER EIGHTEEN

The Writing is on The Wall

Metropolitan Police Officer Alfred Long

At 2:50am, on the morning of 30th September 1888, PC Alfred Long was walking his new beat along Goulston Street. He was one of many policemen who had been transferred from another division to H Division, Whitechapel, to help keep watch of the area in the aftermath of the recent Ripper killings. At the entrance to 108-119 Wentworth Model Dwellings, lying on the floor, Alfred spotted a piece of cloth that seemed to be covered in blood. Above this, on the wall, was a message written in chalk. Whether Jack the Ripper had left this message or not, the piece of cloth was later identified as being the missing piece from the apron which Catherine Eddowes was wearing at the time of her death. This meant that for the first time, it was known roughly the direction that the Whitechapel murderer had taken after a murder...

There has been a question mark hanging over the life of Alfred Long for some time, as there was another officer of that name on the 1891 census, despite it being known that the PC Long who found the piece of apron at Goulston Street had been dismissed from the Metropolitan Police force in 1889 after being found drunk on duty. How can this be? Had he been reinstated?

In looking for an answer to these questions, we need to look both at the service file for Alfred Long and also the census returns to find a connection. If we follow the censuses back to a birth record, the Alfred Long who was a policeman on the 1891 census, and a sergeant ten years later, was born in 1862 in Hertfordshire.[1]

The Alfred Long who found the apron, and whose collar number matches that recorded when he gave evidence at the inquest of Catherine Eddowes[2] and also logged in his service file,[3] was born in 1854/1855 in Berstead, Middlesex. With the regular boundary changes, Berstead sometimes came under Sussex, which is important to keep in mind in further researches.

Taking a closer look at the service file, Alfred Long was a baker before joining the force,[4] and we can find an Alfred Long who was a baker's lad on the 1871 census, born in 1855 in Sussex. The author believes that this is the policeman who found the piece of Catherine Eddowes's apron on that fateful morning in 1888.

Alfred was born in the second quarter of 1855 in Chichester, Berstead in Sussex,[5] to carpenter Henry Long[6] and his wife Fanny.[7] He was the middle child, with an older brother, Henry, born in Farlington, London, in 1853 and a younger sister, Fanny, born in Berstead in 1858.[8]

In 1861, the Long family were living on North Bersted Street, Chichester,[9] where they had a lodger named George Hammon, a widower and a blacksmith,[10] living with them.

---

1   1861, 1871, 1881, 1891 and 1901 censuses and birth record.
2   Coroner's Inquest (L) 1888, No. 135, Catherine Eddowes's Inquest 1888 at London Metropolitan Archives.
3   Summary Service file for Alfred Long 69841 held at Metropolitan Historical Police Archives at Lillie Road, London.
4   Ibid.
5   Birth record.
6   Born 1818 in Berstead, sometimes written Bursted.
7   Born 1828 in Pagham, Sussex.
8   1861 census.
9   1861 census.
10 Aged 78.

Ten years later, by the time of the 1871 census, Alfred had moved away from the family home and was employed as a baker's lad, working and living with John Cox and his wife Sarah in the High Street, Westhampnett in Sussex, Alfred had now turned sixteen years of age.[11] Given how quaint the village is, one can imagine Alfred riding a baker's bike around the streets in his job.

However, looking for Alfred on the 1881 census, he becomes difficult to find. A clue lies in his Police service file, for it states that he was in the army for twelve years and seven days.[12] Considering that Alfred joined the Metropolitan Police force in 1884, twelve years before that would have seen him enlist around 1872, the year after he was recorded on the census as a baker's lad.

Alfred's service file states that he served in the 9th Lancers, but not where. A search in the National Archives gives an Alfred Long of the correct age, who was a driver at St John's Wood Barracks in 1881. However, this Alfred Long was born in Yorkshire.[13] Could the birthplace have been recorded incorrectly?

We are lucky to have a detailed description of the actions of the 9th Lancers at the time in which Alfred would have been a part of the regiment, published in *Regimental Histories 1715-1936* by Major E. W. Sheppard.

The 9th Lancers were stationed at Aldershot in 1872, the year in which Alfred claimed to have enlisted.

In May 1874, the regiment was meant to be in India, but it took another year for this to happen. However, a depot of two officers and 62 other ranks were left behind at the Cavalry Depot in Canterbury, Kent, after the majority of the regiment left England. It is unknown whether Alfred stayed behind and went to Canterbury or travelled out to India, as there seems to be no record of him. If we assume that Alfred was a basic foot soldier - given that he does not mention a rank in his summary service file for the Metropolitan Police - we

---

11 1871 census.

12 Summary service file for Alfred Long 69841 held Metropolitan Historical Police Archives at Lillie Road, London.

13 RG11/165/104/5 (National Archive).

might allow ourselves to think that he may have travelled to India, to help with the numbers needed over there.[14]

The 9th Lancers would become embroiled in the Second Afghan War, which broke out in 1878, and spent an arduous couple of years fighting in numerous locations before receiving orders on 25th November 1880 to leave Afghanistan.

According to the Military Campaign Medal and Award Rolls, Alfred received a Distinguished Service Medal for his part in this conflict. We also find out from the same records that Alfred's regimental number was 1706.[15]

In April 1882, Lieutenant Colonel H.A. Bushman presented soldiers of the 9th Lancers with a medal for their action in the Second Afghan War, with 255 officers receiving the Bronze Star.

Some of the regiment returned to England in 1884,[16] and we can allow ourselves to imagine that Alfred Long was one of these, as he joined the Metropolitan Police force on 6th October 1884,[17] after serving what must have seemed a long twelve years and seven days with the 9th Lancers.

Alfred joined the Metropolitan Police at the age of 30, and was given warrant number 69841 and collar number 254, and placed in A Division, Westminster.[18] He stated that his previous occupation was a baker, and that he had been born in Berstead, but this time, the village is stated as being in Middlesex. He is described as being 5ft 9in tall at the time of joining.[19]

---

14 Regimental Histories 1715-1936 by Sheppard held at the National Archives, references numbers 912L:2088/3/4/42/49/50/55/56/63/70. 912L: 2089/26/27

15 Military Campaign Medal and Award Rolls, 1793-1949: WO 100; Piece 51.984 A Long, which reveal that his regimental number was 1706. The author would like to thank Paul Begg for the information on Alfred's Medal.

16 Regimental Histories 1715-1936 by Sheppard 912L: 2088/3/4/42/49/50/55/56/ 63/70. 912L: 2089/26/27 (National Archives).

17 Summary Service file for Alfred Long 69841 held Metropolitan Historical Police Archives at Lillie Road, London.

18 As stated on his service file, although it is often stated as Whitehall.

19 Summary Service file for Alfred Long 69841 held Metropolitan Historical Police Archives at Lillie Road, London.

A few months later, on 12th February 1885, Alfred married Ellen Yeates at St John the Evangelist church in Lambeth,[20] and the following year the couple welcomed a daughter, whom they named Ellen after her mother.[21]

On the morning of 30th September 1888, Alfred was walking his new beat around Whitechapel. It was a new beat for Alfred, because Sir Charles Warren, the Commissioner of the Metropolitan Police, had ordered other divisions to transfer a number of officers to H Division, Whitechapel.

In reply to the Office Board of Works, Whitechapel District, who had asked for the Commissioner to 'strengthen the police force in the neighbourhood as to guard against any repetition of such atrocities',[22] Sir Charles replied:

> I have to point out that carrying out of your proposals as to regulating and strengthening the police force in your district cannot possibly do more than guard or take precautions against any repetitions of such atrocities so long as the victims actually, but unwittingly, connive at their own destruction.
>
> Statistics show that London, in comparison to its population, is the safest city in the world to live in. The prevention of murder directly cannot be effected by the strength of the police force; but it is reduced and brought to a minimum by rendering it most difficult to escape detection. In the particular class of murder now confronting us, however, the unfortunate victims appear to take the murderer to some retired spot and place themselves in such a position that they can be slaughtered without a sound being heard; the murder, therefore, takes place without any clue to the criminal being left.
>
> I have also to point out that the purlieus about Whitechapel are most imperfectly lighted, and that darkness is an important assistant to the crime. I can assure you, for the information of your Board, that every nerve has be strained to detect the criminal or criminals, and to render more difficult further atrocities.
>
> You will agree with me that it is not desirable that I should enter into particulars as to what the police are doing in this matter. It is

20 Marriage record.
21 1891 census.
22 *The Times*, 2nd October 1888.

THE WRITING IS ON THE WALL

most important for good results that our proceeding should not be published, and the very fact you may be unaware of what the Detective Department is doing is only the stronger proof that it is doing its work with secrecy and efficiency.

A large force of the police has been drafted into Whitechapel district to assist those already there to the full extent necessary to meet the requirements; but I have to observe that the Metropolitan police have not large reserves doing nothing and ready to meet emergencies, but every man has his duty assigned to him; and I can only strengthen the Whitechapel district by drawing men from duty in other parts of the Metropolis.

You will be aware that the whole of the police work of the Metropolis has to be done as usual while this extra is going on, and that at such time as this extra precautions have to be taken to prevent the commission of other classes of crime being facilitated through the attention of the police being diverted to one special place or object.

Notwithstanding the many good reason why constables should be changed on their beats, I have considered the reasons on the other side to be more cogent, and have felt that they should be thoroughly acquainted with the districts in which they serve.[23]

We do not know for certain the beat in which Alfred was given at this time in 1888, as he does not mention his route in his testimony at the inquest into Catherine Eddowes' death. Looking at later beat books for this area,[24] it shows that Goulston Street was dipped in and out of throughout the beat and that a constable did not cover Goulston Street in one go.

Goulston Street would have first been entered from Wentworth Street, with the policeman walking southwards to Whitechapel High Street and walking along this busy thoroughfare until he reached Middlesex Street. He would then follow this road until reaching New Goulston Street, then turning back onto Goulston Street where those two streets met.

Next, turning north to Bell Lane, then finding himself back on Wentworth Street, he would then head towards Castle Alley, walking along this street until he reached Whitechapel High Street again.

23 *The Times*, 4th October 1888.
24 1930s H Division Beat Book.

This meant the constable would then enter Goulston Street from that end, the south end, until he reached the point of New Goulston Street again and Middlesex Street.[25]

There are three points to be made here, if the 1888 beat was the same as the later recorded version. Firstly, the number of separate times Alfred could have been in Goulston Street that morning may well be the answer as to why he did not see Detective Daniel Halse, who claimed to be in the same place at the same time as Alfred.

Secondly, these separate appearances on Goulston Street could also suggest how Jack the Ripper could have walked along that street, which we know he must have done, without Alfred seeing him.

Thirdly, the author has walked this beat. It is still complete and able to do quite easily. During the day it is a very busy place, with public houses and Petticoat Lane market nearby. These would have been there in Alfred's time, and you can easily imagine the stalls lining the streets with the costermongers shouting out their wares. However, in the early hours of the morning, this same place takes on an eerie quietness so that you can envisage what the streets may have felt like for Alfred when walking his beat.

A 2:50am, Alfred had re-entered Goulston Street on his beat. He came across the entrance to 108-119 Wentworth Model Dwellings,[26] when he caught sight of something which he would later claim wasn't there on his previous visit at 2:00am.[27]

He shone his Bullseye lamp into the doorway, and on the floor against the brick wall was a piece of cloth, which, as his light shone upon it, he could see was spotted with fresh blood. Shining his

---

25 1930s H Division Beat Book.

26 Wentworth Model Dwellings were situated on the corner of Goulston Street and Wentworth Street. Comprising of two blocks five storeys high, with four entrances out into Goulston Street, the Dwellings offered over 200 apartments. Surviving the threat of demolition in 1967, in 1990 the apartments were redeveloped and renamed Merchant House. At the same time the Happy Days restaurant opened, and the entrance to 108-119 Wentworth Model Dwellings, where Alfred Long discovered the piece of apron, now forms part of the doorway to Happy Days.

27 Alfred Long's testimony at Catherine Eddowes inquest.

light around the hallway, perhaps looking for more bloodstains, he instead noticed a chalked message written on the wall above the portion of cloth.

This message would become forever associated with the Jack the Ripper case, but we will never know for certain whether the killer actually wrote it. However, the words 'The Juwes are the men that will not be blamed for nothing', as Alfred claimed the message to be at the inquest,[28] has haunted the case in the 129 years since it was first seen by Alfred that morning.

Alfred then checked the stairways on all floors of the building. Seeing nothing else suspicious, he then walked back down to the doorway and into the street, calling for assistance. PC 190 Willie Bettles answered the call, and was told by Alfred to keep watch by the doorway, while he himself went to Commercial Street Police Station to report on his findings.[29] After informing the Inspector on duty, the two of them went first to Goulston Street so that the Inspector could see the message for himself, and then on to Leman Street Police Station.

Alfred would later report what happened there:

> The apron was handed by the Inspector to a gentleman whom I have since learnt is Dr Phillips. I then returned back on duty in Goulston Street about 5.[30]

Although his involvement in the case ended there, his discovery proved to be the only clue in the hunt for the Ripper.

On 13th December 1888, Alfred was suspended for one day, the reason unrecorded.[31] This seems to be the start of a downhill slide for Alfred in the Metropolitan Police force. The next year, on 26th March 1889, his advancement in the force was withheld, or as the

---

28 The spelling has been alternatively given as 'the Juwes are not the men that will be blamed for nothing' or even 'the Jews are not the men that will be blamed for nothing'.

29 Alfred Long's report dated 6th November 1888 (HO 144/221/A49301C - National Archives).

30 Ibid.

31 Police Orders, 14th December 1889.

police would have called it, Alfred was 'retarded'.[32] This punishment, and an accompanying fine of 5s, was because he had been found drunk and away from duty for three hours without permission.[33] His file records that he was 'severely reprimanded and cautioned for the last time,'[34] the phrasing is interesting because it seems to suggest that Alfred had perhaps been cautioned more than otherwise recorded.

Alfred left the force on 18th July 1889. His pension was forfeited due to him being dismissed for being drunk on duty, and he was 'considered unfit for the Police force.'[35]

The 1891 census reveals that he found himself another job, as he was recorded as a 'Clean Porter'. The family was living at 52 Walcot Square in Lambeth. Alfred was now 36 years of age, his wife Ellen was 35 and daughter Ellen was five-years-old.[36]

Five years later, another daughter, Daisy, was welcomed to the family,[37] and although they would have four more children, sadly all of them passed away.[38]

In the 1901 census the family was still living at Walcot Square, with Ellen's mother Mary Yeates, aged 77, now living with them. Alfred's career had changed again and he was now a Fire Stoker.[39]

Ten years later, in 1911, Alfred was now 56 and working as a fireman at the flour mill, which is quite a coincidence given his earlier job as a baker.[40]

Alfred passed away in the second quarter of 1930 at the age of 75.[41] On his death certificate he was described as 'formerly builder's

---

32 Police Orders, 26th March 1889.

33 Ibid.

34 Ibid.

35 Summary Service file for Alfred Long.

36 1891 census.

37 1901 census.

38 The author would like to thank Paul Begg for this information.

39 1901 census.

40 1911 census.

night watchman',[42] which must have been another role he had taken on between the 1911 census and his death in 1930.

41 Death record. In searching for the death record for Alfred Long, the author and Del Purse discovered a problem. There was no record for Alfred coming up in the search engine, because a mistake had been made in the transcription of the record, Alfred was recorded as passing away at the age of 95 rather than his actual age of 75. The mistake has now been corrected by Del Purse.

42 The author would like to thank Paul Begg for this information.

Conclusion

So what conclusion can we come to after reading about the background to the City of London Police force, the history of the area surrounding Mitre Square and Golden Lane, the personal upbringing and experiences of the Eddowes family, and finally the lives of the men who had to cope with the investigation into such an infamous crime, and then go back to work the next day, carrying on with their existences?

Well, only you, the reader can truly decide that. However, the author hopes that by going into more detail about these people they will seem more alive and human to you, rather than just names in various documentation, because they were so much more than that. They were living, breathing people who had their own histories; they were more than what they did on one night or one morning of their lives, and they are certainly more than characters in a play of 'who was Jack the Ripper?', waiting for their turn to take the stage, do their bit and then leave, not to be mentioned again.

Not only have we learned more about those people who are mentioned time and again when describing the events leading to the sad death of Catherine Eddowes on the morning of 30th September 1888 in Mitre Square, but hopefully we have learned something new about the case, whether it be the real first name of the Acting Commissioner of the City of London Police at the time of the Ripper, the first name and life of the policeman who took John Kelly to Golden Lane Mortuary to identify her, or the life of Catherine Eddowes and her family.

Select Bibliography

Official Documents

London Metropolitan Archives
Business Records
CLA/048/AD/01
CLA/048/AD/01
CLA/048/AD/01/014
CLA/048/AD/01/20
CLA/048/AD/01/306
CLA/048/AD/01/360
CLA/048/AD/01/364
CLA/048/AD/01/466
CLA/048/AD/01/478
CLA/048/AD/01/567
CLA/048/AD/01/61
CLA/048/AD/01/651
CLA/048/AD/01/770
CLA/048/CS/02/373
Coroner's inquest (L) 1888, No.135, Catherine Eddowes' Inquest, 1888
H1/ST/MS/G10
SC/P2/CT/01/103

National Archives
HO 144/221/A49301C

MEP021/22

Regimental Histories 1715-1936

RG11/165/104/5

RG8/35-38

W0372/3

WO/12/9080

Other Archives

Births, Marriages and Deaths certificates

Census returns

County of London Battalion records, 1916

National School Admission Registers and Log Books 1871–1914
   (Tower Hamlets Local History Archives and Library)

Old Bailey records

Q476975X (Guildhall Library)

Records of the 45th Regiment of Foot

Records of the Bermondsey Industrial School

Smithfield Conservation Area Character Summary and
   Management Strategy Supplementary Planning Documents
   (City of London Corporation)

St Margaret's Church of England School records

St Mary's Church Parish records

Whitechapel Infirmary records

Workhouse records

Newspapers, Books and Magazines

1888 Business Directory

A Treatise on Bright's Disease of the Kidneys; Its Pathology,
   Diagnosis and Treatment by Henry B Millard

Blackwood's Magazine

Brighton and Hove Herald

Britain in the Hanoverian Age 1714-1837:
   An Encyclopaedia by Gerald Newman

SELECT BIBLIOGRAPHY

Britain Parliamentary Election Results 1832-1885 by F.W.S. Craig

Bulletins and Other State Intelligence by Francis Watts

City of London Police File held at Bishopsgate Police Station

City of London Police Station Number Six Order Book

Copy of a Report on the Probable Duration of Life of the Men
   in the City Police Force, with General Observations on
   the Medical History of the Force, 1863

Copy of the General Report of G. Borlase Childs, on
   the Dress of the City Police Force, 1801

Daily News

Daily Telegraph

Dickens' Dictionary of London 1888

East London Observer

Edinburgh Evening News

Evening News

*Fasti Ecclesiae Scoticanae: The Succession of Ministers in
   the Church of Scotland from the Reformation*

*From Constable to Commissioner, The Story of Sixty Years,
   Most of Them Misspent* by Lieut–Col Sir Henry Smith K.C.B.

Illustrated London News

Illustrated Police News

In Strange Company by James Greenwood

Ipswich Journal

Iron News

Islington Daily Gazette

Jewish Encyclopedia: 1901–1906

Lloyd's Weekly Newspaper

London City Press

London Gazette

London Labour and London Poor byHenry Mayhew

London: The Illustrated History by Cathy Ross and John Clark, eds

Medical Times and Gazette

Morning Leader

New Zealand Herald

News of the World

Nottingham Evening Post

Order Book for Division Six (Bishopsgate)
  (City of London Police Museum)

Pall Mall Gazette

Police Review

Reynolds's Newspaper

Ripperana

Ripperologist magazine

Sir Howard Vincent's Police Code, 1889
  by Neil R A Bell and Adam Wood

Sir Robert Peel, A Memorial Biography by H. Morse Stephens

St. James's Gazette

Suffolk and Essex Free Press

The Aberdeen Journal

The British Medical Journal

The Centaur

The City Bunhill Burial ground, Golden Lane:
  MOL Archaeology Studies Series 21, 2006

The City of London Cemetery and Crematorium Newspaper

The City of London Police Orders and Regulations Book 1839-1894

The City Press

The Echo

The History of Henry Fielding Vol. 2

The Jewish Chronicle

The Lancet

The Life and Memoirs of John Churton Collins

The London Hospital Gazette

The Million-peopled City by John Garwood

The North London News

The Penny Illustrated Paper and Illustrated Times

The Purchase of Officers' Commissions in the British Army

SELECT BIBLIOGRAPHY

The Reading Mercury

The Sanitary Record

The Scotsman

The Shops and Companies of London by Henry Mayhew

The Star

The Times

The Wandsworth and Battersea District Times

The Whitechapel Society Journal

Thomson's Weekly News

Index

INDEX